AMERICAN EXXXTASY

My 30-Year Search for a Happy Ending

John Amero
with Ashley West and April Hall

AMERICAN EXXXTASY
MY 30-YEAR SEARCH FOR A HAPPY ENDING

This first paperback pressing published by FAB Press, November 2021
First published in hardcover only by FAB Press, September 2020

FAB Press Ltd., 2 Farleigh, Ramsden Road
Godalming, Surrey, GU7 1QE, England, U.K.

www.fabpress.com

Text copyright © 2020 John Amero
The moral rights of the author have been asserted

Edited by Ashley West and April Hall
Book Layout and Design by Harvey Fenton
Production Assistance and Additional Research by Francis Brewster
Front Cover Design by Kevin Coward

World Rights Reserved by FAB Press Ltd.

No part of this book may be reproduced or transmitted in any form or by any means, electronic or mechanical, including photocopying, recording, or by any information storage and retrieval system including the internet, without the prior written permission of the Publisher.

Copyright of illustrations reproduced in these pages is the property of the duly credited copyright owners.

A CIP catalogue record for this book is available from the British Library.

ISBN 978 1 913051 13 6

DEDICATION

For my brother and creative partner, Lem Amero,
and my partner in life, Chuck Federico.

ACKNOWLEDGEMENTS

With grateful thanks for all your support and kindness over the years:
Steve and Nancy Gould, Patty Sumner, Richie Weigle, Bill Cosgriff,
Kurt Mann, LaRue Watts, Fabian Stuart, Colette Connor,
Michael Annarumma, Ron and Ronni Scardera, and Ethan Prochnik.

Special thanks to Ashley West and April Hall for overcoming my reluctance to relive my colorful past, making this book a reality.

CONTENTS

    FOREWORD 6

    PROLOGUE 8

1. THE YOUNG MAN AND THE SEA (1939-1958) 9
2. WEST SIDE STORY (1958-1964) 23
3. BODY OF A FEMALE (1964-1965) 40
4. DIARY OF A SWINGER (1965-1967) 51
5. THE CORPORATE QUEEN (1968-1969) 71
6. BACCHANALE (1970-1971) 93

    IMAGE GALLERY 105

7. DYNAMITE, PEPPER AND LORD PERRY (1972-1974) 121
8. EVERY INCH A LADY (1975) 139
9. BLONDE AMBITION (1977-1981) 149
10. THE FRANCIS ELLIE FILMS (1976-1988) 160
11. THE END OF AN ERA (1978-1982) 171
12. THE PLAYBOY YEARS (1984-1989) 181
13. A TIME OF GRIEF (1989-1990) 197
14. PRIMETIME (1991-1994) 203

    EPILOGUE 211

    JOHN AMERO FILMOGRAPHY 212

    INDEX 221

FOREWORD

For as long as I can remember, I've been fascinated with the birth of the adult film industry in New York. The convergence of social, technological, legal, and moral changes in the United States led to the creation of a new, permissive film genre.

In the 1960s, titles like *The Lusting Hours*, *The Curse of Her Flesh*, and *Olga's House of Shame* exploded into theaters across the land, each more graphic than the last, and eventually leading to hardcore box office hits like *Deep Throat*, *The Devil in Miss Jones* and *Debbie Does Dallas*.

When I moved to New York in 2002, I was determined to see if any of the creators of these films were still around. Predictably after such a long time, I found that most of these pioneers had died, and those who were still alive had long moved away from the city, priced out of an increasingly corporatized and gentrified New York.

But one of them was still around and he was the person I was most keen to speak to: the very first adult film director-producer, John Amero.

John was an unlikely figure to spearhead the porn revolution. A self-described repressed gay New Englander, he arrived in Manhattan in the late 1950s, finding a job in the television industry by way of a lowly role in the CBS mail room. From these humble beginnings, over the course of three decades, John had a Zelig-like ability to crop up in every strand of the growing exploitation and adult film industries.

Indeed, the story of his life reads like a history of the New York film industry.

Together with his best friend, Mike Findlay, he made *Body of a Female* (1964), the ground zero film of the modern-day adult business. He then formed a partnership with his brother Lem, directing a series of influential black and white sexual dramas, while also assisting Mike Findlay and his wife Roberta in producing roughies that were big box office hits in the grindhouses of Times Square. In 1970, John and Lem made the hardcore breakthrough movie, *Bacchanale*, a full two years before the landmark porno chic film, *Deep Throat* (1972) was released. Big budget adult film hits followed, such as *Every Inch a Lady* (1975) and *Blonde Ambition* (1981), as well as a series of game-changing gay films John directed using the

FOREWORD

pseudonym 'Francis Ellie'. In the 1980s John moved onto video features, and assisted fellow filmmakers like Chuck Vincent as they moved into the mainstream. And I haven't even mentioned John working for the mob, being thrown in jail for managing an adult theater, producing a television special with Olympia Dukakis, and much more.

In short, John's life is a rollicking and exuberant map of the New York film industry from the 1960s onwards.

Today John still lives in New York City in the same West Village apartment that appears as a set in several of his films. Many of his close friends and former collaborators – such as his brother Lem, Mike Findlay and Chuck Vincent – are long gone, but today his closest friends are still those with whom he worked on many of his classic films.

John's story is much more than just the story of a filmmaker. It's the story of a city, an industry, a movement, a way of life, and many friendships. It's a story that is unexpected, hilarious, moving, groundbreaking, and always engaging. And it's a story that hasn't been told – until now. We're lucky John lived this life, and survived to tell the remarkable tale.

This is the story of John Amero, all the way from porn to primetime.

~ Ashley West, The Rialto Report

PROLOGUE

What am I doing in jail? Not just an ordinary jail, but the notorious "Tombs" in Manhattan. Many dangerous criminals have passed through here, and now me.

If that isn't bad enough, this is my second incarceration. I'm being treated like a common criminal, getting mug shots and fingerprints. My belt and shoelaces have been confiscated as well. It's dark and all I hear are screams from addicts in withdrawal. Sleep will be impossible. I feel an anxiety attack coming on, but they've confiscated my Valium stash.

What have I done to deserve this? I've got to calm down. Try and relax. Go to that Zen place... oh, that's bullshit, that never works. Close your eyes and concentrate on more positive things. But what? I know. Focus on a time and place when you were the happiest.

Slow ripple dissolve to...

CHAPTER 1

THE YOUNG MAN AND THE SEA
(1939-1958)

Gloucester, Massachusetts was a great place to live, and growing up there was wonderful.

By the 1920s, Gloucester was a small but prosperous fishing town. It was popular with the tourists in the summer thanks to a thriving community theater and a lively artist colony. The town had many visitors from New York and Boston which made its residents feel cosmopolitan and sophisticated. The Kennedys may have had nearby Cape Cod, but Gloucester had Cape Ann which locals always called the "other Cape". It was my childhood home and I loved it.

It had large Sicilian and Portuguese populations that had come seeking work in the town's flourishing fishing industry and a better life in America. It also had a lot of Nova Scotians, including my paternal grandfather who arrived in the 1920s when there was a huge influx of fishermen and their families from Canada. Despite this healthy mix of nationalities, the population remained strictly segregated; Italians stayed with Italians, Portuguese stayed with Portuguese, and English stayed with English. These social divisions ran deep, so it was a mystery quite how my parents ever got together as they were from opposite ends of this divide.

My mother, Gladys, came from the English side of the family. She was Protestant, Republican, and a teetotaler. Her mother was well known for having marched down the main street of Gloucester with fellow abstemious townsfolk and taking an ax to the bar rooms where the fishermen gathered. Drinking was a way of life for many in the fishing community, but despite my grandfather being a renowned fishing captain, neither he nor my grandmother ever touched a drop of alcohol.

At the other end of town, my father John Sr., was one of eight children in a family that was Catholic, Democrat, and not averse to alcohol. Socializing, or worse still, fraternizing with someone outside your ethnic group was frowned upon and extremely rare, so the two families were like the Montagues and the Capulets.

As a child I wondered how my taciturn mother wound up married to my garrulous father. To add to my confusion, I couldn't understand why there were no wedding photos anywhere in the house. There were plenty of baby pictures and photos of family and relatives, but nothing from my parent's nuptials.

It wasn't until I was a teenager that the mystery was solved. My maternal grandmother told me that my mother had become pregnant and that my parents felt they had no choice but to "do the right thing" and get married. Slowly the story emerged; they'd hopped across the border to New Hampshire where they could get hitched quickly. This shotgun wedding brought great family shame, especially to someone like my delicate and sensitive mother, who found the experience horrendous. A difficult start to their married life was compounded when Nelson, my parent's first child who was born in 1935, died of a childhood disease only two years later.

Shortly after Nelson's passing in 1937 my brother Lemuel Firth was born, named after my maternal grandfather. I followed soon after in 1939 and was named after my father, John Ellsworth.

Physically my brother and I were at opposite ends of the family spectrum; Lem was blonde, fair, and favored my mother, whereas I was dark and had black curly hair. The family took to calling me "the Portuguee" as I looked like the Portuguese fishermen in town. As the family name ended in a vowel, people would often assume that I was Portuguese or Italian. In reality our name was originally "Amarault" reflecting the family's French-Canadian origins, but the name had been simplified somewhere along the way when the family moved to America.

Life continued to be hard for my parents. Soon after I was born, America entered the war and all the eligible young men in Gloucester enlisted – including my father. He was stationed on a ship near Okinawa and remained there for over three years. I was too young to fully understand his absence but I treasured the regular letters that he wrote to Lem and me telling us to be good boys. When he eventually returned he brought back a bloodstained Japanese flag and two huge empty artillery shells. Or at least we thought they were empty. A few years later Lem and I got bored with the shells and threw them onto our outside firepit where we used to burn trash. The shells exploded violently and blew the cinder blocks in all directions; it's a miracle we weren't killed. So much for my father's World War II souvenirs.

With my father back, Lem and I had our first opportunity to get to know him. He was a strong, handsome man who was a strict disciplinarian. Lem and I responded differently to his stern ways. Once we were sitting at the kitchen table finishing a family meal. My father's rule was that you cleaned your plate or you got no dessert. This was a problem as Lem and I hated vegetables.

THE YOUNG MAN AND THE SEA (1939-1958)

Lem would defiantly say "No, I'm not eating the peas" and my father would yell at him and threaten to take his allowance away. Lem responded by turning and spitting the peas against the wall.

I was more devious. I'd shove the vegetables in my pockets when my father wasn't looking and make an excuse to go to the toilet where I'd flush them away. This strategy wasn't much more successful, as my mother soon became wise to my scheme when she found remnants of mashed up vegetables in my pockets.

Despite his strictness, I adored my father and missed him enormously when he was away fishing. He'd had little schooling and had been going to sea since boyhood. The fact that the fishermen spent long spells away from home meant my mother was left alone to raise the family. She was the smartest and prettiest of three sisters, and was the spitting image of the actress Greer Garson. She was also very fragile and sensitive, and her life wasn't helped by a fearsome set of in-laws, including a domineering mother-in-law.

As for Lem and myself, life was idyllic and the summers were especially magical. We'd visit my mother's parents who had a summer house on the waterfront. For as long as I can remember I loved the ocean. I always had wanderlust and used to sit by the water's edge for hours at a time staring out at the surf. I'd wonder "What's out there?" and then I'd find a map and say "Wow, it's Spain. I'm sitting in Gloucester, but Spain is just across the sea."

There was only one travel magazine when I was a child and it was called "Holiday". It was too expensive for us but I'd seek out used copies and send off for all the free brochures and maps. I'd hang these giveaways on my bedroom wall and pore over them for hours, drawing lines between places like London, Paris, Rome, and Venice.

From an early age I begged my family to let me go to sea but my grandmother always said I was too young and it was too dangerous. Finally my grandfather relented when he felt I was old enough. I was afraid but also excited and desperate not to let my grandfather down. My first concern was that I'd get sea-sick so I didn't eat for the first three days of the trip, thinking "If I don't eat, there will be nothing to come back up."

We stayed out for eight days with a crew of twelve men fishing and talking and joking. I got to sleep in the captain's cubbyhole where I had my own bunk. Humpback whales came right up to the boat. I was fearless, climbing the rigging up to the crow's nest and trying to do everything that the fishermen did. Towards the end of the trip we ran into a tremendous storm and had to dock in Provincetown. As magical as the whole trip had been, it also de-mystified the mariner's life for me and cured me of my desire to become a fisherman.

We lived on a canal and there was a drawbridge that opened up several times a day to let sea traffic through. I'd sit at my window and watch the boats go by, mostly fishing vessels but small local yachts too. The first time an ocean liner sailed into Gloucester Harbor I was awestruck. The stern of these huge ships revealed where they were registered, Bermuda or Nassau – even a European city, and I'd marvel that they had traveled from so far away. In my mind, watching those different ships and trying to figure out where they were going next was like a movie.

But as much as I longed to travel and see the world, I wasn't the type of person desperate to leave their home town. I truly loved Gloucester, and still do.

When we were about eight and six respectively, Lem and I began to notice that our mother would disappear for days at a time. Little was said, but we were never fearful as we'd stay with our maternal grandmother whom we adored. "She's visiting relatives" was sometimes the excuse.

The first time I suspected something was wrong was when my father brought a television set home. He claimed that it was one of the first television sets in town, and the neighbors would all come over to watch shows like "John Cameron Swayze", a short news program, and "Uncle Miltie" on "The Milton Berle Show". The routine when I came home from school was to have dinner and then watch the fuzzy black and white picture on the 10" screen. One evening as we watched TV, my mother walked into the room with some colored cellophane wrapped around her head. She moved the cellophane back and forth in front of her face saying "I'm inventing color television". At first we thought it was funny but she kept repeating it, again and again. After a while, Lem and I exchanged glances and both understood that something was wrong. We didn't find it amusing any more.

For years, nobody told us that the reason for my mother's absences was that she was suffering from mental illness. Later in life I found out that after the death of her first child, my mother had a nervous breakdown and my father had put her in a private sanitarium. This was quite a hardship on a fisherman's income. Each time she came home, and when she did she was the same loving person. But not long after she would mysteriously disappear again. And over time her absences became more and more frequent.

To add to the family's burden, when I was seven Lem and I were both stricken with polio along with hundreds of other Gloucester residents.

THE YOUNG MAN AND THE SEA (1939-1958)

The epidemic occurred during the summer leading the doctors to believe it was transmitted by mosquito bites. Lem and I wound up spending almost a year in the Boston's Children's Hospital. Things were so bad in the beginning that my mother wasn't even allowed to come and visit us; all she could do was call to find out if we were dead or alive.

I had polio in my left leg and right arm, but Lem had it in his lungs so he was placed in a tank respirator – also known as an iron lung – which was terrifying. The prognosis was not good for either of us; but while the doctors thought Lem might not make it at all, they were slightly more optimistic about me – even though they didn't know at the time if I would be permanently disabled. Luckily with time and care, both of us survived – though many of the physical effects of the illness have stayed with me to this day.

Throughout our time in the hospital, my mother seemed to hold up well. It wasn't until we came home, enrolled at school again and everything was back to normal that she had another nervous breakdown. This time she went away and didn't come back for 3 weeks.

Her absence shook my sense of security. One of the immediate effects of the polio was that I couldn't tie my shoe laces. This was something that my mother did for me every morning when I'd get ready for school.

One day Lem said to me "You know, I don't think Mom's going to be here all the time."

I tried to dismiss his prediction, saying "What do you mean? Either she or Gram will always be here". But that night I remember really crying. All I could think was "How will my shoes get tied? And how will I be able to get to school if my mom doesn't tie my shoes? I can't tie my shoes by myself."

Soon after that I was walking to school and one of my shoes came untied. I panicked and ran all the way back to the house. I asked my mother to double knot my shoes because I was so fearful they would come untied again. I still double knot my shoes to this day.

My mother's illness was difficult for all of us including my maternal grandmother. She took care of us when my mother was away and my father was at sea, but she had three older daughters from her husband's first marriage in addition to two daughters of her own. Despite the burden she eventually decided that for our stability she wanted to take us in permanently. She said to my father "The boys should come and live with me because you can't handle them, and because you have a right to a life of your own."

From then on we lived with my grandmother in a wonderful Victorian, three story house with gables. Lem and I adored our grandmother, and living with her gave us a stable home for the first time in our lives.

By this time, my mother had been permanently committed to Danvers State Hospital. My father had opted for a state facility as he couldn't afford to keep her in private sanitariums anymore. Danvers was one of the classic 1940s snake-pit hospitals with corridors of people screaming and carrying on. At first Lem and I weren't allowed to visit. Mother would occasionally come home on weekends, and outwardly she appeared fine. But she started living in the past and seemed unable to look forward. It was good to have her home because she adored us, but at the same time it was awkward because the conversation was so stilted.

As time passed we grew old enough to go to the hospital to visit her. We went on Sundays for visitor's day. We weren't allowed to go into the hospital because it was too noisy so she would come and sit in the car with us. Lem and I would bring chocolates and listen from the back seat while my parents talked. The conversations were often painful. My mother would repeatedly beg my father to have her electroshock treatments stopped. I didn't even know what this was but I could see that it terrified her.

The visits continued every Sunday during my teenage years. The rides home afterwards were particularly depressing. My father would take us for ice cream and try his best to cheer us up, but after a while I started dreading the trips.

By the time I was in my teens it was rare that my mother was even allowed home for the weekend. On one such occasion my grandmother was having friends from the Gloucester Woman's Club over for tea. She told my mother to stay in her room which normally wasn't a problem because my mother didn't like to be around strangers. But on this day, when my grandmother brought some of the ladies into the kitchen, they found my mother. She was dressed in an evening gown, down on her hands and knees with her head stuck in the oven – and all the gas jets were turned on. Without missing a beat my grandmother said "That's alright Gladys, you don't have to clean the oven today" and she went over and turned off the jets. I had such respect and admiration for my grandmother's handling of the situation, but great sadness for my poor mother's condition.

Throughout these years, I had no real idea of what my mother was going through. She never opened up to anyone. Her strict Protestant upbringing discouraged unburdening feelings to anyone else. Many years later I talked to doctors at the hospital and they said "It's the patients that come in kicking and screaming that get out of here the quickest. Sadly your mother came in totally passive."

She spent the rest of her life in that mental hospital.

THE YOUNG MAN AND THE SEA (1939-1958)

So in 1951, my father went to Reno, Nevada, and spent six weeks there to qualify for a divorce, thus ending a marriage that seemed destined for tragedy.

Lem and I knew that Dad had been dating. So we weren't too surprised when one Saturday evening he arrived at my grandmother's house for our weekly visit with his new girlfriend. Her name was Hilda Thome and she was petite, Portuguese and very friendly. Naturally we resented her right away. She was the "other woman", replacing our mother. But we tried to be polite and on our best behavior. My father married Hilda shortly after, and my half-sister Joan was born the following year.

I was a strange mix for a teenage kid. I was a rough-and-tumble, outdoors type and yet I had an unbridled passion for movies. I probably spent too much time at the cinema, but film was always a reliable escape and a safe place to be. I loved the feel and smell of theaters. There were two theaters in Gloucester – the Strand and the North Shore. I practically lived in both of them, going to every change of show, which happened twice a week.

I loved happy endings, but I also liked movies that I probably shouldn't have been seeing at my age. All films in the late 1940s and early 1950s were "G" rated, meaning anyone could see them. These included violent crime dramas, and Joan Crawford and Bette Davis films with mature themes such as adultery and divorce.

Most of all I loved musicals, especially the grand MGM spectacles of the day produced by Arthur Freed. When 3D films and CinemaScope were introduced in the early 1950s, I was beside myself with excitement.

Early on I realized that I had an interest in film aesthetics and mechanics in a way few kids my age did. The first time I saw a producer credit on screen I thought, 'If being a film producer means getting it all together and making it happen, I can do that." I was aware of the editing from an early age too, as well as the styles of different directors. I was fascinated with back lot sets; I first thought they were real locations but Lem said "No, that film is just shot on a lot, it's all phony." With our problems at home, I loved the idea that someone could create a place where nothing could go wrong.

It became impossible to keep me away from the movie houses. Once when I was grounded for a day, I said to my father "At least can you give me some money to buy comic books?"

He gave me two dimes, enough for two comics. It was also enough to cover the 16 cent children's ticket price. My father went out and as soon as he left, I set off to see "Singin' in the Rain" (1952) at the Strand Theater. It was a packed house and the movie had already started, so I took the first open seat

I could find in the dark. I was spellbound watching Gene Kelly and totally oblivious to everything around me. It wasn't until the lights went up at the end that I realized I was sitting next to my father. He was furious, and took away my allowance for a month.

I would go to the movies on my own, but often went with Lem too. He and I were close, but as with all brothers there was a strong sibling rivalry, and we fought and teased each other frequently. I was terrified of electricity so Lem was always trying to get me to stick my finger in a socket so he could turn on the switch. I'd retaliate, once shooting a bow and arrow at him that nearly took his eye out.

He didn't like me hanging around him and his friends. I was a younger snotty kid to him, and he considered himself to be much more sophisticated. He was also far more artistic than I was. He painted from a very early age and learned to play the piano, something I could never hope to do because of the polio.

But Lem was also bullied at school, perhaps because he was fair and didn't look like the other kids. I on the other hand could always take care of myself. Even though I had polio I would beat the crap out of anybody that gave me a hard time. Our high school had compulsory ROTC (Regimental Officers Training Corps) so every Tuesday and Thursday I wore my Eisenhower jacket while military men showed us how to take apart an M1 rifle. I did all the drills and the marching, but the polio meant that I was the only boy in the platoon who wasn't able to carry a gun. That said I made sure I could take apart the trigger housing group as well as anyone.

Polio also made me somewhat self-conscious. I knew people would realize something was wrong when I shook their hands so I became the master of avoiding this. I would create a diversion when I met people, such as commenting on their clothing to move the conversation along. I got good enough at this tactic that most people never realized I didn't shake hands with them. To this day I am still self-conscious upon meeting someone new.

Despite my awkwardness and the fact that I was an average student, I liked high school. I was head of the debating team and also of the drama club. I played the lead in many of the school plays. One year I organized a production of The Glass Menagerie as it had never been done in the school. I took the lead role despite my dreadful southern accent.

Lem loved the theater too and was also part of the drama club. But he was more interested in art direction and was always building and painting scenery or designing lights. I had a grudging admiration for him because he was so independent even when he was young.

THE YOUNG MAN AND THE SEA (1939-1958)

Lem refused to go to church even though everyone was expected to attend and join the parish. I was an obedient Methodist but fascinated by the ornate trappings of Catholicism, especially compared to the cold barrenness of the Protestant church. I loved the depictions of the Virgin Mary, the gold, the gilt, and the smoke.

I also enjoyed singing hymns. I found out from my Episcopalian friends that their choir paid $5, so I devised a scheme to run down to their church after our choir practice. I had to change out of my robes on the way, but I could just about fit both sessions in. It all ended when my grandmother found out; she was appalled and forbade me from doing it again.

I was popular in school, and as a result my social life was happy. In the summer, friends and I would go to the beach at night where we'd have beer parties around bonfires. My grandmother was so anti-alcohol that at first I felt I was doing something very wrong. I was told not to touch a drop, so when I had my first drink I was terrified that the heavens would open and I'd be struck by a bolt of lightning. I was also afraid that my grandparents would smell the alcohol on my breath, so after every party I'd stick my finger down my throat and throw up in the bird-bath in our front yard. Why I didn't do this out in the nearby woods remains a mystery to me. The morning after I'd wake up with a horrible hangover, run out before anybody came out of the house, and flush the bird-bath with fresh water. It was quite the post-party ritual.

In the summer of 1955 when I turned 16, I got my first real job at a wonderful 1920's resort in Gloucester called the Rockaway Hotel. People would spend the entire season there. Wealthy ladies and gentlemen would arrive in elegant cars, unpack their belongings, and spend their days sitting on the verandas rocking back and forth. The properties faced the ocean and were made completely of wood, including the fire escapes. Not surprisingly, they later all burned down.

Despite my young age, I got a job as a dishwasher. The woman who hired me said "All my staff is from Duke University so they're older than you, but I think you'll fit in." I took that as a compliment.

The employees all lived at the hotel; the men were housed in one section separate from the waitresses. I was thrilled to be away from home and on my own. I worked hard and got along well with everyone. In the evenings there were the usual beach parties with plenty to drink. At one of these parties, a waitress chased me around the sand dunes and got me flat on my back whereupon she mounted me. I was so terrified I didn't say anything but I was excited too. In fact I was so aroused by her riding atop me that I came. I was convinced that she never knew, though with hindsight I'm sure she probably did. I felt as though I'd achieved some sort of milestone.

Soon afterwards my sexual education continued. Despite the hotel being on the ocean, it was a few miles from the beach so there was a driver named Gordon who would drive guests back and forth in an old, fishtail Cadillac. I'd noticed him because he was good-looking and beautifully dressed in a classic, movie-like 1940s chauffeur outfit with cap. As a member of staff, I had to walk to and from the beach but one day when I was walking back Gordon stopped and offered me a ride. I was grateful though I felt strange getting into his Cadillac in my swim trunks and t-shirt.

As we were driving back he asked me if I was from Gloucester.

I said "Oh yeah, I've lived here all my life", and he said "Well I'm from Beverly, Mass" which is a few towns up the coast.

He said "I bet I know a spot you've never seen," and I replied "I doubt it" because I knew the area like the back of my hand.

He asked "Would you like to see it? It's really spectacular."

I answered yes and we drove awhile on a deserted road that suddenly opened out onto a spectacular peak overlooking the harbor. We sat there in silence admiring the view, until he asked me "Would you like a blow-job?"

I was dumb-struck. And I was shaking with cold as the sun had gone down and I was still in my wet trunks. So at first I just sat there and didn't say anything.

Then after a few moments I muttered "Okay."

I sat stone still and did nothing, absolutely nothing. I climaxed in a minute. Then he said something that I've never forgotten.

"You know kid... you're gonna have trouble pleasing the ladies later on in life."

I had no idea what he meant so I asked him. It had already been such a traumatic experience and this left me even more confused.

He just said "You'll find out one day."

Prior to this, and to my recent encounter with the waitress, my only sexual experience had been sitting around a campfire with a bunch of friends doing circle-jerks. The object had been to ejaculate into the flames as quickly as you could, and whoever came first got a beer. I always wanted to win the prize and the admiration of my friends. I thought sex was about getting off as fast as you could. I'd heard stories about people who took forever – they were figures of fun.

THE YOUNG MAN AND THE SEA (1939-1958)

The ride home with Gordon was one of the most uncomfortable experiences of my young life. Neither of us said a word. A wave of depression and guilt swept over me; it was the first time I had felt real sadness.

I thought "This guy is queer, does that mean that I'm queer?"

But then I thought "Wait, I didn't do anything...so no, I'm not queer. In fact how dare he?" And then I became incensed. But still I said nothing, and he said nothing.

I thought about the incident all night. I couldn't sleep. I kept repeating "Am I queer? I think I'm queer. But how can I be queer if I didn't do anything?"

The next day I was determined to confront Gordon. I found him out in the yard of the hotel and said "Listen Gordon, I'm not queer. And I want you to know this is never gonna happen again. You had no right to do this. I don't know what your problem is, but it isn't my problem."

I went on and on, and he just stood there with a smile on his face, saying nothing. I finished by saying "Don't speak to me again, and don't offer me a ride if I'm ever on the road."

And that was the end of my relationship with Gordon, the handsome chauffeur. Or at least I thought it was at the time.

During my sophomore year in high school, Dad had me over for the weekly Saturday night franks and beans supper and announced that he, Hilda and baby Joan were leaving Gloucester. Finding no work in town, and not wanting to return to fishing with a new family to support, he had taken a position at Boeing Aircraft in Seattle, Washington.

The ride back to my grandmother's house was a sad, silent ride. As I got out of the car he took my hand and said "Son, we always seem to be saying goodbye."

I would never see him alive again.

While I was working at the Rockaway Hotel as a dishwasher, Lem had a job at Theater Unlimited, a stock company that came to Gloucester every summer from New York. They'd do all the classics like "Pygmalion" and the company was very popular. Lem painted flats and worked on the lighting; it was the lowest of lowly jobs but he loved it. I had a feeling that after high school, Lem would return to New York with the theater company and stay there. And he did, riding all the way in the back of the company's scenery truck.

It was a bold move for him; he didn't know anybody in New York except for a few of the actors in the group. He also had no more than a couple of hundred dollars. But while I was slightly fearful, I was mostly excited for him. I couldn't wait for his letters to hear how he was faring.

He would write detailed accounts of life in the big city. It turned out he loved New York even though he was practically starving. I was sure he was broke so I would send him $5 in a letter whenever I could.

When he could scrape the money together he would go to Radio City Music Hall and for sixty-five cents see both the stage show and movie twice. He wrote that he loved the Music Hall because he felt nothing bad could ever happen to him while he was there.

I lived for his letters and his tales started to inspire me to do something different with my life. Career aspirations always seemed ridiculous to me; lots of women in my family were schoolteachers so up until then I half expected to follow this path. I'd always thought of teaching as a noble profession, especially attractive given the long summer vacations. Now my horizons suddenly seemed broader.

I would visit Lem at Christmas and during spring break, and see as many Broadway shows as I could like "West Side Story" and "My Fair Lady". These experiences made me feel like a true sophisticate as nobody in my high school had done anything like this.

Back in Gloucester I got a job in a bookstore. I became friends with an older lady, Judy Chamberlain, who worked there as well. It turned out that the Chamberlains were one of the most prominent families in town and she lived in a wonderful Edward Hopper-esque house. Despite the age difference between the two of us, I would often stop by her house and spend time with her talking about our mutual love of cinema. Part of the attraction of visiting was also that I loved her house. I dreamt of using it one day as a film set.

I had started dating although it was all very innocent. In the 1950s a girl would only let you go so far; you were never going to get laid. If you unhooked a girl's bra in the backseat of a car, it was a big deal. Nice girls did not put out in 1956 Gloucester. Once in a while we'd hear about a girl who "left town" which usually meant that she'd become pregnant. A girl who became pregnant would never stay in school; she just couldn't. She'd be shunned.

Occasionally I would think back to Gordon, and I continued to have doubts and questions about my feelings. I had friends who talked about queers – the word "gay" had yet to be invented. There was even a kid in my class that people said was queer. I thought 'what's he gonna do? He can't stay in this town because of what people are saying.'

I rarely discussed my feelings, and certainly didn't talk about sex with anyone.

THE YOUNG MAN AND THE SEA (1939-1958)

In my senior year of high school we got a new English teacher named Nancy. English and History were always my favorite subjects, unlike Algebra and Biology which I detested. Nancy was pert and petite, and looked like she wasn't much older than we were. When I stood up in English class and talked about having been to New York and seeing Broadway shows with Rex Harrison and Julie Andrews, I noticed that she was impressed. I liked her immediately.

She soon started driving me home from school, saying it was on her way to Manchester where she lived with her mother. We had long talks about things that you wouldn't think an English teacher and a student would talk about; art, our futures, the meaning of life. She loved theater, film and travel. She'd been to Europe and I was dying to go. I was very comfortable with her and our friendship made me feel very adult. What her feelings were soon came to light.

She introduced me to her mother and started inviting me over to dinner. I had wine for the first time in her home. We fooled around in the backseat of her car but never went all the way. I didn't even know whether I wanted to have sex with her.

At the same time that I was seeing Nancy I was dating Linda, a girl in my class. When it came time for the senior prom, I casually told Nancy that I was going with Linda. There was a deadly pause, and she said "What do you mean you're taking Linda? I assumed that you were going to ask me." I was left momentarily speechless wondering what revenge she might take on my grades. Finally I said "I'm sorry Nancy – but I asked Linda and I'm going with her."

Nancy went straight to the teacher's lounge and burst into tears in front of my history teacher, a very old conservative lady. Nancy then told her the whole story. I thought I would be expelled and that she would be asked to leave the school system. As it turned out, they said nothing to me, but were not so lenient with Nancy. The next year she was not invited back to teach at Gloucester High School.

I was extremely conflicted and felt very guilty. Maybe I had led Nancy on. Out of my emotional turmoil, one aspect became clear. I wanted to live in New York and sort it all out. I said to myself "There's no way I'm going to have a career as a teacher and stay here in Gloucester."

So the day I graduated in 1958, I announced to everyone that I was moving to New York. My grandmother was very supportive and convinced my relatives to help fund my trip. She mustered up a grand total of $200 which was a princely sum for the time.

Two weeks before I left for New York, I checked my 1948 Oldsmobile into the shop for servicing. It was a wreck of a car and needed serious attention before it could handle the journey. While it was there I thumbed rides to get around. One day a guy picked me up and I immediately recognized that it was Gordon. Gordon the handsome chauffeur from four years before. He looked terrific.

I said "Hi Gordon how are you?" and he smiled and said "Hi John, how are you?" We rode in silence for a while and then he asked where I was going. I said "I'm going to New York City." He joked that he wasn't going that far. I said "I don't mean right now – I'm just going to West Gloucester." He said "Well I'm going to my folk's place in Beverly a few towns up" before adding pointedly "They're not home." Then he asked if I'd like to come along for the ride. I knew what he meant. But this time I was less nervous. I was calm, I wasn't shaking. I put my hand on his knee and said "What do you think?" And with that I felt him press down on the accelerator.

CHAPTER 2

WEST SIDE STORY
(1958-1964)

The prospect of moving to Manhattan was exhilarating. The combination of Lem's letters and my own short visits to see him had raised my excitement to feverish levels.

When Lem first moved to New York in 1955, he took up residence in one of the many rooming houses on West End Avenue. Simple and cheap it was the only option considering the small sum the family had collected for his move. He soon got a job at Saks Fifth Avenue fulfilling mail orders for out-of-town shoppers. It wasn't the most exciting job but it did enable Lem to do what would grow to be his lifelong passion – theater production and musicals. Soon after starting work at Saks, Lem joined several of the company's after-hour social groups including the drama and glee clubs. He loved being involved, even reveling in singing Christmas carols in the store lobby which Saks demanded of its employees each year.

He worked 40 hours a week for a dollar an hour, the minimum wage at the time. Promotions and raises eventually allowed him to rent a tiny one bedroom garden apartment for $100 a month, with help from a roommate. Located at 16 West 74th St, it was close to Central Park and just around the corner from the famed Dakota apartment building where John Lennon and Yoko Ono would later live.

Lem was grateful to have his own place but had no money left over to furnish it. So he began to trawl the city streets looking for discarded items. Every piece of furniture, every drape and every decoration in the apartment came from the streets of New York. And thanks to Lem's ability to pick and refurbish second-hand items, his place always looked great.

I left Gloucester for New York in September 1958. Despite the last minute service on my car, I had to accept that the Oldsmobile was a total wreck. But I was determined to drive it to New York because I wanted to take my Hi-Fi system, my collection of 45s and 33s, and all my books. The only problem was that I couldn't put anything in the trunk as it was filled with water containers I needed as the car radiator constantly boiled over.

To make matters worse, I also had to take gallons of oil with me so that I could stop every hour and pour more into the engine. Wherever I went I left a thick smoke screen behind.

Miraculously the car completed the journey to New York. I made it all the way to Amsterdam Avenue – just around the corner from Lem's apartment – where I found a parking space surprisingly quickly. It was at this point I realized that the car wouldn't go into reverse so I had to go all the way around the block and try again. By the time I got back I'd lost the space. Welcome to New York.

I eventually double parked outside of Lem's building, unloaded my possessions and called the first garage I could find: Academy Auto Wreckers in Harlem. They only offered me $25 for the car saying they could only use the battery but I was happy to let it go. I had reached New York City and didn't plan on leaving.

My first few weeks in the city were wonderful. Being reunited with Lem and living with him was every bit as fun as I'd expected it to be. The apartment was a tight squeeze, but after a few months Lem's starving actor roommate moved out leaving just the two of us.

Most exciting of all was having the city at my doorstep. I explored the tourist spots for hours on end. But my favorite place to roam was Times Square largely due to the great movie palaces that were still in operation. There was the lavish Capitol Theater on Broadway, flagship of the deluxe Loews Theater chain where I saw many of my favorite MGM films. The huge Roxy Theater on West 50th Street, known as the "Cathedral of the Motion Pictures". The legendary Paramount Theater, located at 43rd Street and Broadway, famous for its historic swing-era and rock 'n' roll shows. And the palatial Rivoli Theater on Broadway with the enormous curved screen for 70 millimeter films.

Times Square also had a seamier side including a number of sleazy theaters which showed an altogether different type of film. I avoided those theaters like the plague. I was too embarrassed to even go near the marquees. I thought they were disgraceful.

I knew my meager savings wouldn't last long so Lem came to the rescue and found me a position at Saks Fifth Avenue. I was grateful to him but the job only lasted a few weeks because I soon found another, more exciting opportunity. On one of my city walks I'd stumbled upon the offices of CBS at 485 Madison Avenue. The minute I saw the sign outside, I walked straight into the personnel office and applied for a job in the mail room. Much to my surprise I was hired. I told CBS I could start immediately, so I hurried back to Saks to hand in my notice and then rushed home to tell Lem all about it.

WEST SIDE STORY (1958-1964)

I started work at CBS in November 1958 and was walking on air. I couldn't have been more excited about my new job. CBS was at the top of the heap, known as the "Tiffany Network" because of its high quality programming. It was Walter Cronkite, *I Love Lucy*, *Have Gun Will Travel* and *Perry Mason*.

Mine was a lowly mail room job that paid next to nothing but I didn't care. I would rush to work every morning walking all the way from our uptown apartment to the CBS offices in midtown. When I got there I was always full of energy and eager to please. I never took the elevator if I had to go to the 5th floor to deliver mail. I would run up the stairs rather than stand and wait. When my day was done, I would take the largest manila envelope I could find that said CBS on it and carry it under my arm because I was so proud of my new employers.

After six months I got a break. I saw an internal job posting for a film librarian. The position involved cataloging copies of old syndicated TV shows and movies that were shipped in and out. It wasn't much, but it was a promotion and it gave me the chance to have physical contact with actual copies of films for the first time in my life. I applied straight away and got the job.

When I first arrived in the city, co-workers and people I didn't know well assumed I was straight, and I never felt the need to correct them. But I was comfortable with my friends knowing. I was more at ease in New York City than my home town, making me more confident about everything, including my sexuality.

When I was growing up the only time I heard about someone being homosexual was when stories were shared about my Uncle Bobby. Whenever his name came up, family members talked about him in hushed tones. Lem and I were told that he ran a notorious bar in Boston and that we were forbidden from ever going there. Not that there was much risk of that as we rarely went into Boston and wouldn't have been allowed into any bar because we were underage.

Later on I found out that Bobby owned the Napoleon Club, the most famous gay bar in Boston. Apparently he was in constant fear of his mother finding out that he was gay so he lived two different lives, one in Gloucester and one in Boston. The message was clear; being gay was something the family frowned upon and never spoke about openly so I kept my feelings to myself.

When I moved in with Lem, I soon noticed that he never introduced me to his friends. This was strange because we were otherwise inseparable and he took me everywhere, showing me all the sites. But whenever he'd go out at night, I was never invited to join him.

I thought "It's clear that Lem thinks of me as a country bumpkin, the younger brother, the rube" so I'd stay at home or head off to the movies by myself. One night however, I struck up the courage to go to a bar. I walked up Columbus Avenue to West 74th Street looking for a place where I could have a quiet drink. I found a pub called the Park West and went in.

It didn't take me long to realize I'd walked into a gay bar, probably the only one on the whole of the Upper West Side at the time. The interior was dimly lit, full of men and garishly decorated. The walls were painted pink and covered with gaudy paintings of mostly naked Roman gladiators. My heart started pounding and my immediate reaction was to flee.

But I saw an empty seat at the near end of the bar and so tentatively sat down and ordered a beer. The bartender asked me if I wanted a glass. I declined simply because my hand was trembling so much I knew I'd never be able to pick it up properly.

I steadied the bottle with both hands and looked around in trepidation. There were all sorts of strange looking men, and no one seemed to be talking to each other.

I thought "All of these men look like effeminate queens, and I don't like any of them. If this is what being gay in New York is all about, I'm going to have a problem. I know I don't want this." I resolved to drink up quickly and leave but as my eyes became accustomed to the dark, I picked out a figure sitting at the other end of the bar.

It was Lem.

He was with another man and hadn't seen me so I considered leaving. But then a feeling of relief washed over me. I ordered another beer and walked over to where he was sitting.

I tapped him on the shoulder and said "Hi, fancy meeting you here" trying to act casual. He turned and the look on his face showed just how shocked he was. Fortunately the two of us managed to keep up the pretense of a normal conversation.

When we got back to the apartment, neither Lem nor I said anything about our shared discovery. True to our New England, stiff upper lip upbringing, our accidental meeting was never mentioned again. But from that day on we started going to bars together, and Lem began introducing me to his friends.

Back at CBS, I was promoted again. This time I was made Assistant Film Editor and instead of cataloging old syndicated shows, I was now responsible for adding commercials into shows that were sent out to regional television stations. This was a cash generator for CBS who would sell episodes of programs like *Perry Mason* to secondary stations after they had premiered on the network. The regional stations would get the shows at a considerable discount, while CBS earned additional money for old programming that it had already aired.

It was strictly on-the-job training in arduous work because it involved 16mm film which was smaller and more difficult to handle than 35mm. I had to splice four or five commercials into each show. With two breaks per thirty minute program that meant a lot of commercials. How anybody sat through all those ads was beyond me.

In my new job I got to meet respected CBS figures such as Arthur Godfrey and Ed Sullivan. But my real idol was Walter Cronkite.

Cronkite was treated like God in the CBS office. There was an unwritten law that if he got into your elevator car you were required to step out and allow the elevator operator to take Walter directly up to the news floor. I fell afoul of this rule one morning when I arrived at work and bounded into the nearest elevator, jokingly instructing the operator to get moving and take me to my floor quickly. He glared at me and muttered "Get out" under his breath. When I turned around I saw I was standing in front of the venerable Mr. Cronkite. I got out of the elevator quickly. I'd been told people had been fired for much less.

Another larger-than-life figure was Edward R. Murrow who was still doing his radio show when I arrived. One day my boss asked me if I had a pair of black sneakers that I could bring in to work. At that time everyone had to wear a suit and tie to the office, so the next day I turned up wearing my usual black suit – the only suit I owned – and a new pair of black sneakers.

My job for the week was to take teletypes that had just come in from news wires around the world and silently place them in front of Murrow while he was live on air. When I slipped him the teletypes, he'd look at them while he was broadcasting live and decide whether they were noteworthy or not. He would quietly push away the teletypes he rejected, or beautifully incorporate those he selected without missing a beat.

By now I'd started to feel established in New York, my days in Gloucester becoming a distant memory. Then out of the blue I got a call from my former English teacher and paramour, Nancy.

We hadn't been in touch since the discovery of our relationship had caused her to lose her teaching job. On the call she shared that as a result of the scandal, she'd left Gloucester and was now teaching in White Plains, just 25 miles north of Manhattan. Even more surprising was the revelation that she'd moved into an apartment just the other side of Central Park on East 62nd Street and commuted every day to her job.

Hearing her voice brought back a familiar feeling of unease but after a long conversation and much persuading on her part, I eventually agreed to see her. We decided to meet on the East Side at a restaurant called "L'Auberge".

I was nervous about the meeting, and even more concerned about the fact that we were living in the same city again. But despite my fears the meeting went well and, after we'd caught up and drank vast amounts of wine, we agreed to meet again.

Over the next few months we saw each other more and more frequently and always had a good time. She introduced me to the nightclub scene in New York, and wonderful performers like the cabaret singer and pianist, Bobby Short. We'd take long walks through Central Park, then go to the East Side jazz clubs. She lived on the same street as Montgomery Clift, who we saw regularly at the Isle of Capri restaurant where we frequently dined.

I couldn't deny that I enjoyed her company and loved all the activities we did together. I also felt a certain attraction to her and found myself wanting to please her. I wasn't seeing anyone else so before long an affair started up again. This time however, it felt noticeably different; I knew it wasn't what I wanted and it just didn't feel comfortable. To make matters worse, it was clear that Nancy wanted a lot more than I was willing to give. She started talking about getting an apartment together and the wonderful future we could have.

In high school, Nancy had been aware of the doubts I'd had about my sexual orientation but was convinced that I just hadn't met the right woman. She thought a totally satisfying sexual affair was all I needed and was determined that it was going to be with her. The film *Tea and Sympathy* (1956) with Deborah Kerr had recently been released, and Nancy clearly felt a kinship with a "teacher saving a student from a fate worse than death."

As was the case back in Gloucester I started to feel trapped. To make matters worse I didn't feel I could discuss the situation with anyone. In particular I didn't dare tell my brother.

I finally decided that I had to take control and end the relationship for both our sakes. I knew it wasn't going to be pretty. I couldn't think of a way to avoid hurting this person for whom I had so much respect, but I knew

WEST SIDE STORY (1958-1964)

it had to end. I was living a lie. But I couldn't come out and say "Nancy, I'm queer." I just couldn't bring myself to admit this to her, or indeed to anyone. I needed to find a sensitive way to let her down.

One night we were having sex in her apartment living room when her roommate walked in on us. It was like an adult version of a Marx Brothers scene. We both fumbled for our clothes and in the midst of all the chaos, I realized I couldn't find the condom. The roommate, who'd clearly had a few drinks, sat down on the couch and proceeded to talk to us as if nothing unusual had happened. After a few minutes of awkward conversation, I looked down and saw the condom on the sofa between the three of us.

After the roommate left the room, I decided to seize the moment, thinking things could hardly get worse. I said "Nancy, I can't continue this relationship, I just can't. But I consider you a dear friend and I care about you."

As expected, it got ugly. She lost her temper and started screaming hysterically. When she eventually calmed down, she cried "John, I don't believe you. You just don't fuck your friends."

I got dressed quickly and made my way out onto the street where we continued to shout at each other. I finally broke away and with snow falling, walked all the way home. I don't think I'd ever been so upset. Up until that point in my life, I didn't realize I could cause someone that much pain and anguish. I was so distraught I blurted out the whole story of the affair to my brother. He lectured me severely, and said "John, you are what you are. You cannot change it, so don't get involved sexually with any more straight women or men."

It was the first time we'd talked about relationships and sex. I was grateful for Lem's words which consoled me and made me feel closer to him.

After that night, I never saw Nancy again. Years later I looked her up and found that she'd married and moved away from New York shortly after our friendship ended. She remained a teacher until she retired and passed away in 2008.

By early 1961, I started to feel restless at CBS. Being surrounded by film all the time had stimulated my desire to become a filmmaker, but opportunities to join the creative teams never came anywhere near my department.

Christmas was coming up and Lem and I always went home to be with the family. Needing extra money for gifts and travel to Gloucester,

I took a part time job at Macy's. The Thanksgiving Day parade was coming up and employees could volunteer to be in it. That sounded exciting and would give the relatives in Gloucester an opportunity to see me on TV. I showed up at 5AM on Central Park West where the parade started, not too far from our apartment. What they neglected to tell me was that I would be carrying a heavy sign that said: "DOLORES GRAY STARRING ON BROADWAY IN THE HIT MUSICAL DESTRY RIDES AGAIN".

Miss Gray was going to be riding a horse with me walking in front of her all the way to 34th Street. She arrived very late and was not a happy woman. I attempted to say good morning, but she ignored me and started yelling "I've got the hangover of death and THIS is the fucking nag they expect me to ride!" I found her rant in questionable taste as small children were standing close by and their parents did not look amused. Annie Oakley she was not.

This was only the beginning of a three-hour nightmare. The horse kept bolting forward and while I was supposed to stay just five feet in front of her, I kept running out of the way to avoid being trampled to death. She cursed me, the horse, her agent, and her co-star Andy Griffith for talking her into doing the event. I heard her shout "If this gun had real bullets I'd shoot this motherfucking horse!"

I knew the cameras were at 59th and Broadway and was determined not to be made a fool of on live TV. The horse bolted forward again but I held my ground and kept smiling. The poor horse's head was practically resting on my shoulder at this point, but I didn't care anymore. We passed the cameras and the family in Gloucester thought it was all part of the act.

I chose to skip Miss Gray's Broadway show.

In early 1962, I heard through the grapevine that ABC TV on West 56th Street was hiring program editors to work on current ABC programs.

On the face of it, a move to ABC was a step down from my role at CBS, the MGM of television networks. ABC had a largely unimpressive roster of shows, the only exceptions being *The Donna Reed Show* and *Naked City*, a wonderful detective series shot around New York.

Program editors were the lowest level of film editors at ABC and were put to work in musty rooms with ancient equipment. At CBS you'd have your own editing suite with access to a personal assistant; at ABC four editors were jammed into a room of their office building on trashy 56th Street and 10th Avenue.

WEST SIDE STORY (1958-1964)

But as much as I loved CBS I didn't feel I was getting anywhere film-wise. I wanted to learn more about film editing and it just wasn't happening, so I bit the bullet and took the position at ABC.

My initial job was working on the first Sunday night color telecast of a feature film, the Michael Curtiz western *The Comancheros* starring John Wayne. I enjoyed the job immediately because it was hands on and I was actually getting to work with 35mm film. I was tasked with deciding where to insert commercials and then to physically add them into the film. This included creating all the false fades and dissolves that allowed the film and commercials to gradually transition into each other. My work went over well and I received a letter from my boss congratulating me on helping make the first color telecast a great success.

While I was proud of the job I'd done, I also felt guilty for tampering with the work of a great director. We were essentially butchering the film for content, time, and other spurious reasons. This guilt stayed with me on every similar job thereafter. I even found myself hoping that the directors were deceased when their films aired on television as I was sure they'd be mortified to see what we did to their work.

Soon after I started at ABC, I got a long distance phone call from Gloucester. It was my uncle telling me that Dad had died of a massive heart attack at the age of 51. To compound this tragedy, his wife Hilda was nine months pregnant with their second child. His body was being returned to Gloucester from Seattle.

Lem and I drove to Massachusetts and spent three depressing days at the funeral home greeting friends and relatives of Dad's. Hilda returned a few weeks later. With her were my half-sister Joan, and her newly born son, Jeff. Devastated, Hilda moved back in with her family until she could restart her life.

As for how Lem and I felt, we were shocked and surprised. But we had been separated from our father for quite a while at this point. We had just started getting to know each other as adults when he left for Seattle. So we loved him but in reality he just wasn't a big part of our lives.

One thing that does stick out in my mind from those few days in Gloucester was the priest who attended the funeral. When Lem and I arrived he quickly approached us to introduce himself. He took my hand and told me that if I was ever in need, I should stop by the parish.

A few hours later, Lem pointed out that the priest seemed to be paying me quite a bit of attention. Brushing off his comment, I headed into the back room for a drink. Shortly after the priest followed and practically cornered me. Once again he took my hands in his and shared a number of platitudes. When he finally let go, I noticed that I was left holding a business card. The priest let me know that this was his private number and I could reach him any time I needed.

Needless to say, I did not take advantage of the priest's offer at my father's funeral.

A few weeks into my job with ABC, I was assigned to add commercials into reruns of *Naked City* that were being readied for distribution. One Friday night after we finished editing, I noticed that a large number of prints hadn't been dispatched.

I went to the shipping department ready to read the Riot Act to the staff and was met by an awkward, gangly young man. He was tall and was wearing a shirt much too small for his 6' 2" frame. He was just standing there looking unhappy. I confronted him about the shipping problem and he anxiously replied "This is only my first day. I'm sorry but I really don't know anything."

After I finished venting to some of the more experienced staff members, I noticed that the new employee was still standing there. He looked like he was about to have a nervous breakdown. Out of a combination of pity and curiosity, I introduced myself, and he told me his name was Mike Findlay.

I invited him for a drink after work and though he was painfully shy, we hit it off right away. It was clear that he had an enormous knowledge and passion for movies so we talked endlessly about films.

He spoke about Orson Welles and Fritz Lang, and I kept thinking "Why on earth is this guy working in the shipping room?" before remembering that I too had started out in a similar way.

Mike and I became fast friends. We started taking our lunch breaks together and meeting frequently after work at the Crossroads Bar on 57th Street. We'd regale each other with stories about our favorite films, actors, and scenes. I quickly realized that while we both enjoyed many of the same films, I liked the full spectacle of the movies, whereas Mike was often more interested in the racier elements. He told me he'd once skipped school when Rita Hayworth's *Salome* (1953) played at the Roxy Theater – he hoped, in vain, that he'd see a flash of nudity.

We soon moved our film discussions to a wonderful Greenwich Village bar called Emilio's that Mike, a born-and-bred New Yorker, turned me on to. As I got to know Mike better, it became clear that his strange

WEST SIDE STORY (1958-1964)

demeanor the day I met him was not unusual. He was wildly neurotic by nature and full of Catholic guilt and repressed sexual feelings – all of which was tempered by regular doses of Valium. But there was something about him that I found endearing and fascinating.

While I was toiling at ABC, Lem left Saks Fifth Avenue and started working as a stage manager at a classic nightclub on 46th St called the Bal Tabarin. It was the last of the 1940s Jimmy Cagney-style nightclubs where for $7.95 in 1961 you got dinner, dancing, a comic and showgirls. Each of the showgirls was dating a sugar daddy, and judging by the Damon Runyon-esque characters around the stage, the club was entirely run by the mob. Bob Fosse had been the in-house choreographer there early in his career and the quality of entertainment continued to be reasonably high.

I loved the Bal and when I wasn't out talking film with Mike, I'd visit my brother at work. Lem was doing everything; he was running the lighting, changing the scenery, and organizing the performers backstage. He was a one-man-band, and the gangster owners loved him. They particularly appreciated his skill of being able make something out of nothing. If they gave him a budget of $150 for lighting design, they were always impressed by what he was able to produce. He would beg, borrow and steal to try and make the Bal's production design rival that of A-list clubs like the Copacabana and the Latin Quarter.

The Theater was Lem's love, and every dime he made was spent going to Broadway shows. His work was deeply satisfying for him, and something that he excelled at. He wasn't interested as much in films, but I certainly was. As soon as I managed to save a couple of hundred dollars, I purchased a 16mm Bolex camera. It was a wonderful piece of equipment with turret lenses. I was proud of it and looked for every opportunity to use it.

I filmed and edited sequences of the theater marquees at night and sent them back to my family in Gloucester. Of course I always made sure to avoid any shots of the trashy theaters on 42nd Street.

One of the most exciting moments in my early years in the city was discovering that the subway actually went to the ocean. Until then I guess I'd never looked at a subway map – I just went to Times Square and to work. Then one day Lem said "We're going to the beach" and took me to the subway. I thought he was joking but the train emerged from the underground onto the elevated track in Brooklyn and went all the way to

Coney Island. We spent a wonderful day exploring Steeplechase Park just a few years before it was sadly torn down.

I still loved the ocean and hadn't lost my childhood passion for ships of all kinds. I'd read *A Night to Remember* by Walter Lord about the sinking of the Titanic and it mentioned that ocean liners would come all the way up the Hudson River to 50th Street in Manhattan. So in between days editing at ABC, I'd head over to the docks to look out for these great vessels.

By donating 50 cents to the Seaman's Fund you could actually board some of the liners that passed through New York. It was a dream come true for me. On board I would crash "Bon Voyage" parties where I'd mingle and pretend to know people, sipping champagne with an air of authority in my suit and tie straight from work. To this day my wanderlust and love for ocean liners and the sea remain as strong as ever.

My friendship with Mike Findlay continued to grow. His initial diffidence had somewhat receded and he started to open up to me more and more. While our conversations still centered largely on films, we began to talk about work, our families and our personal lives too. I think he assumed I was straight but we never discussed it and no questions were asked.

After knowing Mike for six months, he surprised me by sharing that he'd been dating a girl named Roberta. I was finally introduced to her several weeks later when the three of us went for dinner at Romeo's Spaghetti House on Broadway.

Roberta was several years younger than Mike and attending the City College of New York. She was a child-like girl from the Bronx, who giggled constantly when spoken to, and shyly clung to Mike. They were the only couple I knew who always walked together hand-in-hand or linking arms. Roberta was petite, and hidden underneath the frumpy clothes she always wore she had a great figure. Mike, by his own admission, was obsessed with women's breasts and so his attraction to her was obvious.

Together they were a sight; when they walked down the street hand-in-hand, people looked askance at this lumbering, lanky man and his tiny girlfriend with wild hair invariably carrying a pile of schoolbooks.

They were totally devoted to each other. Their infatuation however was not shared by Roberta's Jewish family who were perturbed at their young girl cavorting with an older, odd Catholic man. Roberta claimed that her father threatened to kill her if she got married at such a young age. But despite her father's threats, Roberta and Mike wed and moved into a ground floor studio apartment on 2nd Avenue in the East Village.

WEST SIDE STORY (1958-1964)

Roberta had dreams of becoming a concert pianist, so they had a baby grand piano even though it took up half of their living area. When I'd go over to see Mike during the summer, it would be stifling hot in their apartment. Roberta would invariably be sitting at the piano in her underwear, a cigarette dangling from her lips. She endlessly played selections from a Schumann piano concerto she hoped to perform with the New Jersey Symphony Orchestra. Roberta had no interest in our film talk whatsoever. Piano playing was her thing.

Mike and Roberta clung to each other emotionally as well as physically. Both had anxious personalities and were terrified of many things, from the seemingly small and inconsequential to larger world affairs. For example, even though every building in New York had roaches, if they saw one in their apartment they would run out, call me from a payphone and not return until I had come over and disposed of it. At the other extreme they were petrified at the prospect of a nuclear attack. During the Bay of Pigs crisis in 1961 they were so paranoid that New York was vulnerable to attack that they left the city and decamped to a New Jersey motel room across the river.

Mike was seeing a therapist at the time and I think Roberta probably was too. He suffered from frequent and severe anxiety attacks. I was with him once when he suddenly had a desire to drive the car we were in off the Verrazano Bridge. It was terrifying but I somehow convinced him to continue to the other side where I took over driving responsibilities.

But whatever their idiosyncrasies, I liked them both enormously and always looked forward to spending time with them. We'd go for drinks most nights after work and Mike and I would talk about becoming real filmmakers one day.

By 1963, I'd become head of the Program Department Editors at ABC. I supervised a team of six doing the work I'd done in my previous job – splicing commercials into shows being sent out across the country. The commercials would change for each regional market so we had to look at the same shows over and over.

All half hour sitcoms consisted of three ten-minute rolls of 16mm film. One of my new responsibilities was to order the prints from Pathé film lab. My team would receive hundreds of rolls of film on Thursdays, then quickly cut in commercials so the shows would be ready to ship on Friday afternoon.

The work was usually mundane but wasn't without its occasional drama. One week, instead of receiving prints of three different 10 minute rolls of film for each episode, the lab sent back two identical copies of the second roll and no third roll. In short I had parts 1 and 2, but instead of part 3 I had extra prints of part 2.

I immediately called the lab to berate them for their oversight and demand that they correct the mistake right away. But the lab boss said it wouldn't be possible, claiming that all his workers had just walked out on strike.

I knew I had to do something quickly. I looked up details of the show in question. It was an episode of *The Donna Reed Show* that had Donna trying to conceal the purchase of a refrigerator from her husband. Her shows were so similar that I immediately thought of another episode about her doing the same thing with a mink coat. I hatched a plan. I would pull the third reel of the mink coat episode and send it out in place of the third reel of the refrigerator show. My editing team wasn't keen on my idea and refused to consider it on the basis that the plot of the episode would make no sense. This was a reasonable viewpoint but what other option did we have?

I stood my ground knowing that ABC would lose tens of thousands of dollars if we didn't find a solution. I pleaded with the team saying that very few people watched these shows. My argument was that the program was on late at night, and thus the audience would likely be too tired or drunk to notice that the episode started with a refrigerator and ended with a mink coat. The editors continued to push back fearing union repercussions but I'd made up my mind, so we shipped 200 prints of the show and miraculously made all the play-dates.

The following day when I arrived at work my boss called me into his office. Apparently one person had contacted ABC to complain. Just one person in all the markets we had shipped to had called in to complain about the massacre of this supposed work of art.

That person? Donna Reed.

Apparently she'd been watching the show in the comfort of her Hollywood home and was livid. She phoned my boss again while I was in his office and could hear her screaming "I'm an artist and an Academy Award winner. How dare someone do this?! I demand this man be fired."

My boss replied "Miss Reed, you're absolutely right" and while she was still on the phone, he told me I was fired.

I asked if I could explain to Miss Reed why I'd taken this course of action but she was not interested in excuses. When he finally hung up the phone I told my boss the whole story. After listening carefully he said "OK

WEST SIDE STORY (1958-1964)

John, you're not fired, but if Donna Reed ever comes to New York, do us all a favor and make yourself scarce."

Ironically that same year, the Academy of Television Arts and Sciences asked me to become a voting member for the annual Emmy awards. I gladly accepted and although members had to spend long days viewing hundreds of shows, the knowledge that there was one show I would never vote for gave me great personal satisfaction.

Whenever Mike and I discussed making our own films, our ambitions differed in one crucial way. While I wanted to make a big budget Hollywood motion picture, Mike was keen on directing an independent feature. What's more, he was convinced that the best way to get started in the business was to make a exploitation film. I was horrified at this idea. I had barely heard of exploitation pictures but knew he was referring to the kind of sleazy movies that played in the Times Square theaters I meticulously avoided.

Mike often went to see exploitation films – in part because he loved seeing films, but also because he found the subject matter titillating. He became familiar with the plots, themes and featured actors and started investigating how the films were made and sold. These films were typically independently produced, low-budget films that had little artistic merit. They were merely vehicles for sexual situations and gratuitous nudity that found an appreciative male audience desperate for risqué content. And they were seemingly very profitable. The films were shown at Times Square "grind houses", named either because the cinemas would "grind" these films out round the clock, or because they had once been burlesque theaters where "bump n' grind" striptease was featured.

Mike began regularly asking me what I thought about making a exploitation film with him but I always said "No way" immediately. Over time however, his arguments began to sound more convincing. He'd say "It's a great way to break into the business because these films are very inexpensive to make. I've seen a lot of them, they're not very good, and I know we could do better."

Eventually Mike turned his attention to just getting me to see a exploitation film with him. For someone who was embarrassed to stand under the marquees, I was naturally reluctant to venture into such sleazy theaters. But his insistence finally paid off.

We decided to see Joe Sarno's *Sin in the Suburbs* (1964) playing at the Rialto Theater. The film was luridly advertised outside the cinema with the tag line "The Sensation Clubs! Partners in Pleasure! Wild Bottle Parties!" I found this promotion distasteful but was impressed to learn that the film had been playing at the Rialto for ten weeks. I figured that such a long run meant that it must be making serious money.

Mike and I went to see it alone leaving Roberta to her piano practice. The cinema was full of eager, expectant men. We sat at the back, as I didn't want to mix with what I assumed to be the degenerates watching the film.

The movie told the story of a bored housewife drawn into a suburban mate-swapping ring and succumbing to the temptations of illicit sex. But if I expected it to be a scandalous, gaudy piece of trash, I was proven wrong. Shot in black and white with an ever-present jazz soundtrack, the film was a gloomy, heavy sexual melodrama with surprisingly little outright sex or even nudity. And rather than an exciting expose of the joys of swinging, sex was shown as a release that results in unhappiness.

The film starred an actress called Audrey Campbell. The name meant nothing to me, but Mike was in complete awe of her. Audrey Campbell was like Lana Turner to him. Mike told me she'd recently starred in another exploitation film called *Olga's House of Shame* (1964) as a madam who presides over a network of prostitutes and criminals. With the tag line "Bodies Racked by Unspeakable Tortures! Captive Girls Used for Experiments in Lust!" this notorious film had capitalized on the increasingly popular trend of sexual violence – a trend that was becoming a staple of many exploitation features.

When Joe Sarno's film finished and we stumbled out into the daylight, Mike immediately turned to me in expectation and asked "OK, what did you think?!"

I hadn't been impressed with the film itself. But rather than being shocked by the subject matter I was intrigued by the fact that someone could make a successful movie without the resources of a Hollywood studio.

I had to admit, Mike was probably right; maybe we could make something better than this. My previous reference points had been the big budget films I loved. But movies like *Sin in the Suburbs* opened up new possibilities. We went for a drink and reviewed the film scene by scene, gradually convincing ourselves that maybe we could, and should, make a exploitation film.

In the end Mike said "Why don't we just sit down and try to write a script first?"

WEST SIDE STORY (1958-1964)

I agreed, but insisted that we keep both our jobs at ABC and write on the weekends. We had absolutely no money for equipment, locations, or a cast so it was important that we maintained our regular salaries if we were going to make this work.

Our first task was to come up with an appropriately sleazy title. It didn't take us long. We decided on *The Sins of a White Slaver,* and our careers as budding exploitation directors had begun.

BODY OF A FEMALE
(1964-1965)

As we embarked on our first film, Mike and I agreed that we'd share the responsibilities of writing, producing and directing. We set up a production company called "Amlay Pictures", an amalgamation of our names, to reflect our collaboration. I wanted to include Lem as he was so creative and resourceful but he'd become stage manager for the Lake George Playhouse and was living in upstate New York at the time.

By now some of my prudishness had abated, and I was actually going to a few grind house theaters on my own to analyze the films. It was clear that the topic of sexual violence was popular, and white slavery was particularly hot, so we decided to work both themes into our story. We crafted a plot about a wealthy man who hires a thug to drug and kidnap girls in New York City, then transport them to New England so his employer can abuse them for his gratification. But the thug falls in love with a stripper he's been paid to transport and "trouble ensues" as they say.

We set part of the story in New England so we could shoot back in my hometown of Gloucester. Filming would have to be done very discreetly of course, but I figured my knowledge of the local area would add some much needed production value to the film.

We finished the script in a couple of weeks and were very pleased with it. We incorporated the seemingly obligatory scenes for an exploitation film and created plot devices so we could include nude bathing, a shower scene and even a strip tease.

The way these titillating scenes were woven into the story was important. The censor had to consider the premise totally natural to allow nudity to be included in a film. We figured that as a woman has to get undressed to get in the shower or to go for a swim, we'd probably be able to get away with that. It was all very mild but we knew that seeing even a woman's back with no bra would be worth the price of admission to a Times Square grind house patron. As for violence, there seemed to be a lot more leeway so we figured we could push the envelope as long as we didn't go completely over the top.

Once the script was done we ran into our first significant challenge – casting. Despite Mike's interest in exploitation films he didn't know a soul in the business, and we were too intimidated to approach the familiar actresses

CHAPTER 3

that other directors like Joe Sarno used. We also didn't have much money to lavish on talent as the whole enterprise was being funded by our lowly jobs at ABC.

As we scratched our heads for options, the idea of using Lem came to me. I mentioned it to Mike and said "I'm sure we can talk him into coming back for a few days and playing Spencer, the wealthy sadist in New England. And he wouldn't cost us a thing." Mike agreed, and then volunteered himself to play Bruno, the man whose job it was to procure the girls.

With the two male leads cast, Mike suggested Roberta for the leading female role, Cindy the stripper. In all honesty it never occurred to me that Roberta could play this part. She looked nothing like the exploitation stars of the day – such as Audrey Campbell, the smoldering sexpot who had appeared in the *Olga* films. In my mind Roberta was still the classical pianist, a shy and neurotic girl who showed no interest in film.

I hesitated but was surprised by Mike's insistence. In the end I said "Okay, but how is Roberta going to feel about being on screen in a state of partial undress?"

We ended up discussing it with Roberta, who sat giggling like the teenager she was. Despite my thinking "this is never going to work," Mike insisted that she'd be fine so I relented. We had our leading lady.

We still needed to fill the other acting roles so in desperation we turned to friends and acquaintances. This worked well for the male parts but not for the female roles. The truth was we didn't know that many women, especially ones that would be willing to undress on camera. And as a casting team Mike and I were so uptight, shy, and repressed that it was difficult to even know where to start. But eventually we found two or three girls who reluctantly agreed to take their tops off, so long as we agreed to shoot their nude scenes from behind. One of these actresses, a stunning woman named Gigi Darlene, had recently started making a name for herself on the exploitation scene.

Given the difficulty of finding girls willing to disrobe, we were concerned about one scene in particular that called for a whole group of near-nude women. I couldn't imagine how we'd be able to film it. The sequence had the rich sadist played by Lem out on the prowl in New York when he comes across a club featuring girls in various states of undress. The only places I could think of where we might find such a setting were the "camera clubs" popular in New York at the time. For a price these "clubs" allowed men to bring still cameras and photograph girls who would sit on a small stage in bikinis or skimpy stripper outfits and strike poses. The "photographers" weren't allowed on the stage itself but they could get pretty close, snapping away at the models in open-mouthed awe. I couldn't believe these men were so desperate to see partially naked women that they would pay for such a limited thrill – but the camera clubs seemed to have an endless stream of keen patrons that kept them busy.

While the setting seemed promising, motion picture cameras were strictly forbidden in all the clubs. I wondered if there was a way we could sneak our camera in and secretly film the girls. Mike agreed it was worth trying.

For equipment, we bought a primitive 35mm World War II camera, which had to be seen to be believed. It was a Bell & Howell Eyemo camera, first designed and manufactured in 1925. Its small size and durability made it the preferred choice for newsreel and combat cameramen. It was also ideal for us as it was inexpensive and unobtrusive, perfect for our more clandestine shooting. The downside was that the camera only took one-minute rolls of film and was spring-operated so had to be wound up before each shot. In reality you didn't even get a full minute of usable footage because the shutter speed changed towards the end of each take. But the camera only cost $100 so it was our best – and really our only – bet.

In order to shoot in the camera club, we devised a rig to make everyone think we had a strange looking still camera. Wearing large raincoats to hide extra rolls of film, we set off to a notorious club on 44th Street. Our plan paid off – we wound up with some acceptable, though grainy, footage of girls in bikinis parading around and sitting in swings. We were extra careful to avoid shooting any of the models' faces as we knew we couldn't get releases from them.

The next scene we decided to shoot was Roberta's striptease. Full nudity would never be allowed by the censor so I went out and bought Roberta a peignoir – a sheer robe-like garment. I took the peignoir up to Mike and Roberta's apartment and suggested she put it on so that Mike and I could see if it fit the bill.

It was an embarrassing moment for all of us as it was the first time I'd seen Roberta's breasts. I tried to bring a degree of levity to the proceedings by exaggerating my enthusiasm, saying "That looks great; that's gonna' be terrific. You're never gonna' have to take it off because we can see straight through it."

But on the heels of my comments, Mike bolted out of the apartment and slammed the door behind him. I had never seen him act that way. I asked Roberta "Was it something I said? Was he offended?" Roberta answered "Oh don't worry, he's just crazy because you've seen my tits now. He's probably gone to get drunk in a bar some place. He'll be back eventually."

BODY OF A FEMALE (1964-1965)

I was mortified, and concerned that I may have hurt Roberta's feelings as well. I asked "Are you sure you have no qualms about doing this?"

She appeared unaffected, saying "Oh no, not at all, it's not me, it's him." Then she lowered her voice and said "You know, he still thinks you're straight."

I was shocked. I'd spent the previous six months with Mike raving about Joan Crawford and Bette Davis movies so I figured he had to know by now.

Roberta and I agreed that she'd tell him I was gay when he returned, and I left their apartment feeling confused and a little depressed. But when Mike and I next met up we returned to being the best of friends. He never brought the incident up or asked me about my personal life, not even to find out if I lived with anyone.

The main shoot for the film proved more difficult than we expected. Mike, Roberta, Lem and I were the whole crew, performing all the tasks ourselves because we couldn't afford anyone to help out. We could only shoot on weekends because we didn't get paid until Friday and the extra money didn't last more than a couple of days. We didn't storyboard anything in advance though we did come up with a simple shot list to follow. I liked to think it was very John Ford, nothing complicated, very "meat and potatoes". We filmed plenty of master shots, some medium shots and close-ups where needed.

The whole film was shot MOS, meaning we didn't record a synchronous audio track. Some say MOS stands for "Motor Only Sync" or "Motor Only Shot", while another popular theory was that it stood for broken-English "Mit out sound", just as a 1920s German émigré director such as Ernst Lubitsch or Fritz Lang might have said it.

Shooting without capturing sound was good for us as it saved time and money. It also meant we didn't have to remain silent during a take, so we could shout out instructions as we filmed. We recorded the dialogue afterwards and added it in post-production together with any music and sound effects. In many cases we didn't even use the actors' own voices.

We eventually made it to Gloucester to shoot the scenes I'd scripted with specific locations in mind. We all stayed with my maternal grandmother, which took Lem and I back in time. It felt strange to be back filming a sleazy blend of sex and violence in our hometown while staying with the family matriarch.

But I got to fulfill my teenage dream of filming in Judy Chamberlain's house. When I was a teen, Judy had been my co-worker at the local bookstore and we'd stayed in touch. And when I asked her if we could film in her beautiful home, she agreed. We even cast Judy in a small part, giving her the glorious screen credit name "Kate Swanson" after Katherine Hepburn and Gloria Swanson.

It was at Judy's house that we shot our first sex scene, a key sequence with Roberta and Mike. Of course in reality it was just simulated sex consisting of a lot of writhing and rolling around, but nevertheless it was a milestone in the shoot. The two of them got into bed and we shot very carefully with a sheet pulled up to their necks. We were all embarrassed by the whole business and keen to be done as quickly as possible.

We had also scripted an outdoor nude swim scene for Roberta as I knew of a reservoir that would make an ideal location. Access to the reservoir was severely restricted however. There were signs everywhere warning trespassers to keep away and a foreboding barbed wire fence to reinforce the message. We knew that if we got caught, we'd be in big trouble. And if we were caught filming a naked woman, things would be much worse.

Fortunately, Roberta was a good sport and quite fearless so we snuck the equipment past the obstacles and set up. Unfortunately, the water was freezing cold and Roberta really couldn't swim.

Once Roberta was submerged we instructed her to turn around so we could film a hint of bare breast. But she couldn't control her movement in the water, so it was a matter of feast or famine with Roberta either exposing far too much flesh or not enough. We shot as carefully as we could and finally called it a day, hoping we'd got some usable footage.

We returned to New York to shoot the movie's climax. We spent a day at Coney Island filming scenes against the backdrop of landmarks like the Wonder Wheel, the Boardwalk and the Carousel. The plot's denouement had Mike's character finding Roberta tied to a bedpost in Lem's New England mansion, freeing her and escaping to New York. Lem's character follows in hot pursuit and in the film's final sequence, Lem fights Mike on the beach and in the water. To complete his redemption and prove that love conquers all, Mike emerges victorious and leaves Lem for dead.

To commemorate this final day of shooting, Lem, Mike, Roberta and I had our picture taken standing behind the bars of a mock-up jail cell in the Playland Arcades. We were still carrying our old World War II camera and tripod from the day's shoot. Little did we know the scene was a harbinger of things to come.

The budget for *Sins of a White Slaver* was just over $5,000, though it was difficult to track the exact amount because our ABC paychecks went piecemeal towards making the film. We made it work; the only time we were stretched financially was when we shot in Gloucester because we were there for several days.

Being first-time filmmakers, we were surprised by the cost of film stock and processing. We had chosen to shoot on 35mm because we thought 16mm looked cheap and tacky. But as they say, "Champagne taste, beer budget", and 35mm film was expensive. To save money, Mike struck upon the idea of buying what we called "baby film" from professional portrait photographers. It was actually called "Var-I-Pan", but we called it "baby film" because photographers would often buy the film to shoot pictures of babies. Each session required hundreds of individual pictures because it would take ages to get a good shot of a squirming child. What we failed to grasp was that much of the stock was old, giving the film a really dark look. The problem was compounded by our lack of skill in the lighting department.

Then we had to rent editing equipment, which added to our costs. We created the film's title sequence ourselves, and Mike handled most of the editing. Certain sequences proved to be problematic to edit, most notably Roberta's scene in the reservoir. Roberta had exposed herself too much, giving us only short clips to work with. They were a nightmare to splice together into a watchable sequence, so we had to keep cutting to endless reaction shots of Mike ogling her.

For the music soundtrack we came up with the cost-saving idea of "borrowing" everything, lifting songs off albums from our local library. "Francesca da Rimini", a work by Tchaikovsky I'd always liked, was prominently employed. The final score was a mish-mash but it seemed to work, giving the film a much needed air of respectability.

Mike and I decided we would adopt pseudonyms for the credits to disguise our involvement. We had no idea what the film's reception would be, but we knew that to give it a chance of being successful we would have to market it in the most lurid and sleazy way. And we were concerned about the impact exposure might have on our future career prospects.

I adopted my middle name and became J. Ellsworth. Mike called himself "Julian Marsh", paying tribute to the lead character from one of his favorite films, the Warner Brothers musical "42nd Street". Marsh delivers one of the film's most memorable lines that we hoped would apply to our own careers: "You're going out a youngster, but you've got to come back a star!"

We combined our middle names for a shared writer's credit as "Francis Ellie", and I took a credit for "camera operator" as John Firth, using my mother's maiden name. Mike and Roberta took the names Robert West and

Anna Riva respectively for their acting roles, names they would continue to employ on future film projects.

Mike wanted to pay tribute to the pin-up model Bettie Page, famous since the 1950s for her jet-black hair and trademark bangs, so he included the name "Bette Page" in the credits. Bettie had nothing to do with the film and I thought she was sheer camp, but Mike adored her. I'd often look for pictures of her in movie bookshops whenever I wanted to buy him a present. At the time, I was unaware of the bondage and sadomasochistic pictures Bettie had done for New York photographer Irving Klaw, but with hindsight I'm sure Mike was a huge fan. He would often drag me to burlesque shows featuring some of the great names of the day like Tempest Storm and Blaze Starr. He loved the whole spectacle that, even at the time, felt old-fashioned to me.

When we saw the first print of the completed film, we were cautiously optimistic we could get a distributor. We'd heard of other filmmakers who would start to make an exploitation film and never finish it. They just couldn't get it together – but we did.

That said, we didn't have any illusions that our movie was a masterpiece. In fact, parts of the movie were stupefyingly boring. One of the problems lay with the direction. For example, when Roberta was washing herself in the bathtub, we'd told her "Move the soap very slowly" because we wanted to create some erotic tension. But in the final cut this seemed to have the reverse effect and the scene verged on the comical.

Another issue was the pacing. I had naively liked the fact that we had to restrict ourselves to shooting only one minute at a time due to the limitations of our ancient camera. I thought it would result in a faster-paced, more exciting final cut. But boy was I wrong. There were sequences that seem interminable with nothing happening for minutes on end.

However despite the deadly pacing, I didn't think our film was any worse than others that were playing at the time. And it certainly didn't look like the kitchen sink melodramas that directors like Joe Sarno were making. It had a beginning, middle, and an end. It had nudity and a little bit of action. In other words, it was a bona fide exploitation film.

The first distributor we reached out to was William Mishkin. He'd made a fortune distributing burlesque films in 1950s New York. He was also notorious for importing inoffensive films from Europe and transforming them into U.S. successes by adding sordid titles and lurid advertising campaigns.

BODY OF A FEMALE (1964-1965)

Mike and I set up a screening for Mishkin. He turned up by himself and watched the film in silence. At the end he stood up, told us he liked it but said "It's gonna need a lot of work and I'm not willing to put up the money for the re-shoots. If you guys want to fix all the stuff I say needs fixing, I'll re-evaluate it."

We thanked him for coming but told him we didn't have the money or appetite to re-shoot anything. Besides, we believed the movie was perfectly good as it was.

We then turned to Joseph Brenner, a major distributor of horror and exploitation films. Joe's reaction was more positive, though he did insist on one change. He said, "It needs another sex scene in the middle of the film and Roberta should do another strip. I'll pay for the changes and take the money off the top. If you're open to that, we can talk."

We were excited, especially given his offer to pay for the additional scenes, so we went to his office on 42nd Street and drew up a contract. He was a great salesman and promised us the moon; a wonderful ad campaign, a first-rate press book, good theaters. And much to our surprise, he actually delivered on most fronts. Sure, he also promised us untold riches which we never saw, but we were off and running.

Mike and I agreed we'd shoot Roberta's additional strip tease in their apartment. But before I knew it Mike went ahead and filmed the scene without me. It seemed the issue was that he was still uncomfortable with me seeing Roberta undressed. So he just turned up one day and presented me with the footage. After everything we'd been through in making our first film, I was deeply disappointed to be excluded. And the scene he shot was a tame sequence of Roberta swaying back and forth, holding her hands over her breasts. But while it wasn't "Salome", it would do.

Despite my disappointment, the film was now almost done. Only one issue remained – the film's title. During the shooting of *The Sins of a White Slaver* we decided that too many films already had the word "sin" or "slavery" in the name. So we went back and forth and somewhere along the way, one of us came up with *The Body of a Female*, which we subsequently shortened to *Body of a Female*. I thought it was ironic given there wasn't a single great body in the entire film. But Mike and I were happy with it, and so was Joe Brenner, so the new title stuck.

Body of a Female premiered November 4th, 1964. Our excitement was tempered by the fact that the film opened at the Studio Theater in Philadelphia and not in Times Square or anywhere else in New York. Nonetheless, Mike, Roberta and I drove to Philadelphia and, after taking pictures of the marquee, went in to watch the movie in the presence of an audience. We were surprised and impressed that the theater was three quarters full on opening day. When the lights went down, we giggled – and groaned – throughout the movie. Roberta in particular spent most of the showing laughing at all the wrong moments. We didn't care – our little film was on a big screen in a big theater, and it was a tremendous thrill. We celebrated afterwards by going to a bar and getting completely hammered.

The film's New York opening was January 7th, 1965 at the Globe Theater on Broadway and West 42nd Street. The theater occupied the best corner in the area, and had a great big marquee. It was so exciting to see our movie title in big cut-out letters, not the stock letters they slapped on cinema fronts in later years. We thought, "This is it, we've arrived. We've really made it." For someone who'd been so embarrassed to be seen in front of a grind house less than one year earlier, I'd sure changed.

As promised, Joe Brenner pulled out all the stops for our New York premiere. The one sheet he produced was particularly trashy boasting "Body of a Female…boldly explores the bizarre twilight world of abnormal sexual behavior! A Story of the whip and the flesh!"

Joe also took out suitably lurid newspaper ads showing a nude Roberta peering out from beneath the sheets. She had a look on her face that somehow managed to be both sultry and fearful. The ads boasted:

"Until now, the screen did not dare.
Until now, the theme of this picture was talked about only in whispers.
Until now."

In some other cities, newspapers refused to print the ad unless the artwork was toned down and the film title changed to just *The Female*.

Joe Brenner also sent out a personally signed release to exhibitors extolling the commercial value of the movie. He wrote, "The production techniques used in the film enhance the story in a remarkable way. Fluid camera work, fast cutting, unusual shooting angles and lighting of scenes, as well as a good deal of location shooting, all work together to give the film plenty of impact." He concluded that it was "the kind of film the public has been looking for."

It wasn't the kind of film Boston, MA was looking for however. The local Mayor described our film as "hardcore pornography and completely objectionable," and ordered the city's censor to take action against the film.

BODY OF A FEMALE (1964-1965)

Shortly afterwards, a court judge spoke with the manager of the State Theater where the film was being exhibited, and it was withdrawn.

Nevertheless, the film enjoyed a long run and made a great deal of money. Our deal with Brenner called for a 60/40 split after expenses, 60% in our favor and 40% in his. The first ten to fifteen thousand dollars all went to Joe because he'd paid for the ad campaign, the prints and the shipping. But after that, we were supposed to start receiving our share of the revenue. We sat back and waited for the money to roll in.

We started receiving calls from people saying the film had opened in Detroit or Chicago or any number of other cities. The problem was none of these cities were showing up on the monthly statements that were supposed to list all gross receipts and deductions. Mike and I began to think that Joe wasn't reporting all of the grosses to us. Other filmmakers told us that this was commonplace, but it was nonetheless discouraging to have to go to our distributor on a regular basis and accuse him of not reporting dates.

After a year of seeing precious little financial return, I decided something had to change. I thought it would be a good idea to sell my half of the film to Joe while it was still doing well, and use the proceeds to form a production company. I was ready to leave ABC and start life as a full-time filmmaker.

Mike and Roberta also talked about forming a production company. Roberta decided that while she didn't want to star in any more films, she wanted to work on the production side.

We all shared a desire to make more films, but our ideas about subject matter dramatically differed. By this time, I'd seen a few exploitation films that were lighter in tone and my preference was to move in that direction. But Mike and Roberta were clearly drawn to the darker elements of the genre, and talked about writing scripts that contained all manner of comically sadistic exploits. So we decided to go our own ways.

Our friendship was unaffected by the split and remained as strong as ever. We continued to see each other regularly and swap film ideas. And Mike and Roberta were a good team. They started to collaborate on scripts, and Roberta expressed a desire to be the camera person on their films. We each had a vision and resolved to help out on each other's sets in the future.

Mike and Roberta were dead set against selling their share of *Body of a Female* and tried to dissuade me from selling mine. But my mind was set so I approached Joe Brenner and asked him if he wanted to buy my half. He offered me six thousand dollars, which I thought was wonderful money at the time. And most importantly, I knew that with six grand I could fund another movie.

Body of a Female continued its successful run all over the country. And Joe Brenner went from strength to strength, enhancing his already profitable distribution empire with a slew of successful home grown and imported horror films. Eventually I lost track of both him and *Body of a Female*.

Over time, all copies of the film seemed to disappear. To my knowledge, *Body of a Female* was never released in any other medium and I am sadly resigned to the idea that the negative, which was on very inexpensive film stock, has been lost forever. I was always sorry that I didn't keep a copy of a 35mm print but fortunately I did retain a copy of the trailer which I treasure. Being my first film, it's like a first child. I still hope against hope that one day a print of the film will come to light.

With my payout from Joe Brenner, I suggested to Lem that we make a film together. Though Lem's first passion remained the theater, his career as a stage manager had stalled. I thought he'd be a great director and I fancied trying my hand at producing. Lem had seen the fun Mike and I had making *Body of a Female* and he liked the idea of directing, so he agreed.

So we hired a lawyer, set up a corporation, and "Amero Brothers Inc." was born.

CHAPTER 4

DIARY OF A SWINGER
(1965-1967)

With our production company established, Lem and I needed a work space. We soon found one in Tribeca – a great old loft on the middle floor of a three-story building at 134 West Broadway. It was a large, open-plan space that had been a doll manufacturing factory at the turn of the previous century. Tiny porcelain eyes were still embedded in between the floorboards, staring up at you as you walked around.

The landlord told us the building was strictly for professional use and no one was allowed to live there. But we soon found out that an artist named Terry was residing upstairs with his wife. We figured if they were getting away with it, why couldn't we? So I came up with the bright idea of building a set resembling the inside of an apartment. If a building inspector ever turned up, we could claim that the set was for a movie shoot. Lem liked the idea so we gave up our apartment and moved into the loft.

Building out the studio however was going to take money. I was determined not to use up the six grand I'd made for *Body of a Female* so I looked for some temporary work. I didn't want to go back to the networks as I needed something less complicated and shorter term. I knew a couple of people that worked as movie theater managers and thought that their work sounded interesting and might fit the bill. So I leafed through the New York Times and found a wanted ad for a manager at the Trans-Lux company that operated cinemas up and down the East Coast. I applied and got the job.

My first assignment was as assistant manager at the Trans-Lux newsreel theater on Broadway and 49th Street. The mid 1960s was the twilight for the newsreel theaters that had been so successful in the 1930s and 1940s. Back in their heyday, these cinemas offered a one-hour show consisting of a cartoon, a travelogue, a short, and a newsreel digest that most major studios – including MGM, Paramount, and Universal – produced. The show changed twice a week on Tuesdays and Thursdays and the admission price was 65 cents.

The job was a lot of work but I loved it, and it still gave me time to write scripts and build out our studio. My co-managers – Steve Gould, Ron Scardera, and Jack Ballard – would become lifelong friends. And Steve and

Ron would go on to work on many future Amero Brothers productions. But before long Trans-Lux bowed to the inevitable. Television had made newsreel houses redundant, so the theater switched to showing first-run features and re-branded as the Trans-Lux West. Ironically, the theater would become the Pussycat Cinema in the 1980s.

With the newsreel gone, I became a roving theater manager for Trans-Lux. I moved from theater to theater as the company either fired managers or had a sudden vacancy when someone quit without notice. From the Trans-Lux West, they sent me to their theater on 85th St, and then shortly afterwards to their movie house at 52nd and Lexington. This last theater is where the iconic scene in *The Seven Year Itch* (1955) was filmed. As Marilyn Monroe exits the theater, her white dress is blown upwards as she stands over a subway grate.

One evening at the Trans-Lux on Lexington, an usher came to my office at the end of the night's program. He complained that there was someone asleep in the balcony and, as hard as he'd tried, he'd not been able to rouse the man. Mildly irritated at having to sort out a problem the usher should've been able to handle, I headed up to eject the comatose customer. As I approached his seat, I immediately recognized the sleeper. It was the actor Montgomery Clift.

I'd seen Clift before several times at the Isle of Capri restaurant where I used to dine with Nancy, and as any keen cinema goer of the time, I was a big fan. He'd been nominated for several Academy Awards and was responsible for memorable performances in films like *A Place in the Sun* (1951), Hitchcock's *I Confess* (1953) and *From Here to Eternity* (1953). His stellar career had been interrupted when he'd suffered a disfiguring car crash ten years earlier, which led to alcohol and prescription drug abuse. Now in his mid-40s, he'd become erratic and his professional reputation suffered.

I managed to wake him and it was clear he'd been drinking. He immediately started complaining about missing the end of the film, a war movie called *King Rat* (1965). I calmed him by promising him a press book and we made our way back to my office. He seemed happy with the promotional materials I gave him, and soon we were engaged in conversation about the film industry. By the time we got back to the lobby, Clift had sobered up and asked if I'd be interested in getting something to eat with him. I agreed and so after locking up the theater for the night, we set off to the Isle of Capri.

DIARY OF A SWINGER (1965-1967)

I was an avid reader of movie industry trade papers and was aware that Monty had a reputation for being a different kind of Hollywood star. For a start he avoided movie premieres and parties, and rarely made himself available for interviews. Rumors about his sexuality circulated and he was widely thought to be bisexual. I also knew that he was embroiled in messy legal proceedings over his role in the John Huston film *Freud: The Secret Passion* (1962). Universal Studios claimed that Montgomery's self-destructive lifestyle and frequent absences had caused the film to go over budget.

In person however Monty was good company and, despite the car accident, still very attractive. He had wonderful, expressive eyes and a beautiful quality to his voice. He spoke about his close friend Elizabeth Taylor, and how she was keen for him to star in the upcoming *Reflections in a Golden Eye* (1967). He also spoke of plans to star in *The Defector* (1966) which was due to shoot in Germany later that year.

I usually drank beer, but I ordered wine, feeling it more fitting for the lofty company I was in. But I needn't have worried as Monty drank vodka and ignored his food altogether. After the meal he invited me back to his townhouse on East 61st Street where he lived with his personal secretary, Lorenzo. After all the wine I drank, I was nervous but excited about the prospect of being intimate with someone I had idolized from afar all my life.

Over the following months, I saw Monty on a semi-regular basis and our dates usually followed the same pattern. We'd meet at the theater and go on to the Isle of Capri restaurant, before retiring to his bedroom. I never mentioned the relationship to anyone, including Lem, for fear that it would hit the grapevine and end up in the tabloids.

Monty eventually left town to film *The Defector* and I didn't see him again. The following year Monty died at the age of 45 of heart disease, thought by many to be the result of his drug and alcohol abuse.

After six months in my new role, Trans-Lux asked me if I'd be interested in serving as interim manager of the State Theater in Boston. They referred to the State as a "problem operation" and were looking for someone to turn it around. Because I was from Gloucester, they assumed I'd be grateful for the chance to be closer to home for a while. I also was promised a good pay raise and a room at the Avery Hotel just around the corner from the theater on central Boston Common. I felt bad leaving Lem to work alone on the studio but hoped the temporary job would enable us to save more money for our next film.

The State Theater was in the notorious "Combat Zone", the adult entertainment district in downtown Boston filled with exploitation theaters and sleazy bars. The name of the area had a double meaning as the zone was known for crime and violence, but also for uniformed sailors on shore leave frequenting the area's strip clubs and brothels.

Prior to its troubles, the theater had been a reasonable moneymaker, showing a steady diet of exploitation films. *Body of a Female* had played there, so one of the first things I did when I arrived was look up our box office figures. I was pleased to see that the Trans-Lux numbers matched those reported by Joe Brenner, and those figures confirmed that the film had done very well.

The State had been an elegant, legitimate theater back in the 1920s and 1930s, but by 1966 its glory days were long gone. The balcony was condemned due to age so we only had the orchestra seats left to accommodate the audience. Everything felt ancient, even down to the concession stand lady who was in her 80s and had been working there since the golden age of Jean Harlow. She was quietly appalled at the film fare the theater was now playing.

But I was there to do a job and immediately got to work. I fired the manager, re-painted the theater and generally cleaned it up. I also reviewed the finances and made sure we had more control over our costs.

I hired a new assistant manager named Robert Parker, and one day in conversation I told him about making *Body of a Female*. He was a bright kid who struck me as straight-laced and fairly repressed, so I was surprised that he showed interest in our experience and in exploitation films in general. He told me that he'd started work on a script he called *Diary of a Swinger*. I told him to let me know when he finished it as I'd be interested in taking a look.

I also met a young, good-looking local named George Delemos, another person interested in exploitation films. He often came to the State as he was good friends with Martin Avedisian, a photographer Trans-Lux hired to take pictures of every marquee we put up. George and Martin expressed an interest in financing a film and indicated they'd be able to round up other people to join them on the money side. I was pleasantly surprised at their interest as I'd assumed we'd only be able to find backers for exploitation films in New York.

Before long the State was back on its feet and making money again. We continued to show exploitation fare like Doris Wishman's wonderfully sleazy and inept *Bad Girls Go to Hell* (1965) and Robert Downey Sr.'s *Sweet Smell of Sex* (1965).

DIARY OF A SWINGER (1965-1967)

My entire time on assignment, I didn't tell my family in Gloucester that I was in Boston. I didn't even go back to visit them as I didn't know how to explain my presence. What I did know was that they certainly wouldn't approve of me managing an exploitation theater in the Combat Zone.

Lem was anxious for me to get back to New York, but I stayed another couple of months to complete the State's turnaround. And I enjoyed my time in Boston. I'd typically hang out in the neighborhood bars, many of which were owned by local mobsters. I got to know these mobsters because I'd give them passes to the State Theater in exchange for free drinks.

Before I knew it, it was New Year's Eve at the end of 1966. I decided I wanted to do something different to mark the event so I headed over to my Uncle Bobby's Napoleon Club. I didn't go there often as I didn't want Uncle Bobby to feel he had to spend time with me, but fortunately that New Year's Eve he was nowhere to be seen.

Bobby had turned the Club into a highly successful bar and a staple of Boston's gay community. It was a huge complex spanning several buildings and named for its faux Napoleonic style. As we used to say in those days it was "piss elegant" – you had to wear a suit and tie just to get in. Downstairs was the main piano bar with a second bar room behind it. Upstairs was the "Wrinkle Room" which had a sizable dance floor and a white organ. It was known as the "Wrinkle Room" because the lighting was dim enough to encourage those of a certain age, usually employees of the Jordan Marsh department store, to gather on Friday nights. Needless to say, younger men wouldn't be caught dead in that room.

Despite the party atmosphere that New Year's Eve, I was lonely. But I got into conversation with a guy sitting at the opposite side of the bar. His name was Chuck Federico and he looked like a young Robert Morse, an actor who had recently become famous for his portrayal of J. Pierrepont Finch in the Broadway musical "How to Succeed in Business Without Really Trying". Chuck had a cute little turned up nose and was sporting a semi-drunken grin. I can still remember to this day that Frank Sinatra's "Strangers in the Night" was playing in the background. Sinatra probably never realized it but his song had become a gay community anthem. Chuck asked me to dance and while normally I wouldn't, I made a New Year's Eve exception.

As we danced we talked, and I learned that Chuck was Italian through and through and loved cooking his native fare. In fact, he spent most of the time talking about the proper way to prepare and serve Italian food.

Normally I had little interest in discussing food but I'd been eating at cheap restaurants in between theater shifts and hadn't had decent home-cooked fare in months. So when Chuck invited me back to his place for a meal, I jumped at the opportunity. To this day I remain convinced that Chuck's invitation was based on the sincere aim of cooking for me, not fooling around. And I have to say I too was thinking more about food than the possibility of sex at the time.

Chuck prepared a full Italian feast for me that night. He was a wonderful cook, and as we ate he told me how he'd started out in the Navy and now worked as a dispatcher for a large trucking firm in Brookline. We talked for hours and for the first time ever I felt that maybe I had met someone whom I could have a relationship with.

Chuck and I continued seeing each other, and soon he convinced me to move into his apartment. So I rented out my room at the Avery Hotel that Trans-Lux was paying for and moved my meager belongings into Chuck's place. It felt good to have a partner to share daily life with, but I kept thinking "I've got to get back to New York to make films – how is Chuck going to fit into that life?"

I also worried about what would happen to him if I did invite him to come to New York. Moving would be a big commitment, tantamount in my mind to asking him to marry me, and I wasn't sure I wanted to feel responsible for him. Though he liked movies, and was supportive of everything I was involved in, Chuck had no interest in film-making. He was a hard-working, blue-collar guy, not driven to pursue a creative dream.

I told Trans-Lux that I'd have to leave the company unless they found me a job back in New York. Happily, they gave me my old job back managing the Trans-Lux on Broadway. Then I sat Chuck down and explained the situation. I encouraged him to stay in Boston saying "I think we should slow things down because while I care for you, we've only known each other a few months. Let's see if when I'm done working on the film we still have the same feelings for each other".

Chuck was crestfallen by my suggestion and pushed hard to come with me. But while I had strong feelings for him, I wasn't ready for that deep a commitment yet. I headed back to New York alone.

Before leaving Boston I made an agreement with my assistant theater manager, Robert Parker, to shoot the script he'd completed for *Diary of a Swinger*. Then I struck a deal with George Delemos and Martin Avedisian to finance the film. Lem was on board so we were ready to start planning the production.

I moved back into the studio with Lem on West Broadway. While I was gone he'd done a tremendous job building film sets, and had also been helping out Mike and Roberta. They were keen to exploit the grind house market for "roughies", films that portrayed an imaginative mix of sex and sadistic violence, and Lem was part of the crew on their first feature film, *Take Me Naked* (1966). Lem also assisted them in assembling a collection of stock footage to create the pseudo-documentary *Sin Syndicate* (1965) for Joe Brenner, and built sets for *Satan's Bed* (1965) starring a young and then-unknown Yoko Ono.

Settled back in New York, I got a call from a reporter at the World Journal Tribune asking to interview me for a piece on exploitation films. This was the first time I'd been approached by a legitimate publication. And as I read the Tribune regularly at the time, I was excited at the prospect of being interviewed. I didn't stop to think about whether the article would have a favorable or negative slant, I just thought "Hell – it's the Tribune; we've made it into the mainstream!"

I met the reporter several days later and he told me that he was thinking of calling the article "Making Money in the Goon Trade". I found this strange as we never referred to the industry by that name. But then he turned to the basics, asking about the standard elements of a exploitation film. I told him there was usually an orgy, a girl being taken advantage of and, if you thought you could get away with it, a hint of a lesbian scene too. I mentioned that a nude swimming scene was always a winner and told him about shooting Roberta in the reservoir in Gloucester. I felt the interview went well and looked forward to reading the resulting article.

The story appeared in the Tribune the following Sunday, January 1967. In addition to my input it featured an interview with Joe Brenner who spoke at length about the profitability of exploitation films. He initially estimated the grind house market to be worth $10,000,000, but the Tribune disagreed. The paper reckoned it was more like $60,000,000, and Brenner admitted to downplaying the figure for fear it would attract more competition. Brenner also shared that the average picture cost less than $20,000 to make and realized a profit of over $100,000. *Body of a Female* was cited as being made for $8,000 and grossing $250,000 to date.

I was disappointed to see that I came across as a little contemptuous of the industry. I was quoted as saying, "Nobody wants nudies any more, they've had them. So we go in for violence and orgies. Orgies are very big. But we give it to them in small doses, like maybe 15 minutes out of a 90-minute picture, and the rest of the time we bore them with the worst stories and the worst actors. In this business, quality will kill you. You can't think low enough. And they come back for more." Though mildly irritated by this, I ultimately decided that any publicity was good publicity.

A couple of months after the article was published I received a long letter from my grandmother in Gloucester. She included the front page of the Gloucester Daily Times bearing the headline "Who is John Amero?" The article referenced the Tribune piece, stating "John Amero said he filmed a sex film in Gloucester using our reservoir for a nude swimming scene, and that he gives the public orgies in small doses." My grandmother gravely concluded her letter by saying "John – I don't think you better come home for Christmas this year."

I was appalled and beside myself with anger. I showed the letter and article to Lem who, much to my dismay, found it all amusing. But seeing I was less than entertained, Lem said "Well, you're just going to have to write a rebuttal to the editor of the Gloucester Daily Times and deny, deny, deny!"

So that's exactly what I did. I penned a letter stating the article was incorrect on various fronts. I asserted that *Body of a Female* was not a nudie, but a low budget melodrama about wild teenagers. I proclaimed indignantly that "It did NOT have an orgy in it". And I closed by stating "the finished article was so full of half-truths and distortions...that many involved are considering legal action. In the future I will not consent to publicity without the presence of my lawyer."

My statements were all completely untrue of course, but faced with the disapproval of everyone I knew in Gloucester, what else could I do? Fortunately the paper printed my letter in full. More importantly I learned my lesson. I would make damn sure in the future to stipulate that any article I was quoted in received my approval before publication.

The following week I was approached by a local Gloucester newspaper asking if I wanted to set the record straight. The article would be a profile of Lem and I, complete with pictures and quotes. After the sobering experience with the Tribune, we were both very careful. I said our first film was sold to Joe Brenner who edited the movie and named it *Body of a Female*. I stated, "Joe Brenner may have added a few spicy scenes, I don't know. Our name isn't on it. I haven't seen it since we delivered it to him, and I have no desire to."

The article included a glowing tribute from our high school principal. In terms of damage control, it was about the best we could hope for.

DIARY OF A SWINGER (1965-1967)

Lem and I both thought the script for *Diary of a Swinger* represented exactly what we wanted to do next. It had all the elements needed for a perfect exploitation film. The plot centers on Jeannie, a sweet girl from the country who becomes cynical after men take advantage of her. She's driven out of her hometown and leaves to find fame and fortune. With luck finally on her side, she becomes a successful model in the big city and meets a wonderful guy. But soon she is preyed upon by her boss and, after an orgy, ends up in the arms of another woman. It had a little bit of sex, some nude bathing (again) and plenty of melodrama.

We were keen to make a Douglas Sirk-type film. Sirk made a number of melodramatic soap operas in the 1950s, like *Magnificent Obsession* (1954), *All That Heaven Allows* (1955) and *Imitation of Life* (1959). They all focused on love, death and societal constraints.

In many ways we saw *Diary of a Swinger* as the antithesis of *Body of a Female*. We wanted to portray people who were generally happy rather than sinful or sleazy, and who didn't all end up dead or drug addicts. It couldn't have been further from what Mike and Roberta were doing.

Most of the film's plot is revealed in flashbacks with the lead character telling the story via voice-over. The film opens with Jeannie going to her psychiatrist to share her tragic tale but soon ripple-dissolves to the past and doesn't return to the present until the very end. This approach minimized the need to capture live sound, allowing us to shoot most scenes MOS as we'd done with *Body of a Female*.

When it came to casting the film, I was slightly more experienced this time. We placed an ad in Backstage and used one of our favorite hangouts, the Haymarket restaurant on 8th Ave between 47th and 48th, to conduct our casting sessions. The restaurant had a payphone which was handy for making and receiving casting calls. And we became close to an actress who worked as a waitress there, Patty Finnegan, who helped us with the casting process and went on to become a life-long friend.

One of the first actresses we auditioned was a Mary Tyler Moore lookalike named Jeanette Banzet. Jeanette was a Texas-born actress in her early 30s who, unlike a number of other women in exploitation films at the time, was neither a dancer nor stripper. She'd appeared in a small role in *Breakfast at Tiffany's* (1961) a few years earlier while she was attending Bill Hickey's acting classes at the HB Studio in Greenwich Village. Unable to land many mainstream roles, Jeanette started appearing in New York exploitation films in the mid 1960s using pseudonyms such as "Pat Barrett" and "Marie Brent", or the abbreviated "Janet Banzet". She was clearly good with dialogue and we liked her, but she lacked the glamour we wanted for the leading role, so we found her another part.

After interviewing several other actresses who didn't fit the bill, we finally met our ideal Jeannie. Rita Bennett was a stunning Long Island girl with a successful modeling career and a host of magazine appearances under her belt. At the time, her face appeared on the side of New York buses promoting cigarettes and she was a regular in print ads for perfume, clothes and household products. Rita was also a stripper and night club dancer and, under the name "Joanna Cunningham", had been crowned Miss Cavalcade 1967 in the magazine of the same name, a cheaper imitation of Playboy.

With her background we felt confident Rita would have little problem disrobing for simulated sex scenes. We immediately told her we were making an exploitation film and that semi-nude scenes would be required. She agreed because, like many actresses in early exploitation films, she convinced herself that parts like this could lead to bigger and better films. Privately I disagreed, but who could tell at the time? It was a different era and many believed that exploitation films would eventually converge with more mainstream movies. So Rita accepted the role for the sum of $850, which was good money in those days.

We cast Ron Scardera, my fellow manager at Trans-Lux, as the vicious predator who early on attacks Jeannie on the family farm. Ron was extremely supportive of us throughout the production, lending us money and dubbing many of the voices in post.

Ironically, we cast a gay couple as two of Rita's love interests – one as a farm hand, the other as Rita's boyfriend in New York. Other parts were played by exploitation regular Rose Conti and SAG actor Ronald Durling. In a display of great confidence, Ron took an ad out in Variety advertising his part in the film.

Rita Bennett, while beautiful and physically appropriate for the role, had a rather flat manner of delivering lines. We quickly realized that we needed an alternative for the voice over as most of *Diary of a Swinger* is narrated by Rita's character. While casting at the Haymarket we had met a Canadian actress named Cara Duff-McCormick who had a wonderful voice. When she realized the kind of film we were making, she quickly lost interest in an acting part. But when we phoned her back offering her a voice-only role, Cara agreed. After our film Cara went on to have an acclaimed theater career, including a Tony Award for her supporting role in the 1972 Broadway production "Moonchildren" which also starred Christopher Guest.

DIARY OF A SWINGER (1965-1967)

I was particularly excited that we could build sets in our own studio and have more control over the creative process. I was the cinematographer and lighting designer, responsible for giving *Diary of a Swinger* a truly professional look. One stumbling block was that I was going to have to learn to operate a 35mm Arriflex. It was the standard camera used for motion pictures at the time but I'd never worked with or even seen an Arri before. And while I'd been the cinematographer on *Body of a Female*, we'd just used our World War II Eyemo camera that anyone could operate.

As I stood in the camera rental store, I was hugely embarrassed at how little I knew. I asked the store manager "Have there been any changes to the standard Arriflex 2C in the last couple years?" hoping he might let slip valuable information on how to operate the camera. He looked at me suspiciously, so I said "As I'm not the DP and I thought maybe you have some instructional materials I could take along to show him."

The manager replied curtly "Look buddy, anybody who is a DP is gonna know how to operate an Arri 35." I was just going to have to do my best.

Unlike the grainy old film we used for *Body of a Female*, this time we purchased brand new Eastman Stock. It was called Double-X and was a real step up in quality. The downside was that it was expensive so we would have to find other ways to save money.

At last we had our script, our cast, our sets and our equipment. We were ready to begin production on our first Amero Brothers film.

We shot *Diary of a Swinger* in late spring 1967. I worked out a detailed budget that totaled $8,250. It was going to be tight so we did almost everything ourselves. Lem was the director and editor, I was the producer and cameraman. On the days that Ron Scardera was around and not acting, he pitched in as an additional crew member.

Remarkably we did have a person responsible for wardrobe. Jack Benson was a friend of Lem's and had been a dancer on Broadway. He now had a company called "Brock Frocks" and designed costumes for shows at the Bal Tabarin super club where Lem used to work. In addition to wardrobe, Jack also let us use his apartment to shoot some interior scenes. We even persuaded him to play the part of a rapist. He was initially reluctant to take on the role but eventually agreed on the condition that we didn't show his face. We shot his scene entirely from behind him while still trying to show plenty of the damsel in distress –no small feat.

We filmed all the exteriors first. The opening scene takes place on a farm where Rita's character is raped. I hired a rental car and we all drove to

Dover, New Jersey where I'd secured a suitable location from a farmer who was completely unaware of the nature of our film. We spent most of the morning shooting Rita walking around the farm – not as easy as it sounds as Rita proved to be afraid of horses and refused to go near them.

In the afternoon we filmed the start of the sexual assault. The assault was scripted to take place in a shed but we didn't dare shoot it on the farm. So after filming the lead up we collected plenty of hay and drove back to the studio in New York where we replicated the inside of a shed. The scene was shocking for its time with Rita's assailant ripping off her clothes and exposing her breasts.

Another scene called for a jazz club where Rita's character is taken by her boyfriend to watch a racy strip-tease. We managed to persuade the owner of Arthur's Tavern at 57 Grove St in the Village to let us shoot there after hours. This was a coup for us as it was a great location with a storied past. Arthur's had opened in 1937 and was known as "Home of the Bird" since it had regularly hosted the legendary Charlie Parker back in his heyday.

Chuck was visiting from Boston and I asked him to play a bar patron. Unlike many of our friends, Chuck was not enamored with the idea of appearing in films, but I persuaded him. We placed him at one of the tables with a drink. He looked glum throughout the whole scene, no doubt wishing he was at home cooking. But free talent is free talent.

In addition to Chuck's grumpiness we also had a problem with the stripper we hired. When we filmed her shimmying out of her top, we noticed she was wearing huge pasties over her nipples which she adamantly refused to remove. Fortunately, our friend Darcy Brown, who had a part in the film as a nurse, allowed us to film close-ups of her breasts and insert them into the stripper's scene. Darcy was a serious performer – a great tap dancer and singer who regularly appeared on Broadway. She had a beautiful feline appearance and was always in demand. Lem and I had seen her once when she took over the starring role in a production of "Guys and Dolls" when Betty Grable was injured. That night Darcy went from the chorus to the lead, and was fantastic.

Rita was a lot of fun to work with. I liked her, and she liked me. I used to drive her home from the shoot every day and we'd stop at a bar before I dropped her off. She could drink most people under the table, and our evenings together would often end in the early hours. After the first few days of this routine, she called to say "I want you to come over this evening for drinks." Normally I would have loved to but on this occasion we had an early shoot the following morning. So I said "I really don't think we should. You've got to be up early and you've got to look your best. And I cannot face the day with another hangover." She persisted, but started not to like where things were going.

I assumed Rita knew I was gay although this wasn't something we'd explicitly discussed. After what seemed like an hour on the phone trying to be extremely diplomatic, complimenting her beauty and telling her what a great actress she was, she finally blurted out "John, if you don't get over here and ball me, I'm not showing up on set tomorrow morning" and then hung up.

I panicked. What to do, what to do? I called my brother and said "Lem, she's the star of the film. All our money is sunk into this movie and she wants me to come over there and have sex with her! What am I gonna do?" There was a pause on the phone, and then Lem quietly said "John, go over and screw her."

But I couldn't do it. So I called Rita back and told her I felt it would be unprofessional on my part to accept her invitation. I told her I adored her and that she was wonderful, and that once the film wrapped maybe we could explore a relationship, but I begged her to show up the next day. Thank goodness she did – and acted like nothing happened.

Outside of my negotiations with Rita, our most difficult task was shooting an orgy for the end of the movie. We'd never attempted to film a scene with a large group of people before. Since our studio had limited space, I decided we'd shoot in the art deco lounge at the Trans-Lux on Broadway I managed at the time. We planned to film in the middle of the night after the cinema patrons had all left. Once they cleared out, we decorated our makeshift set and let in the thirty or so extras we'd asked to turn up.

The scene depicts an after-hours party Jeannie is taken to by the man she's fallen in love with. The party soon gets out of hand and she's appalled by the debauchery she witnesses, causing her to become fatally disillusioned. To convey the extreme decadence, we had wild characters including go-go dancers with bare breasts. In an act of unparalleled ludicrousness, a woman – played by Janet Banzet – is brought out by muscled men who spread caviar on her breasts for party goers to lick off. Due to budgetary restrictions we used jam instead of caviar hoping viewers wouldn't be able to tell difference. Sadly I don't think we pulled it off.

Finding extras that wouldn't balk at appearing as a backdrop to an orgy had been difficult, especially as we were unable to pay them for their participation. And just one person expressing doubt could risk a mass desertion. So we promised that as it was a party scene we'd serve free cocktails – which helped abate some of the reluctance.

Men were reasonably easy to convince as their eyes lit up at the prospect of female nudity. And some of our male investors jumped at the chance to hang out on set with girls willing to take their clothes off. I even persuaded Chuck, who was visiting again, to take part.

But it was more difficult to persuade women to act in a nonchalant fashion while people are doing all manner of lascivious things in front of them. We appealed to people like Cara Duff-McCormick, who'd signed up to provide the narration, and Darcy, who by now already had two roles in the film, and slowly convinced enough people to join in.

But we ran into problems with the scene ending when Jeannie discovers her boyfriend sexually engaged with another woman on the main circular staircase of the theater. The actress meant to play the hussy on the stairs failed to show up. True to form we asked Darcy if she would take on yet another role in the film. Fortunately for us she agreed to nosh it up with Jeannie's beau.

Then Rita went missing toward the end of the evening. She'd been liberally helping herself to the alcohol on offer and was nowhere to be found for her horrified reaction shots. By this time we'd let most of the other actors go home, so Lem and I conferred and came up with the only solution we could think of: Darcy yet again. We cobbled together a makeshift wig and filmed Darcy mimicking Rita's response, hoping no one would notice the difference.

In the end we got our footage and finished filming our exterior scenes, including some great street shots of New York City. We were ready to move into our studio and film the interiors on the three sets we'd proudly built. After four days of event-free filming in the studio, we wrapped the shoot on schedule and on budget.

The couple of times Chuck came to visit while we were making *Diary of a Swinger* I checked him into the Taft Hotel on West 51st Street since my apartment was our studio. It felt wonderfully illicit to meet him there, and when I wasn't filming we'd have a great time going to shows together and dining out.

By now I realized that I really missed Chuck when he wasn't around. So as he was about to return to Boston after his second visit, I asked him if he'd like to move in with me. I was excited at the idea of living with him, but felt I had to warn him about what he'd be letting himself in for. For a start he'd be living illegally among our film sets in a studio with no hot running water (we only had a cold-water shower hidden in a corner where we stored lumber). And he'd be sharing that space not just with me but with Lem as well. It was pretty grim and hardly a case of "come with me to New York and I'll give you this wonderful life." But Chuck was keen to move in together despite the conditions. So, several weeks later, he came back to New York for good and moved in with Lem and me at the West Broadway studio.

It was great to have Chuck with me, even though our new living arrangement was no bed of roses. It was fairly cramped with three people sharing about 1,500 square feet of space. Chuck and I slept on the floor of a set using a mattress he said "some scuzzy actress probably just performed a sex act on." To make matters worse, I knew that in several months the space would become freezing cold. Lem and I had barely made it through the previous winter using sleeping bags next to an open flame gas heater.

And every so often we'd get word that the police or a building inspector was coming to check the premises so we'd hide all our personal items and pretend we were shooting a movie. The raids were completely unannounced but we could usually hear them climbing up the stairs and had enough time to hide anything that would give us away.

But finally we caught a break. After hearing about my experiences as a theater manager, Chuck thought he'd also be interested in that line of work. So he wrangled a job at Radio City Music Hall as assistant manager and with the extra money, we were able to afford a place of our own. We started looking in the West Village and soon found a sweet one-bedroom apartment with a wood beam ceiling and working fireplace on Cornelia Street. It was petite but charming, not expensive and we loved the location. So we moved out of the studio, leaving Lem the studio space for himself.

When we completed post production on *Diary of a Swinger*, Lem and I were really pleased with the results. Technically it was a step up from *Body of a Female*, showing we'd clearly learned a lot since those first days.

The film premiered at the State Theater in Boston in September 1967. The supporting feature with a potboiler called *Kiss Me Quick* (1964). I was very proud to return to my previous place of work as a filmmaker rather than as a manager. I still had friends at the theater and so I got to see the film grosses. *Diary of a Swinger* opened to even better business than *Body of a Female* had done.

The film was billed as "A significant new approach in motion pictures, the kind of film Hollywood doesn't dare make," and the one-sheets blared the tag lines "Memoirs of One of Today's Turn On Girls" and "A Generation in Heat!" The poster also played heavily on Rita's provocative good looks.

Box Office, a legitimate trade publication that reviewed exploitation films at the time, gave it an excellent review. Even better, Variety ran a column on opening week's business headed "Swinger Boffo $15,000". The article proclaimed that the only big winner in town was "locally made exploitation film, *Diary of a Swinger*, which was torrid in first week." Publicity in Variety for *Diary of a Swinger* wouldn't always be that good. The following year an article would cite the movie as one of the few films banned outright in Ontario, Canada, where the local censor described it as "an offensive feature of unknown origin."

Diary of a Swinger went on to play all the major cities across the country and proved to be very profitable. George Delemos had been a good ally and supporter to us during the making of the film. He clearly had confidence in us and left Lem and I completely alone to make the film. This was somewhat surprising considering I'd admitted to George that this was the first feature Lem and I had made together. But his trust was amply repaid when the company he set up to produce the film, "De Lem Films", made a great deal of money. George distributed the movie through the West Coast exploitation specialists, Box Office International Pictures. The company was owned by Harry Novak, the so-called "Sexploitation King" of the time and a prolific producer and distributor of softcore films from the early '60s to mid-'70s.

After we delivered *Diary of a Swinger* to George our paths didn't cross again. But he remained active in the exploitation world, going on to work on a couple of films with Gerard Damiano in the early 1970s, *Teenie Tulip* (1970) and *Changes* (1970).

Sadly, we never saw Rita again either. She appeared in a few other exploitation films and continued stripping in New York throughout the 1970s until ill health forced her to retire in the early '80s. Two of her last acting appearances were small parts in big budget mainstream films, *All That Jazz* (1979) and *Raging Bull* (1980). Rita went on to live in subsidized housing just off Times Square in reduced circumstances and with a rather bad alcohol problem, and passed away in 2017. I remain eternally grateful for her lead performance in *Diary of a Swinger* and see it as a testament to her beauty and luminous presence.

Unlike *Body of a Female*, *Diary of a Swinger* is widely available today on video and DVD. But I've been saddened by the quality of what I've seen.

DIARY OF A SWINGER (1965-1967)

At the time the film was first released, it was expensive for a distributor to make many copies for cinemas. This often meant that when a print was damaged say by a rip caused by a projector, it had to be quickly fixed by cutting either side of the offending frames and roughly reattaching the undamaged ends together. At best this would result in disarming jump cuts; at worst entire scenes were removed. These butchered prints seem to have been used for many of the reissued versions. Recently however I was happily sent a high-quality copy of a French DVD reissue by Artus Films. In addition to the visual caliber I was impressed by the first-rate dubbing of this French language version.

As we were making *Diary of a Swinger*, frequent letters from my grandmother in Gloucester let us know that our mother's health was deteriorating at an alarming rate. She had been diagnosed with cancer and when we visited her at Christmas, it was obvious that her days were numbered.

Driving home from the sanitarium one Sunday after a visit, my grandmother told us that she used to try and cheer my mother up when she was a girl by saying to her "Gladys, if the first half of your life is hard, the second half will be wonderful". It was one of the few times that I saw my grandmother cry.

Our mother died on December 16th, 1967. She was only 57.

Though we hadn't worked with Mike and Roberta for a while, Lem and I continued to see them on a regular basis. By now they were married, and we'd drink together, often too much, and swap stories about our film productions. They were very supportive of us and we of them.

Through their work, they'd forged a good relationship with Stan Borden, a New York producer and distributor of low-rent exploitation films. His company, American Film Distributing, had its offices on the mezzanine of the Paramount Hotel on West 46th Street. Stan specialized in the "roughie" genre and had been behind the enormous success of the *Olga* series of films. He was a larger than life character, over 6' tall with multiple chins and an old cigar always hanging out the side of his mouth. He was entertaining, funny and jovial which somewhat made up for the fact that he always wore the dirtiest clothes and seemed to be drooling. He had an equally entertaining and considerably more attractive wife named Lorraine.

Lem and I met Stan through Mike and Roberta, and thought of approaching him at some point to fund a future film of ours. The problem was that the amount he offered was always appallingly low. We'd spent just over $8,000 on *Diary of a Swinger* and Stan rarely offered more than $7,000 which left little room for making a profit.

Mike and Roberta happily worked with Stan though. They wanted to shoot an avant-garde, experimental exploitation film that they tentatively titled *Eroticon*. Somehow they convinced Sam to finance this "art" film. They even talked him into letting them go to Belgium to shoot and insisted on traveling on the Queen Mary because they were both terrified of flying. Given my love of ships, I was hugely envious of their voyage but also excited for them. I made sure I saw them off when they left on a bitterly cold February day. They had reserved a very inexpensive cabin but because it was February the crossing was under-booked. They ended up with a free upgrade to a first class stateroom.

While in Europe they stayed for a time in London and decided to buy a classic black taxicab to bring back to New York. Remarkably they managed to get it onto the Queen Elizabeth with them for the return journey. I was there again at the pier to welcome them and their amazing new purchase back home.

I was throwing myself into all aspects of the film business and having the time of my life doing it. This sometimes created problems with Chuck who had no real interest in film-making. He was just a very down-to-earth guy who was happy with a low-key life. So when I went out at night it was often to meet Mike at a bar to discuss movies. I seldom invited Chuck as he just wouldn't have enjoyed the conversation.

On the work front, Chuck accepted a new position as personnel director of the Brandt Cinema chain on 42nd Street. The chain was founded by Bernard B. Brandt and his brothers in 1930, and they eventually had more than 150 cinemas, mostly on the East Coast.

Chuck's main role in his new job was to hire cashiers, ushers and managers for the cinemas. This was actually easier than it sounded as the main criteria for deciding if someone was suited to a position was whether the cinema in need had a uniform that fit the applicant. Needless to say, this led to a variable standard of employees at best.

Chuck was told by his management not to hire black people. He was even given a guide on how to treat patrons, which stressed that black people should be ejected "with care" due to their "excessive sensitivity". Chuck found this difficult to cope with so he eventually left to work for the Post Office. Although the work was boring, there was job security, a pension, and decent pay. And this predictable day job allowed me to live the life of a filmmaker. Often times Chuck would become the main breadwinner, supporting us both between my films.

While I worried he wouldn't be happy in such a low-stress job, it seemed to fit Chuck fine. Unlike me, he lived for our home life. I loved Chuck but didn't look forward to just staying home the way he did.

And I was thrilled with the work Lem and I were doing. The experience of building up the studio and making *Diary of a Swinger* had made us even closer. Not that we didn't fight tooth-and-nail. As producer, my financial responsibilities often conflicted with Lem's directorial vision. It was a typical, complicated fraternal relationship. I never wanted Lem to outshine me, but at the same time I never wanted to overshadow him.

Unlike me, Lem was often a real loner. While I was at Trans-Lux, he was constantly working by himself in the studio. He was carpenter, electrician, and decorator, slavishly devoted to making the studio better. When I fell in love with Chuck, it bothered me that there was no one similar in Lem's life. At night when I'd go home to Chuck, I'd often feel guilty wondering what Lem was doing. Was he in the studio? Had he gone out for the evening? Why didn't he have his own apartment?

In fact, Lem spent most of his evenings at the Big Spender. "The Spender", as it was affectionately known, was a wonderful small theater bar on West 48th Street frequented by dancers, actors, and singers. We both passed a lot of time there but Big Spender was really Lem's whole social life. It was his club, lounge, and where all his friends were.

I always wanted Lem to find someone to settle down with but he'd never had a significant other. While Lem was easygoing and gentle and everyone adored him, he was also extremely sensitive – probably too much so for his own good.

Chuck and I started to travel whenever we had some free time and spare money. I felt guilty whenever we left thinking "I should invite Lem", but I don't think he would have come. Still it broke my heart every time to leave him alone. I just wanted him to feel settled and content in his private life. Lem probably wanted the same thing but being two uptight, gay, New England brothers, we seldom talked about it.

Lem's laid-back character meant I often had to lead and play the heavy when necessary in business dealings. We were never "starving artists", but we certainly weren't commercially minded hustlers either. At the time, there were no percentage deals for film makers. And even if there were, we probably wouldn't have been interested fearing the thievery of distributors. It was strictly a flat fee to deliver a finished film. And as we were constantly trying to improve the finished product, we would often eat into our profits. With no income to tide us over between projects, I was extremely grateful that the Trans-Lux Theaters always seemed to need me when I needed them.

The bottom line however was that we were making films and, for better or for worse, we were living the life we wanted. Lem and I even stopped paying much attention to what our competition was doing. We knew the films we wanted to make and, sometimes foolishly, we were going to make them. We were fiercely independent that way and bullish about the future.

CHAPTER 5

THE CORPORATE QUEEN
(1968-1969)

Our experience making *Diary of a Swinger* had been good; Lem and I were pleased with the movie and learned a lot more about film making. But we wanted to try something new with our next film so we decided to make an R-rated suspense thriller.

We wrote *Violent Summer* about a Senator's daughter who goes to a small fishing town as an investigative reporter and uncovers a drug smuggling ring. Russian trawlers are placing drugs inside phony bricks used to weight lobster traps; unscrupulous local lobster men are picking them up and selling the illicit goods.

The idea of lobster traps came from our upbringing in Gloucester, so we decided to shoot the exteriors in our hometown for authenticity. I knew we'd be able to get some great footage of lobster men retrieving traps that we could inter-cut with staged shots of crooks and contraband.

Filming in Gloucester also let us return to Judy Chamberlain's beautiful house to shoot. We decided to spice up the plot and turn Judy's home into a house of ill-repute. We changed the movie name to *Bordello* and cast Judy as the madam.

We intended to film all the other interiors back in our studio in New York. But as much as we loved the studio, the situation there was becoming untenable. We were increasingly worried about the fire risk due to the open flame gas heater among our wood film sets. On top of that, the City Buildings Department had started harassing us as they suspected someone was living in the studio.

So Lem and I started looking for another place where we could work and Lem could also live. I was disappointed Lem didn't want a proper apartment of his own as I thought this would improve his social life, but he was set on the studio.

We lucked out and found a wonderful space at 24 East 22nd Street. At $450 per month plus two months' security, it was twice as much as our West Broadway studio and probably more than we could afford. But the space could fit a two-tiered set, supplied ample electricity, and had an elevator to bring up heavy props from the street. We figured we could save some money by setting up an editing suite there as well.

We loved the space and got straight to work renovating it. This time it was legal for Lem to live there, so when we built a set to double as his apartment it was by choice, not necessity. The space was open-plan so we used large dividers to create rooms. We sectioned off an office at the entrance to the apartment set. Lem and I each had a desk and we adorned the front wall with posters from our two films. We placed our editing equipment in the corridor just by our office and used most of the remaining space as a film stage.

The studio soon became the center for all our activities. We held many parties there, and invested in a 35mm projector so we could screen our films for friends and potential investors. We were ready to take our filmmaking careers to the next level.

We were keen to finance *Bordello* ourselves. This was no small undertaking as the increased production values had pushed the film's budget to just under $20,000. And since we saw it as a more professional production, we decided we needed serious actors for the lead roles. We placed an ad in Back Stage and after a series of auditions found our cast.

For the male lead we chose Ted Pugh, an accomplished theater actor who trained – and later taught – at the Mike Chekhov Studio in New York. Ted had performed in all manner of productions on Broadway, off-Broadway, and in regional theaters across the United States. We gave the female lead to Nan Courtney, a talented singer and dancer who had appeared in "Finian's Rainbow" on Broadway a few years earlier.

Despite the higher cost – or maybe because of it – we quickly realized that *Bordello* had to be an exploitation film if we were going to make any real money. So to up the ante we changed the name (again) to *Circle of Lust* and started looking for actresses willing to undress on screen. We also recruited Mike and Roberta to help out behind the scenes, and got Roberta to act in a role that called for her to play the piano.

In late spring of 1968 we took everyone up to Gloucester and moved them into Judy's mansion. Judy adored having us there. Her acting was no great shakes, but in appreciation we made sure we shot plenty of footage of her as the haughty madam.

It was a bit more difficult this time to keep our presence under wraps as the number of people involved had grown. Before long we were visited by a reporter from the local Gloucester Daily Times and asked to do an interview. After our experience with the Herald Tribune the previous year, we politely but firmly declined saying "We'd love to, but only once the film is completed." Needless to say, we never called them back.

THE CORPORATE QUEEN (1968-1969)

Lem and I once again split the production duties – I was the cameraman and producer; Lem directed. The shoot was more ambitious and difficult than anything we'd done before. We'd scripted a lot of action, including a fistfight on the cliffs where one of the villains is thrown into a local landmark, Rafe's Chasm, and washed out to sea. We also shot a storm sequence, all faked, but using a real lobster boat we hired at some expense. To maximize our investment we filmed a love scene between the two leads in the cabin of the boat. And for good measure we changed the title again, this time to *The Girl on Nightmare Island*.

By the time we filmed all the exteriors, we were completely broke. We were happy with the footage shot in Gloucester, but we'd gotten carried away and were now wildly over budget. To make matters worse, both our leads had theater commitments and couldn't wait for us to find the money required to finish. Ted said, "I've got to take gainful employment, I just can't let the whole summer season go. I won't be able to work with you again until the fall." Then Nan told us she was up for the lead in a summer stock road tour of the musical "Anything Goes". For the first time in our careers, we stopped production and shut down. And without more money, completing the film now seemed an impossibility. We needed to come up with an alternative plan.

At first I thought "we'll show what we filmed to people in New York and see if anyone will buy it, so at least we can get the financing back." The trouble was that we only had half an hour of footage so nobody was interested. To compound our problems, the rent on the new studio was crippling us. It was soon clear that Lem and I both needed to take day jobs. So I went back to the Trans-Lux company.

I heard that the Tivoli Theater on Eighth Ave was looking for a new manager. The Tivoli was a notorious cinema opened in the early 1920s, now owned by Chelly Wilson. Chelly was a Greek immigrant who'd started off importing and distributing Greek films. Soon realizing how much more lucrative the exploitation industry was, she formed Chellee Films and financed a number of Joe Sarno pictures. She ran her business, which included the Cameo Theater on Eighth Ave and the Mykonos diner on West 46th Street, out of a smoke-filled office near Times Square.

As we couldn't afford to do anything for a few months, I convinced Lem to take the manager's job at the Tivoli. The assistant manager was a guy named Bob Sumner, and Lem and Bob quickly became good friends. Bob looked like a small Steve McQueen, possessed great imagination and energy, and had a unique flair for promotion and publicity.

The Tivoli didn't seem to require much management because Lem and Bob spent the better part of every shift at the Blarney Stone bar next door. They would talk for hours about the film industry and their ambitions. Soon Bob started hanging out with the rest of us at the Haymarket, which still doubled as our casting office. We'd all go and see off-Broadway productions together, a number of them featuring Patty Finnegan, the actress-come-Haymarket-waitress who'd become a regular in our group of friends. Soon Bob and Patty were an item.

As luck would have it, the apartment across from Chuck and I became available, so Bob and Patty moved in. With so many interests in common we lived in each other's pockets, often leaving our front doors wide open to create one big apartment.

I was still determined to do something with the footage we'd shot for *The Girl on Nightmare Island*. After much deliberation, I decided our best option would be to shoot some additional scenes and add it to the existing footage to create a complete film. The problem was finding money, so we had to shoot cheaply and use all the free resources we could get our hands on.

We had leftover footage from *Body of a Female* and *Diary of a Swinger* so I figured we could weave some of that into the new film. I was nervous about re-using the footage as technically we'd sold the rights to the distributors, but we couldn't afford to do anything else. And with hindsight I'm happy we did as the resulting film contains the only surviving footage from *Body of a Female*. This includes parts of the reservoir scene we shot with Roberta in Gloucester, and shaky guerrilla-style footage from when Mike and I shot in the camera club. We also included parts of the scene that Mike shot on his own of Roberta stripping.

We soon realized that the final product was going to be a Frankenstein monster. It cross cuts between old and new footage and uses a hodgepodge of different film stocks, lighting approaches, and shooting styles. But we were desperate to get our money back so we were willing to try anything.

We needed to link the footage together with a framing device and decided that a pseudo-documentary on prostitution would be the most marketable idea. So the film that started as *Violent Summer* before becoming *Bordello*, then *Circle of Lust* and *The Girl on Nightmare Island* eventually became *The Lusting Hours*. Lem did his best to edit it all together but the final cut made little sense.

I wanted to start the film with some contemporary news footage to set the tone of the times. So I went to the Trans-Lux theater library and took some film of the Beatles coming to the U.S. to cut it into the beginning of the movie. Then to signal that this was not a typical documentary, we had flames burning over the title sequence. In reality I just held a burning copy of the Daily News in front of the camera, but it seemed to successfully convey a sense of danger and the forbidden.

The opening of the film begins with a passionate embrace between Ted and Nan that we'd shot for *The Girl on Nightmare Island*. I avoided using footage that showed their faces as we didn't have their permission. I also feared that being associated with such a cheap production would negatively impact their theater careers.

The scene had been shot in a romantic, sensual style but we knew that a documentary about prostitution would need to be much sleazier. Enter Roberta to the rescue again. We persuaded her to perform a striptease on a little stage we built, and got a friend to ogle her lasciviously from the audience. While Roberta was game, she was also absolutely insistent that she would not act for free. In this respect she differed from Mike who, like us, wasn't great with money. Roberta always demanded to be paid in advance for any acting performance. And on the rare occasion we owed her money she would hound me constantly.

Times had already changed since we shot *Body of a Female* and we were conscious that audiences now expected more explicit content. So we also shot a lesbian scene with our friend Janet Banzet and Sheila Britt, an actress favored by director Joe Sarno. Not surprisingly Mike volunteered to help us with this shoot; he loved lesbian scenes and would have filmed nothing else if he'd had the choice.

To satisfy audiences, I was keen to push the envelope. I wanted to show one of the girls putting on a strap-on. There was nothing particularly explicit about the scene, but the mere fact that we were showing a girl with a dildo was daring. To soften the scene and raise the tone, I used the Max Steiner soundtrack from *Parrish* (1961), a film with Troy Donahue and Connie Stevens.

Another daring inclusion was a pick-up scene we filmed in the men's room of a Trans-Lux theater. We shot Chuck and good old reliable Ron Scardera, and I jiggled the camera behind a grill to create a voyeuristic impression. In reality it was more of a massage between the two, but the gay subtext was risqué for a exploitation film at the time. Equally risky was a sequence of a man – in this case, Lem – in drag. Lem never had any interest in cross-dressing but entered into the spirit of the occasion.

As before no one wanted to have their real names associated with the film so we had fun coming up with alternatives. We used Lina Lamont and

Don Lockwood – characters from *Singin' in the Rain* – for our leads. For our new friend and fellow Trans-Lux manager, Steve Gould, we used Satch Gould. For the film lab, we listed grain effects by Pathé, music editing was credited to Ruth Less, merkin production by J. Crawford (what would Joan have made of this?!), and even a stray Dick Feeler.

With a finished product ready, we finally had a chance to recoup our costs. So we set about shopping *The Lusting Hours* around the usual motley array of East Coast distributors.

One person who was keen to own the Boston distribution rights was Richard McLeod, a Massachusetts wheeler-dealer I met at the State Theater. He'd seen the success of our previous films and made it clear that he wanted a piece of the action. Dick was a unique character to put it mildly. He was highly intelligent and articulate, but also excitable and a little scary. Basically, he was a snake oil salesman, always on the lookout for anything that would make him money. He constantly hounded me to invest in his latest harebrained and barely legal get-rich-quick scheme. He set up companies selling everything from cosmetics to organic bread that all had one feature in common – customers were invariably ripped off.

He had recently hired *Diary of a Swinger* star Rita Bennett to do her old time striptease and burlesque routine in Boston theaters that he rented for variety shows. At the same time, he was playing Santa Claus at the Jordan Marsh department store in Boston and entering Hemingway lookalike contests. He even got involved in local politics, backing a Boston politician and managing his campaign.

Dick really wanted to direct and fancied himself as Orson Welles. He'd made two exploitation films, *The Last Semester* and *Kitten in a Cage* (1968), that were both terrible. The former was notable only for the fact that its star, 20-year-old Vito Aras, was arrested in 1969 trying to steal a copy of the Gutenberg Bible. Aras had hidden inside the Widener Library at Harvard University where the Bible was kept inside a secure glass case. After the library closed he lowered himself out of a second-floor window with the Bible stored in a knapsack. Unfortunately for him, the rope snapped and he was found unconscious on the ground with the knapsack torn open and the Bible next to him. When the case went to court, Vito was found not liable due to mental illness. Vito also had *other* talents...but more about that later.

Dick ultimately decided that distributing versus directing films would be the easiest way to make money. But being wary of Dick's wayward methods, Lem and I decided to go a different route. We'd met up with Mike and Roberta's distributor, Stan Borden, and described *The Lusting Hours* to him. Stan growled "you'd better not take it to anyone else," so we arranged a showing for him.

Selling Stan wasn't going to be easy. For a start he was nervous about the lesbian scene with the strap-on, telling us we'd never get away with it. So we re-edited the sequence so the audience could only see the actress strap on the sex toy from behind. But Stan wasn't enamored with the gay scene either, delicately stating "I think that fag shit should go." And he practically had a fit when he saw Lem in drag. He hated any suggestion of homosexuality, which made it all the more surprising that he eventually consented to leaving those scenes largely intact.

After the screening, Stan offered to buy the film outright for $12,000 and we were overjoyed. We hadn't expected Stan to offer anything above $10,000 as he'd never given Mike and Roberta more than that for a film. A sale at this amount would let us get back to making films.

The sale terms were fairly standard. We would receive four payments of $3,000 – the first upon signing the contract, the second when we finalized the edit, the third once we delivered a trailer, and the final payment six months after the film opened. As we were signing the contract Stan said "If you ever tell the Findlays how much I've paid you, I'll cut your balls off".

My grandmother was visiting as we worked through the sale. Having her stay was always tricky, even at the best of times. For a start Chuck had to decamp to our friend Steve Gould's apartment as we only had one bedroom. And then there was the subject of our work. Thanks to a few recent newspaper profiles of Lem and me, this time there was no getting away from the films we made. Fortunately, our grandmother took a pragmatic view.

"Do they make much money?" she asked.

When I assured her they were highly profitable, she said "Good – just make sure no one back home hears about them."

With that, the subject was dropped and she never asked another question. I loved her for her true New England hypocrisy.

Stan handled all the promotional materials for *The Lusting Hours* (1968) and sent the one-sheet and press book over to my apartment for review. I considered showing the materials to my grandmother if they weren't overtly sexual. But much to my amusement, and Lem's horror, the one-sheet prominently featured Lem in drag with Ron Scardera crawling through his legs. We were terrified that she'd see it so we quickly shipped the materials back to Stan, and shipped grandmother back to Gloucester.

Dealing with Stan meant frequent trips to his office at the Paramount Hotel. I'd often take Mike with me as it gave us a chance to catch up on all the film industry gossip. And Stan always had such an array of characters hanging out that we'd make up excuses to go and spend the afternoon chatting with whomever happened to be there.

Our favorite was an old film industry character named George Weiss, best known as the producer who funded the infamous 1953 exploitation film *Glen or Glenda* directed by Ed Wood. The film was originally conceived as a fictionalized account of Christine Jorgensen and her sexual reassignment surgery, but in Wood's hands became a more autobiographical tale about his struggle with being a closet transvestite.

Mike and I knew George better as producer of the sadistic *Olga* films such as *Olga's House of Shame* (1964), *White Slaves of Chinatown* (1964), and *Mme. Olga's Massage Parlor* (1965), the film that inspired us to make *Body of a Female*. We called him Georgie and would sit in Stan's outer office for ages listening to his stories. He looked old beyond his years and perennially stooped over, but was always elegantly dressed. He had a dry sense of humor and was often unintentionally hilarious too. It was difficult to tear yourself away when he was holding court.

George was still interested in drumming up business for new film projects, and would approach me whispering "I got a great title." Invariably that's all he had, and all he was interested in. Just like an old-school carny, he was after the sizzle, not the steak.

Sometimes George's old partners in crime, like Ed Wood and Joe Mawra, would be there too. Mike and I heard of Ed because of the daring low budget films he'd made in the 1960s. By the time we met him he cut a sorry figure; sweaty, unkempt and unhealthy. His disposition was quiet and morose, and he seemed permanently under the influence of too much alcohol and God knows what else.

Joe Mawra on the other hand was a shady associate of Georgie's who owned a number of cinemas including the Avon 7, the Doll, and the Hudson. He was credited with having directed the *Olga* films but we didn't believe he had the creative vision to put them together.

Despite its tortured genesis, *The Lusting Hours* was surprisingly successful and enjoyed a long run in New York and across the country. To this day I can't believe we got away with it.

As soon as we sold the film to Stan, Lem and I started on a new script. We came up with *The Corporate Queen*, a return to the exploitation melodrama.

THE CORPORATE QUEEN (1968-1969)

We were determined to learn from the mistakes we'd made on *The Girl on Nightmare Island*. We set ourselves a budget of $12,000 and since we wanted to continue shooting on 35mm, decided to use fewer sets and as many free locations as possible to keep costs down.

The plot of *The Corporate Queen* was a rip-off of the typical Joan Crawford rags-to-riches story. I adored Crawford and had seen all of her movies. Many of them had her playing a girl from the wrong side of the tracks who makes good in some way. So, in homage, our heroine starts out as a hooker.

The script featured a character named Crystal Laverne, a flamboyant woman who runs a call-girl service from her Manhattan penthouse. Her agency provides every type of sexual service from straight to gay, employing both gorgeous women and men. She recruits her team from the New York streets with the appeal, "Why work the corners or the bus terminal when you could be sitting in a plush office just waiting for the phone to ring?"

She hooks up with a handsome man named Chino and they start to run the agency together before she finds him in bed messing around with her assistant and she's forced to take drastic action. In the words of the press book, "No one crosses the Corporate Queen!"

We assembled a great cast of actors. Renay Clair Granville played Crystal Laverne. Renay was elegant and beautiful and perfect for the character that runs the whole operation. By the time Renay appeared in *The Corporate Queen* she was in her late 30s and had a good amount of acting experience under her belt. She was the niece of Bonita Granville, a prewar Hollywood star and Academy Award nominee for William Wyler's *These Three* in 1936. Renay made sure everyone knew about her distinguished aunt. On set she was full of airs and graces and kept her distance from the rest of the cast.

The part of Chino went to our friend and fellow theater manager Ron Scardera, concealing his identity behind the pseudonym Tony Vito. We also turned to Janet Banzet again, this time offering her a leading role as Chino's secret lover. By now Janet had become a staple of the New York exploitation industry, appearing in films directed by regulars Mike Findlay, Joe Sarno and Doris Wishman. Lem and I always wondered what happened to her mainstream career that had started out so promisingly a few years earlier. But by the time of *The Corporate Queen* those parts seemed to have dried up completely and her work was restricted to the increasingly cheap sex films being churned out. For our part we were happy to be able to work with her again; she was fun, lively and great to have around. The role we gave her in *The Corporate Queen* was one of her best parts and she was fabulous in it.

A new actress we cast in the film was Uta Erickson. Her exotic name, combined with her high cheekbones and blonde hair, suggested she was Nordic. But in reality she was Artie Giannini from Atlantic City, New Jersey. Lem and I loved Artie from the first time we met her. Apart from being a beautiful woman, she was always professional and a joy to work with. We gave her the pseudonym Ulla Kops and cast her as one of the hookers in a fumbling lesbian scene that ends in a threesome when Chino arrives.

As was becoming the norm, we cast everyone we knew in one role or another. This meant a non-sex role for Bob Sumner, and another small part for my partner, Chuck. Bobby was excited to take part as he was keen to get involved in the industry. Chuck on the other hand was lukewarm at best.

The only problem we encountered during the filming dealt with our lead actress Renay. She was in complete denial that this was an exploitation film, and doing everything she could to convince herself this would lead to mainstream acting roles.

When it came to Renay's first sex scene, I talked her through what Lem and I were expecting. The sex was all strictly simulated of course but I'd made it clear that nudity was absolutely required. But I could tell she was becoming uncomfortable and sure enough, when it came time to shoot, she turned up wearing a large feather boa intended to cover her modesty.

When Lem and I took her aside and insisted she abandon the prop, she started crying and hid in the kitchen. In an attempt to comfort her, I insisted that she was beautiful and talented and that this scene would in no way hamper her career prospects as no one who mattered would ever see it. Eventually I persuaded her to come out, and though she kept hold of the feather boa we managed to shoot around it and film her scene.

As with *The Lusting Hours*, we wanted to include gay as well as straight sex in our film. But once again we were discouraged by people like Mike who insisted that gay sex would be a commercial kiss of death. In the end we stuck by our guns and included another pick-up shot in the men's room at the Trans-Lux Broadway, and a sex scene between two men.

When we required a more opulent setting, we shot again at Lem's dancer friend-come-costume designer Jack Benson's apartment. For less luxurious scenes we filmed back at my apartment on Cornelia Street.

Outside of our issues with Renay, shooting went smoothly, and this time we kept to the budget we'd set for ourselves. With filming wrapped, Lem and I eagerly returned to the studio to start post production.

THE CORPORATE QUEEN (1968-1969)

Whenever Lem and I were working in the studio we'd go to Max's Kansas City for lunch. Max's was a great restaurant on Park Avenue South that opened in 1965 and quickly became a gathering spot for musicians, poets, and artists.

It was a favorite hangout of Andy Warhol and various members of his ever-changing entourage. We'd met Andy at some of his film screenings in the mid 1960s, and so when we saw him at Max's we'd frequently engage in conversation with him. He was a strange character, often diffident and aloof, but when he found out who we were, he opened up. He'd seen *Diary of a Swinger* and was interested in what we were doing so we'd end up sharing film making anecdotes. The police frequently shut down his films for obscenity so we also had that risk in common. I'd give him passes to the Trans-Lux theaters as I still had connections there. He was especially interested when there was any kind of special event taking place. If there was one thing Andy loved, it was attending premieres, openings, and private screenings. As the saying goes, he would turn up for the opening of an envelope.

While we were editing *The Corporate Queen* Andy came by our studio and looked at some of the footage. We were sure he'd find it campy and uninteresting, but he said he liked it a lot.

One day there was a knock on our studio door. It wasn't locked so after a few moments a rather nervous looking woman in her early 30's stepped in and said "Hi, I'm Valerie, and I have a script that I think would be right for you."

We weren't looking for anything at this point and I was busy. Also she conveyed a rather unstable demeanor. I was keen to get rid of her but she sat straight down and placed her script in front of me. I tried to convince her that I didn't have time to read it but she was insistent. She said "Just read the first four pages and you won't be able to put it down. I know you're gonna' want to make this film." It was titled "SCUM Manifesto".

She was looking more deranged by the minute, so I relented and started reading. I could tell straight away that the material was appalling. It was ugly and violent and something we'd have no interest whatsoever in filming. I stopped and said, "I'm sorry, but this really isn't our type of subject matter." She stared back and in an ever more adamant tone said, "Keep reading." I was becoming frustrated and somewhat rattled so I mentally scrambled for a way to get her out of our office.

A light bulb finally went off in my head. I said, "Look – this is the kind of material that I know Andy Warhol loves. Have you shown it to him? He's a dear friend of mine and he's just around the corner."

Shaking her head, she looked hopeful for the first time. I continued, "Well, you have to get it in front of Andy. This is exactly the kind of edgy fare that is perfect for him." She grabbed the script away from me and rushed out. I headed into the editing room to tell Lem the story. He laughed and said "That was a cruel thing to do. Be ready for Andy to be pissed off at us now."

We soon forgot about the whole affair. Then one day in June 1968, I noticed a blazing headline in the Daily News: "Actress Shoots Andy Warhol". I bought a copy and learned that the actress in question was Valerie Solanas, the very girl who had come to see us. Apparently, she'd made it to the Factory to present her script to Andy and he'd turned away the work. Sometime later, frustrated by his rejection, she'd returned and shot him. Andy was recovering in the hospital but I didn't dare go and see him. I was afraid members of his entourage would ask "Was it you who sent her over? Couldn't you see how crazy she was?!"

It wasn't until I read that Andy was going to make a full recovery that I relaxed a little. Still, we didn't venture into Max's Kansas City for a while for fear we'd run into him. Eventually we did see Andy at a screening and shared a few words. He never mentioned Valerie so I can only hope she never mentioned the Amero brothers.

And, fortunately, we never saw Valerie Solanas again. Though diagnosed with chronic paranoid schizophrenia, she was deemed fit to stand trial for Andy's shooting. She represented herself without an attorney and plead guilty to "reckless assault with intent to harm". She was sentenced to three years in prison and in 1988 died in San Francisco at the age of 52. In 1996 a film called *I Shot Andy Warhol* was made, focusing on her assassination attempt and starring Lili Taylor as Valerie. I guess you could say that in the end, she was in fact responsible for an interesting and successful film.

When *The Corporate Queen* was ready we decided to screen it for Times Film, a quasi-mainstream distribution company specializing in foreign movies. It was owned and run by Jean Goldwurm, a film distributor who had imported neo-realist classics like *Rome, Open City* (1945), *Bicycle Thieves* (1948) and *Forbidden Games* (1952) from Europe. More recently Jean had been involved in two significant censorship lawsuits – "Times Film vs. Chicago" (1961) and "Times Film vs. Maryland" (1965) – regarding attempts to bar the showing of a number of Times' films.

I'd always admired Times Film because they owned two theaters I loved – an art house cinema called the Little Carnegie Playhouse on West 57th Street and the World Theater on West 49th Street.

THE CORPORATE QUEEN (1968-1969)

Times Film had a subsidiary – Victoria Films run by Felix Bilgrey – that handled racier fare. These were ostensibly low budget art house films but offered enough nudity for the grind house market. Victoria Films had recently started to show an interest in New York exploitation movies.

We arranged a screening for Felix. He was a small, slightly creepy man with a sleazy appearance. But he was known as being honest and fair and had the reputable Times Film company behind him.

As we prepared to show the movie to Felix, I became more concerned about the gay sex scene. Though it was tame and innocuous, I still feared it would be a turn off for distributors. When we got to the scene, I said to Felix "You can cut this out as it's not going to affect the plot line". But I needn't have worried. Felix thought the film was great and wanted to buy it as is. He offered us $27,000; of this $5,000 would be paid to us immediately and the remaining $22,000 once we delivered the materials. We tried to push for some residuals but this was one area where Felix flat out refused.

Needing money after the debacle of *The Girl on Nightmare Island*, we accepted the offer without any of the usual haggling. We felt it was an excellent profit on a film that had cost us just under $12,000 to complete. And more importantly, the money would allow us to make another film. This would become our professional pattern – make a film and sell it with the hope that we'd then be able to make a bigger and better one.

We were so pleased with the deal, we decided to throw a celebratory party at our studio. It ended up being a huge affair – probably the largest party we ever hosted. We wanted to create a wild nightclub feel so we had our new friend LaRue Watts help us with decorations. We'd met LaRue at Big Spender – he was an aspiring playwright working at the Meadowbrook Dinner Theater in New Jersey to make ends meet. The Meadowbrook was one of the biggest and best dinner theaters that featured prestigious touring groups. Chuck and I frequently went to see productions there.

For our party, LaRue suggested we blow up photo stills from the film and build large arches with dramatic lighting for extra effect. LaRue topped things off with a large disco ball at the center of the revelry. We were so impressed with his work that we wound up hiring him for our next production.

We invited everyone we knew from our extended group of friends, including Mike and Roberta, Bobby Sumner and Patty Finnegan, and two of our film's stars, Ron Scardera and Janet Banzet. LaRue turned up in outrageous semi-transparent white bell-bottom pants. Even Felix came along, although that may have been because he'd fallen for Janet despite the fact that he was married. The aloof Renay was the only notable absentee, as we hadn't kept in touch after the film wrapped. The whole shindig was a raucous affair broken up by the cops at 4am when a neighbor complained about the noise.

The Corporate Queen opened at the Times Film-owned World Theater in April 1969. Felix took out large ads in the local newspapers announcing the premiere. He created a great campaign for the film, prominently splashing the sleazy tag line "No Desire Went Unfulfilled!" all over the one-sheets. Janet Banzet even made personal appearances to meet fans and promote the movie. *The Corporate Queen* ran for many weeks with showings starting at 8.30am and continuing into the night. Lem and I were very happy with the exposure the film received and its huge success.

The Corporate Queen was our first film reviewed by Screw magazine, newly founded by Al Goldstein and his partner, Jim Buckley. The review was authored by Al himself who, after complimenting us for having made a "good skin flick, with respectable acting and careful production", asserts "There is one point of major importance to *The Corporate Queen*. That is, this is the first truly bisexual film I've seen in the exploitation class… This one doesn't even get embarrassed about guys with guys. The whole sexuality is nicely uncomplicated and non-moralizing. Very healthy, actually."

Despite our positive experience with Times Film we never wound up working with them again. But we – and other exploitation filmmakers – continued to have reason to be grateful to them. Jean Goldwurm and Felix Bilgrey devoted much of their remaining careers to fighting local and state censorship of motion pictures, and were involved in many notable court cases.

The Corporate Queen was the last of the black and white films Lem and I cut our teeth on and I'm proud of it. Sadly, to this day, it remains a lost film – no known prints exist and, as far as I know, none of the Victoria Films have been re-issued. It seems strange to me that it disappeared since it was owned by the reputable Times Films. I live in hope that a print is stored away somewhere and that one day *The Corporate Queen* will emerge.

As Lem and I continued to work, so did Mike and Roberta. They were prolific and very successful. Their dark and sadistic stories reached a wildly popular climax with three films referred to as the "Flesh Trilogy" – *The Touch of Her Flesh* (1967), *The Curse of Her Flesh* (1968) and *The Kiss of Her Flesh* (1968).

All shot for Stan Borden, the "Flesh Trilogy" had Mike in the lead role of all three films and featured many of the usual players such as Uta Erickson,

THE CORPORATE QUEEN (1968-1969)

Ron Scardera and Janet Banzet. In addition to fetishistic scenes of bondage and torture, a key to the trilogy's success was the imaginative way in which victims were dispatched, from blow darts and a crossbow to a buzz saw and poison-tipped rose thorns.

Richard Jennings – Mike's character in all three films – is a misogynist killer who stalks, maims and murders prostitutes and strippers. Mike always insisted that he appeared in his films because it was cheaper than having to pay someone else – but I knew he wouldn't have done it if it made him at all uncomfortable. I'm convinced there was an element of enjoyment and pleasure he got from acting out such crazy scenarios.

Off screen, Mike still came across quiet and repressed and certainly wasn't a violent or sadistic person. He wasn't sexually promiscuous either, and to my knowledge he never cheated on Roberta. He kept his wildest and most extreme thoughts for his scripts and we would have long, intense discussions about them over beer. But I never felt he took the strange and bizarre plots seriously in any way.

He had a conventional speaking voice but developed a wonderfully sleazy and guttural Richard Jennings persona that he used to great effect in the trailers for the films. He would describe acts of "unspeakable depravity" in this over-the-top voice that cracked me up every time I heard it.

Mike would often consign his lead character to a wheelchair, ostensibly to show feebleness and inadequacy but also to highlight Richard Jennings' desperation, bitterness and self-loathing. Mike even chose the name Jennings because that was the brand of wheelchair he used.

Around the time of the trilogy, Mike and Roberta rented a big beautiful old New England house in Manchester, Massachusetts. They'd first visited the area when we shot *Body of a Female* in Gloucester and had fallen in love with it. Roberta was now pregnant, and they decided to move up there for the rest of the year with the intention of having the child in Massachusetts.

Mike and Roberta were rarely idle however, and had started thinking about pre-production for their next film, *A Thousand Pleasures*. They decided to shoot it in their Manchester house during the winter months. They contacted me to ask if I would cast the film in New York and bring the actors and crew up to their Manchester house to shoot. They also wanted me to be production manager and on-set still photographer. I was game, though my first concern was how cold it was going to be in the house at that time of year. It was going to be difficult to persuade people to sign up for a frigid Massachusetts winter.

By now I was an old hand at recruiting for an exploitation film and knew immediately who to contact. One of the first people I called was Janet Banzet who was keen to be part of the adventure. I then secured the services of Uta Erickson and her close friend Linda Boyce, another stalwart of the scene. They both ended up wearing slightly comical wigs on camera, in Uta's case because she was self-conscious about her thinning hair.

A Thousand Pleasures followed the "Flesh" trilogy pattern in that it portrayed another breathtaking array of sadistic moments conjured up by Mike and Roberta. Also, as with the trilogy, most of the characters meet their end in absurd ways, including whipping, torture, and even suffocation by breasts. As usual Mike added his demented film noir voice over, including nuggets such as "The drug in that tea hit me like a concrete lullaby".

Mike and Roberta took full advantage of the ever more sexually permissive environment. For example, pubic hair no longer had to be concealed, though male nudity was still by and large a no-no.

We filmed the interiors in the drafty old house and the exteriors in the surrounding areas. As expected it was freezing cold, and the girls we'd brought up from New York were profoundly miserable because of the conditions. What's more the script called for them to be scantily clad and walk around in lurid spiked heels. To keep warm we spent most of our time indoors crowded around one of the few heaters available in the house.

Even though Manchester is close to my hometown, I avoided going to see my grandmother and the rest of the family. I knew they'd ask why I was staying in Manchester instead of with them and I'd have to lie to cover up the film shoot.

On occasion, however, I had to go into Gloucester to pick up props or equipment that we couldn't find locally. For these trips, I decided to concoct a disguise to avoid being recognized. I found a wool knit cap that I pulled down over my head and turned my collar up as high as I was able. I then borrowed Roberta's large glasses that had such a strong prescription I could barely see. Fortunately, I didn't run into a soul I knew.

Back on the set, my role turned into more than I had bargained for. Mike and Roberto convinced me to take on some acting and in one scene, Janet's character tries to seduce me. I react by violently stubbing a cigarette out on her bare breast and leave her on the floor writhing in complete agony. Not that this did much lasting damage as Janet appears nude in the following scene with no hint of a burn. In the climactic scene of the film, Mike and I fight to the death on the beach at Gloucester Harbor, the same beach where I had spent much of my time daydreaming as a boy. Sometimes life comes full circle.

THE CORPORATE QUEEN (1968-1969)

Despite the freezing temperatures, the shoot was fun and it was enjoyable working with Mike and Roberta as always. Never ones to miss an opportunity, they quickly decided that shooting another film in the house was in order. So they embarked on making *The Ultimate Degenerate*, largely a remake of *Body of a Female* with Mike in the lead role. I rounded back up Uta Erickson and Janet Banzet and roped in another exploitation regular, Kim Lewid.

I also cast a strong, ambitious young actor named Earl Hindman in the film. His fresh-faced look was a welcome addition to some of the paunchy actors that appeared in these movies. We stayed drinking friends for a time after the film but eventually lost touch. Earl wound up moving to Hollywood and had a successful film and television career, including a recurring role as the kindly neighbor on the hit sitcom "Home Improvement".

Shooting of *The Ultimate Degenerate* went fairly well, even though by that point Roberta was very pregnant and seemingly shot every scene with an Arriflex camera perched on her belly. But her work rate put the rest of us to shame and by this time she'd developed into a talented camerawoman, with a good sense of lighting and creative flair to her work. This in an era when just carrying the heavy equipment was a challenge and the camera operator often had to be strapped into an Arriflex brace. But many movies were filmed hand-held which meant getting a smooth shot was arduous with lengthy takes only increased the degree of difficulty. It was exhausting work, but Roberta was always up to the challenge.

After we wrapped shooting on *The Ultimate Degenerate*, Roberta gave birth to a daughter at the local hospital; the same hospital where I was born.

After I cast Janet Banzet in Mike and Roberta's Massachusetts films, we started seeing less of her. She'd sometimes stop by the studio when she was in the neighborhood but her visits became less frequent until gradually we lost touch with her completely. It was a shame as we always loved spending time with her and considered her a close friend.

A couple of years later we were shocked to learn that Janet had hung herself. She was due to go out with friends one night and when she didn't turn up they went to her apartment and discovered her body. We heard rumors that she was distraught over a bad relationship with someone in the film industry, but we never found out the truth.

It was tremendously sad as she was a wonderful person and a very talented actress. She'd been so good to us in *Diary of a Swinger*, *The Corporate Queen* and the other films that we'd cast, and we missed her greatly.

Back in New York and returning home late one night, I stopped at the well-known Village bar, Julius', for a nightcap. Julius' served a straight clientele during the day and a gay crowd at night and was notable for having established the right of homosexuals to be served in licensed premises in New York State in 1966. This advancement cleared the way for the opening of many new legitimate gay bars.

I was not an activist and rarely went to rallies but I was living in the heart of Greenwich Village at a critical and exciting time for gay rights and was fully supportive of the movement. I would often drink at the Stonewall, which became newsworthy after a police raid in June 1969 that prompted a week of sometimes violent confrontations.

There were other flash points too, such as at a Howard Johnson restaurant on 6th Avenue and 8th Street that refused to serve gay men. Management claimed this was largely due to drag queens that would congregate there at night-after parties, but the story hit the press and soon there were pickets outside demanding equality.

That night at Julius' when I stopped for a drink, everyone seemed hammered. I met up with friends at the bar and they mentioned that Anthony Perkins was in the back room. This wasn't a surprise as he often could be found at Julius'. Rumors about Tony's sexuality had persisted for years. I later learned that he was in psychoanalysis attempting to eradicate his homosexual desires. It deeply saddened me that people like Tony were so conflicted by their sexuality. Despite this being the era of sexual permissiveness, being gay was still clearly a difficult burden for many. This was particularly acute for a Hollywood leading man whose career could be terminally damaged if his sexual orientation was made public.

But that night, I was excited as I'd been a big fan of Tony's since I'd seen him in *The Matchmaker* (1958) ten years earlier. He had the most beautiful eyes, both sensitive and expressive. His physique on the other hand was unusual in that he was bony and slender yet had broad, athletic shoulders.

After a couple of drinks, I made my way back to the restroom. It was a tiny space with barely enough room for more than one. Soon another person entered the cramped space and complimented me on my lambskin coat. I turned around and saw Tony. He too was wearing a good-looking jacket so I returned the compliment. Before I knew it we were locked in a drunken embrace. The coats came off and zippers came down.

It was over fast and in just a few minutes I was back at the bar sobered and guilt ridden about Chuck. I never told Chuck or anyone else about my encounter with Tony. A few years later Tony married and had children.

THE CORPORATE QUEEN (1968-1969)

But by all accounts his mental anguish continued until his passing in 1992 as a result of complications from AIDS.

One day, Lem called to tell me about an incident that happened to him the previous night. He'd been working late at an editing suite we were leasing at 1600 Broadway, a building where many filmmakers did post production work. The walls between the offices were paper-thin and you could always hear conversations between editors swapping battle stories.

This time Lem heard a man sigh and groan continually in an adjacent office, and then finally begin sobbing convulsively. Lem went to investigate and came across a young filmmaker named Jack Bravman, sitting forlornly at a Moviola. When Lem asked what the matter was, Jack mumbled "They're going to kill me."

Jack explained to Lem that he was trying to edit his first film, a exploitation potboiler called *Blonde on a Bum Trip*, but that he didn't have a clue how to do it. Lem offered to help but soon learned he was taking on more than he bargained for. Jack had cut out the film frames that contained the slate details, thinking they wouldn't appear in the final cut so he didn't need them. Lem explained that without the slates, syncing shots would be impossible. So with painstaking patience Lem showed Jack how to re-attach the cut frames and edit the film. Lem and I found this story hilarious, probably because it reminded us of how far we'd come since being clueless first-timers only a few years earlier.

Despite his lack of knowledge, Jack was a sweet guy and we soon became friends with him. He was from a lower middle-class family in the Bronx and had left school to work for MGM in the early 1960s. An aspiring filmmaker, he quickly learned about the industry but grew frustrated as he wanted to make his own movies. He heard from friends about an underground industry for black-and-white exploitation films and just like Mike and I had done, he went to Times Square to check them out. He was immediately convinced that this was his chance to make films.

Movies like Jack's *Blonde on a Bum Trip* (1968) had even lower budgets than anything we'd been making. People started referring to these films as "One-Day Wonders" as they were shot from start to finish over the course of a single day. Producers sometimes shot enough footage in a day to assemble more than one movie – which gives a good indication of the production values involved.

In many ways Jack was ideally suited to this bargain basement strand of film making; he was an energetic hustler, always on the lookout for a moneymaking opportunity. He was also very neurotic and saw an endless number of shrinks over the years. He was often unintentionally funny and had a habit of rubbing his head comically whenever he was stressed – which was all the time. He had no interest in sex, but loved films and film history. We spent many hours chatting about our favorite cinematic scenes.

A few months after we became friends, Jack called to ask if I wanted to help him on his next production. He told me he was going to make two films over one weekend: *Lovers By Appointment* (1960) and *Everything for Everybody* (1969). Jack, always casual about his business dealings, asked me if I would "kinda" write, direct, produce, be the cameraman, the sound man, and the production manager. Oh, and could I find the locations too? He was already thinking of his girlfriend Linda to feature in the films. And he said he had a crew ready, but it turned out to be a rag-tag group of NYU film students willing to work for free.

Needless to say, Jack was never overly concerned with the quality of his pictures. In that respect he was probably wiser than Lem and I were. He recognized that the way to make money was to churn these films out at speed and release them to the grind house market with lurid ad campaigns promising the most daring action ever. He rarely used his real name on his films, concealing his involvement behind fanciful pseudonyms like "Wizard Glick", "Seaman Losch" and "Looney Bear".

It was a far cry from an Amero Brothers production but it sounded like fun so I agreed to the work. I didn't necessarily want my name associated with the films though, so my one stipulation was to use a pseudonym in the credits. Jack mostly respected my request but once or twice there's a reference to my name, or at least a derivation of it. For instance, in a later film I helped on called *The Ballers*, Jack gave me the name John Meroa.

I wrote the scripts pretty quickly. They were flimsy works but I inserted a little character development to make sure they were a cut above simple stag films. To save Jack money both films needed to be shot in one location, so I opted for my good friend Steve Gould's apartment on Christopher Street. Of course, we paid Steve nothing, and for the same non-existent fee even convinced him to make a cameo appearance as the landlord. For the other roles I turned to two of my reliable favorites, Artie and Linda, and cast a French girl who'd just arrived in New York. It was always a risk to go with someone new, but I crossed my fingers and hoped for the best. Rounding out the cast was our friend, Bob Sumner.

When I'd arranged all the details, I phoned Jack to set up the rendezvous the following day at Steve's apartment. But Jack overruled me, stating we'd all

THE CORPORATE QUEEN (1968-1969)

need to meet in front of the Brill building on Broadway at 49th Street. When I asked why, he casually admitted "Because that's where I'm gonna get the funding for the film." This was the first time I realized he didn't have the money to make the film yet. He said "Just bring the cast and equipment, park on Broadway and wait for me. I'll come downstairs when I'm ready and then we can go to the location."

Early the next morning, I found myself jammed into an Econoline van with a group of exploitation actresses and a bunch of film equipment. Parked on Broadway as instructed, I was sure we looked incredibly suspicious. I told the girls not to get out of the van as they were already dressed for their roles as hookers. After what seemed like an eternity Jack appeared carrying a soiled paper bag. He got into the car and proudly announced "I've got the funding." He pulled filthy, crumpled bills from the greasy bag and proceeded to pay everyone there and then as I drove down Broadway. He simultaneously reached into his jacket pocket and pulled out stained release forms he got everyone to sign. By the time we arrived at Christopher St, all formalities had been dealt with. We set up the equipment and started to shoot.

The fact that we had to shoot both films back-to-back that day left little margin for error. But the problems started early with a love scene between Bob and the French girl. Though it was strictly a simulated sex coupling, our actress seemed to doubt Bob's intentions and spent the whole scene wailing "Don't stick it in me! Get it away from me!" As usual we shot around her protestations.

Another of Jack's idiosyncrasies was his love of basketball. He was crazy about the sport and insisted on watching games on TV even when they conflicted with our filming schedule. I was familiar with Steve's building so I warned Jack, "This building is very old so I need you to refrain from turning on any electrical appliances while we film or you'll blow the fuses."

Later that day when we were in the middle of shooting a lesbian scene I noticed our lights becoming dimmer and dimmer until suddenly they cut out completely. As I anticipated, Jack was watching a basketball game and had blown the electricity. He yelled from the kitchen, "Don't cut, don't cut. Keep shooting, I'll go and fix the fuse."

After a few minutes in near darkness, Jack was successful and the lights came back on. The girls were still noshing it up and I thought to myself "When Jack gets this into the editing room, he's going to have a real job putting a decent segment together." But I needn't have worried. Rather than edit the sequence, Jack released the film with the scene going dark and then suddenly, miraculously, returning to normal.

At one stage, I was so exasperated with the shoot I excused myself so I could sit on the toilet and get away from the craziness. I was still strapped into the heavy Arriflex and didn't even bother to take it off. I just sat there wondering, "Has it really come to this?" Working on cheap exploitation films, trying to get away by sitting on the toilet with the camera still attached? Fortunately, I couldn't help but see the funny side, and was soon back on set directing the action amid the madness.

We started at 10:30am and wrapped late the following evening with two feature films in the can. I never wound up seeing *Everything for Everybody* and *Lovers By Appointment*, and, thankfully, believe they have joined the list of lost films.

I continued to work with Jack on his films for many more years. They were always cheap and quick and crazy, but they were also easy money and usually fun. Jack had a sense of humor that could always puncture the ridiculousness of a dire situation. And he laughed all the way to the bank.

CHAPTER 6

BACCHANALE
(1970-1971)

The 1970s started out with a bang – literally. On New Year's Eve 1969, Chuck and I were partying with Mike and Roberta at Steve Gould's Christopher Street apartment. As the festivities wound down we all piled into Mike's car, the same one featured in his film *A Thousand Pleasures* (1968). Mike clearly had too much to drink but insisted on driving, and foolishly we let him. He ended up crashing the car into the 6th Police Precinct on 10th Street. We all wound up in the emergency room, in Mike's case having glass removed from his head. But luckily we all survived and amazingly Mike never faced any legal or criminal repercussions.

Apart from this bit of unwanted excitement, I was feeling good about life. The exploitation industry had taught Lem and I every aspect of filmmaking and enabled us to make a string of movies that pulled in more money than we expected. This income allowed us to live reasonably well and invest in our 22nd Street. studio, which was now fully equipped and ready for our next picture. My personal life was happy too, though our various film projects meant I didn't get to spend nearly as much time with Chuck as I would have liked.

Lem, Chuck and I would go see the latest movies and live performances whenever we got the chance. We had a particular soft spot for Radio City Music Hall. For the price of admission, you'd get a first run feature and a stage show. We'd view the stage show and the film from the balcony, then rush down to the first row of the orchestra to see the stage show again. Our favorite live act was called "Music Box Mine" about a little girl who brings a doll to life. Once animated, the doll dances on point and then proceeds to play the violin with incredible skill while continuing to dance. The performer was older than those usually featured but she was hugely talented. She was clearly classically trained, had tremendous grace and was in fantastic shape. We were always thrilled when she was on stage and would marvel at her. Little did we know at the time that our paths would cross again in the future.

Unlike in the early days, film work was now abundantly available to Lem and me. The extensive network of people we knew in the industry meant we were always being asked to help out on sets or in cinemas.

Our friend and fellow filmmaker Jack Bravman decided to make a horror exploitation movie about a psychotic teen girl murdering her way across the country. This time he was willing to spend a little more money than he had in the past and paid James Foley, an author who was friends with Mike and Roberta, to write the script. He then enlisted Mike, Roberta and myself to help with production, which he titled *Janie*.

Jack wanted to cast his girlfriend Linda as the lead, even though she had almost no acting experience. Linda was a dark, attractive Italian woman who had done some nude photo spreads for local men's magazines and Jack had completely fallen for her. She agreed to do the movie but wanted to conceal her identity so Jack christened her Mary Jane Carpenter. To further disguise Linda's identify we filmed her in a number of wigs for the first few scenes but none of them did her any favors. Eventually we decided she should dye her hair blonde, but Linda refused to go to just any old salon. Jack was so enamored of Linda that he agreed to pay for her to see George Masters, stylist to the likes of Marilyn Monroe and Ann-Margret. But while Jack was willing to shell out money for a famous hairdresser, he was not willing to re-do the initial scenes we'd shot with a wigged Linda. To make matters even worse Linda was keen to showcase her own extensive wardrobe, sometimes insisting on costume changes in the same scene. Needless to say continuity went right out of the window.

Linda wasn't the worst actress in the world and the film had a decent budget, but it was still a typical Jack Bravman shoot plagued by a complete lack of organization. Jack started out directing but soon handed those responsibilities over to Mike. Both Roberta as cinematographer and I as production manager struggled as Jack made up much of the story along the way. Jack also asked Mike and Roberta to take on acting roles on top of their other production duties. But despite this usual Bravman set chaos, I didn't mind terribly as it was always fun to work with Mike and Roberta and we got to shoot at Enrico Caruso's summer home in East Hampton. I never asked Jack how he arranged that location because with Jack's somewhat questionable connections I wasn't sure I wanted to know.

When we finished with production Jack struck on the idea of having Linda appear on the then popular Joe Franklin television show. We scoffed at the suggestion as television coverage of exploitation films was unheard of, but to our amazement Jack made it happen. While I never saw the show, or the film for that matter, Linda's appearance earned *Janie* (1970) good publicity and a decent box office showing.

BACCHANALE (1970-1971)

The start of the '70s also saw our friend Bob Sumner take the plunge and direct his first film. He would often hang out with Lem and me and would have liked to play a bigger part in Amero Brothers productions. But in truth Lem was more enamored with Bob than I was, and I was wary about Bob's fairly aggressive approach and tendency to take over. I was keen to keep him at arm's length when it came to our films.

So on his own Bob came up with a script titled *The Sidewalk Cowboy*, a blatant rip off of the box office hit *Midnight Cowboy* (1969), and hired exploitation actress Linda Boyce as the female lead.

Making the film put Bobby in contact with Sam Lake, a veteran distributor in his late 50s. Born Sam Lakernick, he had started his career at Universal Pictures and was now one of the most significant New York distributors of exploitation films. His company, Sam Lake Enterprises, had fueled the success of many New York directors such as Joe Sarno, Doris Wishman, Ron Sullivan and Graham Place.

Sam was a larger-than-life figure, always elegantly dressed in a suit and tie but with a reputation for being one of the biggest shysters in town. He was socially awkward, rude, crude and lacked any sense of humor. He would always interrupt whomever he was talking to and then drone on interminably about his latest film project. He would take credit for anything he was remotely connected with. And he was dishonest if he felt it benefited him to be so.

Looking for a distribution deal, Bobby showed Sam his completed film. Sam liked *The Sidewalk Cowboy* enough to buy it outright.

Helping friends out on their productions paid the bills and could be fun, but we wanted to get back to making our own films. We were keen to make a more ambitious movie, which we knew would also mean a bigger budget.

Enter Bill Perry. I'd met Bill a few years earlier when he was an assistant manager at the Rivoli Theater in Times Square across the street from the Trans-Lux West where I worked at the time. Bill would come by and share stories of his upbringing in the Deep South. Bill was proud of the fact that he was born in a log cabin in the Ozarks and spent the first 15 years of his life without a pair of shoes. The combination of his southern drawl, his warmth and his cornball sense of humor reminded me of Andy Griffith and endeared him to me.

Even though Bill never made it past the 7th grade, he had a good head for business. And being gay like me, Bill saw firsthand the growth of the same-sex movement and was convinced there was money to be made from it. He was confident that a gay cinema was a gold mine waiting to be exploited, and lobbied me to pursue the idea with him.

Bill was acquainted with two men who became interested in opening a straight X-rated theater in Times Square when they witnessed the booming business of other exploitation cinemas. Bernie Rose and Lenny Clark seemed to work well together but could not have been more distinct. Bernie was a short Floridian with a dark complexion and thinning hair; Lenny was a tall, fair, good-looking New Yorker. Bernie's disposition was as relaxed as Lenny's was severe. Bernie was happily married, whereas Lenny kept his family in upstate New York so he could house his mistress, a delightful Las Vegas showgirl named June Valentine, in Manhattan. What they did have in common was that they were both serious businessmen. Bernie owned a successful string of theaters in Miami; Lenny made his money producing printer paper for early computers.

Bernie and Lenny took a long lease at considerable cost on a former jewelry store on Broadway between 49th and 50th. Their plan was to convert the space into a straight adult theater and they approached Bill to manage the transformation. Bill viewed working with Bernie and Lenny as practice for when he could open a gay cinema of his own and so agreed. Bill then asked for my help and, since it sounded like a good way to raise additional money for the next Amero Brothers' production, I jumped at the opportunity.

Bernie and Lenny were open to our ideas but they had three requests that were set in stone. They wanted to call the theater "Circus Cinema", they wanted a huge marquee, and they wanted to open as soon as possible. So Bill and I quickly began converting the jewelry store into a clean, well-lit 35mm projection theater that could seat 200. It was a difficult, round-the-clock job and we were on ladders with staple guns attaching drapes just hours before the theater was due to open. The Roxy it wasn't.

I was convinced that we would fail the building inspector's checks as we used every trick in the book to make the theater appear further along than it actually was, a dangerous deception as the fire escapes and emergency doors didn't actually work. But remarkably we passed the inspection, the theater opened on schedule, and we had a hugely successful first night. To express their gratitude, and probably more to reduce future film exhibition costs, Bernie and Lenny promised to show any adult films I made in the future.

BACCHANALE (1970-1971)

Even though Circus Cinema was in its infancy, the money started rolling in straight away. Bill and I stayed on for a time to hire the staff and stabilize operations. It was an interesting, well-paying job and being part of creating a new theater was exciting. I could see that Bill loved it and that his involvement only increased his appetite to open a gay cinema. The idea still seemed far-fetched to me, but seeing how quickly Circus Cinema had found its footing, maybe Bill was on to something.

With the additional earnings from Circus Cinema in our bank account, and a small loan from our friend Ron Scardera and his new wife Ronni, Lem and I turned to the next Amero Brothers' production. As we began conceptualizing our project, we thought of the foreign films we'd seen at the Apollo Theater on 42nd Street. For two dollars we enjoyed pictures ranging from early Peter Sellers and Ealing Studios' films through to the work of Italian directors like Antonioni and De Sica. We loved all of these movies but gravitated most towards films by Fellini such as *Variety Lights* (1950), *I Vitelloni* (1953), and *Nights of Cabiria* (1957). I became aware of Fellini when I was manager of the Trans-Lux West. Hanging on my office wall was an un-retrieved New York Film Critics Circle Award that Fellini's *La Strada* (1954) had received for Best Foreign Language Film in 1956. Fellini's movies showed tremendous imagination and were absolutely unique. We also admired the way he worked, refusing to accept any funding unless he had complete control over every creative aspect of his productions.

Lem was heavily influenced by Fellini's *Juliet of the Spirits* (1965) and, inspired by that film, set about writing a script. While *Juliet* wasn't the best of Fellini's works, its impressionistic approach to female sexuality impressed Lem. To this day I don't really understand the story that Lem came up with but it centered on a woman who leaves her body and floats through a series of strange circumstances around New York. People often ask if the story was drug-inspired, but while we sometimes smoked a little marijuana the answer is no. We wound up calling the film *Bacchanale*, for no better reason than we liked the sound of it.

The movie starred Uta Erickson and as always Artie was both wig-clad and a delight to work with. She convinced her friend Linda Boyce to join us for a few days of filming as well. And as usual we leaned on our other regulars. Darcy Brown took on two roles, this time as a fashion model and an announcer, once again using the Phoebe Dinsmore credit in homage to *Singin' in the Rain* (1952). Michael Burns played a crazed pianist and Steve Gould, Ronni Scardera, Mike and Roberta all had small acting parts.

Bacchanale featured some newcomers as well. A friend of mine from high school had moved to New York and shared an apartment with an up-and-coming East Village artist named Neil Jenny. My friend mentioned that Neil was looking for a fast way to make some money and was just crazy enough to consider an exploitation film. We met to discuss the idea with Neil and straight away thought he would be great thanks to his striking looks and sharp sense of humor. He wound up in a "pillar and fog" fantasy sequence with Artie and did a wonderful job, especially considering Artie insisted Neil tape back his genitals for fear of an unwanted erection. While to my knowledge he never made another film after *Bacchanale*, we'd run across his name now and again in the local newspapers when he had a gallery showing.

Bacchanale also marked the introduction of LaRue Watts' partner Fabian Stuart to our film family. Both were regulars at our go-to watering hole Big Spender and wound up designing the sets and costumes for *Bacchanale*. In a strange twist of fate it turned out Fabian had danced with Darcy Brown in the Betty Grable production of *Guys and Dolls*. We even convinced LaRue to make a brief appearance in the film as a deranged harpy, dancing with Darcy.

We had a budget of $15,000 for the film. While we wanted to make *Bacchanale* our first color production we couldn't afford color film for the whole shoot. So we used Eastman color stock for the more straightforward scenes and had the lab color tint black-and-white film for the dream and nightmare sequences. This wasn't the only creative workaround we employed to manage costs. Lem and I shot almost every scene in our studio and tried to re-use as many of the props as we could from our previous film *The Corporate Queen*.

The opening scene of *Bacchanale* is a perfect example of our "do-it-yourself" approach. The story opens with Artie leaving her body. To avoid paying for an optical special effect, we spread black cloth around Artie's body and filmed her sleeping. We then rewound the film in the camera and used the same stock to film Artie waking up. It wasn't a very sophisticated approach but it served its purpose.

For another scene we wanted to shoot in a cemetery without leaving the studio. So we set to work building grass mounds and tombstones and rented a casket, our most expensive prop of the production. We also used fog machines we'd hired for scenes throughout the film. The machines

BACCHANALE (1970-1971)

were impossible to control and seemed to spew loads of fog whenever we wanted a subtle effect, and then barely cough out a puff when we wanted something more significant. The cemetery set took ages to build and demanded great patience as we worked. When we finally finished construction and were ready to film, we sprayed water down to imitate rain. As cold water poured over the actors I could hear Roberta muttering under her breath, "Yeah, these are exploitation films all right... and we're certainly being exploited."

We did get to shoot several scenes outside of the studio. Influenced by Hitchcock's stair scene in *Vertigo* (1958), we filmed one passage on the fire escape of our studio building. We shot some exteriors at the Morton Street Pier on the west side of Manhattan. And it wouldn't be an Amero Brothers' production without a scene at the Trans-Lux cinema, complete with Ronni Scardera in a sexy brassiere.

We wanted the closing scene of the movie to take place in a cave. So we took a bunch of two-by-fours, newspaper and paste and created an elaborate paper maché set of stalactites and stalagmites. We thought it came out great, but unfortunately so did the mice. Attracted to the sweetness of the glue, they seemed to eat the set as fast as we could build it so it was a constant battle to hold the line. To simulate a sand and dirt floor in the cave, I asked everyone to bring bags of kitty litter to the set. The mice found it a comfortable place to leave their droppings so the litter took on a life, and odor, all its own.

The script was so surreal the actors didn't understand what they were meant to be doing. Fortunately, we were shooting MOS so we could provide instructions as we filmed. The actors were asking us questions like, "Was she in love with her brother, or not?" and "Was this terribly perverse?" I told the actors they didn't understand because they hadn't been in all the scenes. But in truth, I wasn't sure what Lem had in mind. I was just the happy cameraman shooting it all, thinking to myself, "when Lem edits this together, it will make sense."

When it was finally time to break down the cave set and dispose of it, I decided to have a few drinks and do it myself. As I started working my way down from the top, I noticed that I was basically creating a giant ball of sticky, smelly paper. By the time I got to the bottom of the set, the ball was about 8 feet in diameter and too big to fit in the elevator. So I rolled it down the steps, out onto 22nd Street and left it leaning against the front window of a fancy shop nearby. The next day, the ball was covered by bright orange Sanitation Department violation stickers. Some people thought an artist had created a conceptual piece. Goodness knows what kind of fine I cost the store owner.

We shot *Bacchanale* with relatively little sexual content compared to other exploitation films of the time. But since standards had become more relaxed, male and female nudity were plentiful in the film. And, of course, we included a signature Amero Brothers simulated male-on-male scene.

As we were about to enter post-production, I got a call from my friend J.J. Coyle. He said, "John you'd better get to the Tivoli Theater in Times Square, they're showing something you won't believe." I dropped everything and headed over to meet J.J. and see a film called *Mona: The Virgin Nymph* (1970) directed by Howard Ziehm. I walked in to see a woman giving a man head on the big screen. This wasn't a case of clever angles and backs of heads that hint at fellatio without ever actually showing it. This was a full-on blow job with no punches pulled.

I couldn't believe my eyes. Gay and proud of it, J.J. leaned over and jokingly said "This is bad. If they start teaching women how to do this, we're in big trouble!" But I wasn't in a joking mood. While we'd been making sex movies for years, I never expected the political and cultural establishments to allow hardcore sex out in the open like this. As I watched, I thought the police would burst into the theater any minute and arrest us all for even witnessing such a thing.

The writing was on the wall. I immediately knew that if hardcore sex was going to be the new norm, nobody would pay for imitation. I rushed back to the studio to tell Lem that from this day forward, softcore would not be enough. In fact, to avoid losing our shirts, we would have to add hardcore sex to *Bacchanale*.

We approached Artie first to see if there was any way she might consider shooting hardcore scenes to insert in the film. Artie told us that while the industry may be moving to hardcore, she was not willing to have actual sex on camera. So we asked her how she'd feel about us shooting someone else as a stand-in for her during sex scenes. Artie was a good sport and had no qualms about hardcore inserts being added to scenes she was in. She was fine for people to think she was having sex, just as long as she didn't have to do it. We approached several other actors in the film but all shared Artie's point of view. We had to find other people and hope that their "parts" matched with our leads.

Artie's friend Linda Boyce had become an agent for adult acting talent so we asked for her help. Her first suggestion was a married couple named

BACCHANALE (1970-1971)

Tina and Jason Russell who'd made a bunch of explicit loops for peep show machines and under-the-counter sales. They agreed to be filmed and also put us in touch with Herb Streicher, a handsome theater and fellow loop actor who would gain notoriety the following year as Harry Reems in the groundbreaking film *Deep Throat*.

Now that we'd found our hardcore performers, it was time to film them. As cinematographer I was basically on my own for these scenes and I didn't find the work easy. I had to identify points in the movie where it would make sense to insert hardcore sex, then set up the shots to provide as much continuity as possible with those previously filmed sequences. This was one time where Lem's fantasy story actually served us well as I could use fog and film-tinting to obscure the fact that those having actual sex were not the original actors.

I shot the first hardcore sequence with Tina and Jason. I found Jason humorless and not particularly attractive, but Tina was dark, beautiful and easy-going, almost making up for Jason's dour disposition. I wasn't nervous to shoot my first hardcore scene but I wasn't confident either. I wound up shooting the sex close up and clinically. I also had to stop and start a good deal to make sure I was getting what I needed, an approach that caused Jason some performance challenges.

When I finally got the footage with Tina and Jason, I replaced Jason with Herb to film some more inserts. Then to complete the hardcore transformation, we shot one more explicit insert for a scene with Artie and an actor named Ron Babin. We wanted to place Ron's body in a coffin, have him play dead, and have Artie give him a hand job. But like Artie, Ron wasn't willing to perform explicit sex on film. Since all we needed was a close up of a female hand and a male member, Darcy and LaRue stepped up to the plate and helped us out.

With the inserts finally completed, Lem edited them into the movie. We had to cut out some other scenes to not increase the film's total running time but overall we were relatively successful. Though years later re-watching *Bacchanale* I did notice that you can see Harry and Tina's faces for a split second.

We completed the sound dubbing with help from Roberta and LaRue who used his best campy voice. And we "borrowed" music as usual – this time from Bernard Herrmann's *Psycho* (1960) score.

And that was it. It had been fun making exploitation movies, seeing what we could get away with but never quite crossing the line. Now that there was no line to cross, things seemed like they'd be less exciting. It was strange to be doing something I never dreamed we'd do. But the market had changed, seemingly overnight, and we needed to change too if we wanted to make more films.

From that day forward, we were no longer exploitation filmmakers. We were now John and Lem Amero, pornographers... whether we liked it or not.

It was time to screen *Bacchanale* for distributors, and we needed promotional materials to share. I wanted to try something different from the standard, sleazy ads so I chose a luminous close-up photo of Artie's face that I loved, and featured it on the posters. Everyone tried to discourage me saying it was the wrong style for the grind house crowd we were trying to reach but I held firm.

We took the rough cut and the poster to Lenny and Bernie first to see if they'd honor their promise to play any of our movies at Circus Cinema. Lenny liked it a lot and offered us an advance in exchange for granting them exclusive distribution rights. We feared Lenny didn't have the right contacts to effectively distribute the film but we needed money to pay the labs so we accepted his offer. We signed an agreement for seven years with ownership of the movie returning to us after that.

On July 22, 1971 *Bacchanale* had a tremendous opening night at the Circus Cinema, accompanied by a lavish premiere and a review in Variety. The reviewer Eric Spilker wrote "*Bacchanale* gives equal time to all the basic human sexual possibilities." We didn't understand what he meant but since the quote was from a Variety review we printed it on all subsequent promotional materials, including on an enormous banner we hung in front of the theater.

As the money rolled into Circus Cinema from *Bacchanale*, Lenny and Bernie began to look for a national distribution partner and struck a deal with a company called Distribpix. Arthur Morowitz and Howie Farber, two young friends, used their bar mitzvah money to start Distribpix in 1965. They quickly found success distributing exploitation films and like us, saw the writing on the wall as hardcore sex crept into films. But while Lem and I found the idea of hardcore to be a necessary evil, Arthur and Howie appeared to view it as a great opportunity and were ready to jump in feet first. Their approach seemed to be one of quantity rather than quality so they released a tremendous volume of cheap films as the market transitioned to hardcore. But they seemed to appreciate the quality of *Bacchanale* and did very well with it as evidenced by the regular pay statements we received.

BACCHANALE (1970-1971)

Bacchanale had a long run at the Circus, but the quality of the film might not have been the primary reason. Now that hardcore was available people were lining up in droves to see it and theaters couldn't get enough product. New theaters were popping up to capitalize on the transition, including the World Theater, which would become famous in 1972 for premiering *Deep Throat*.

Throughout production of *Bacchanale* I was in the studio day and night instead of at home with Chuck. And when I was able to make it home, I often brought the problems of work with me. Chuck never complained; he was always there to offer his encouragement and love as he had for all the years we'd been together.

Chuck had always wanted to go to Europe, as did I, so with *Bacchanale* in theaters we planned our first trip across the Atlantic. We had old friends that had moved to Amsterdam, so we went there first, then Paris and finally London. This would be the first of many trips to Europe which became some of the best times in our relationship.

Back in New York, Bill Perry had not given up on his idea of opening a gay movie theater. While setting up Circus Cinema, he'd eyed a large space upstairs he thought might fit his needs. Accessible by a small elevator and staircase, the location was formerly home to China D'Or, a nightclub where Lem had stage-managed review shows several years earlier. Arthur Morowitz and Howie Farber now owned the space but were willing to lease it to Bill. I have no idea where Bill got the needed funds as it must have cost a pretty penny, but he made it happen. It was a huge undertaking but Bill had the cojones to take it on.

Inspired by the Circus, Bill named his theater the Big Top Cinema. He showed new hardcore gay films every two weeks, mostly loops from San Francisco as there weren't a lot of gay films being produced in New York at the time. The cinema configuration was terrible, with no seating slope to allow for good sight lines. But the Big Top also had a large concession area, an office, a sex accessory store, several party rooms and a nightly disco where gay men could come and dance – basically a bathhouse without the baths. Open 24 hours a day, it even offered a continental breakfast between 6.00-11.00am. Its tag line was "Broadway's first and only male showcase – We doze but we never close".

The Big Top wasn't really my scene so I rarely went, but some of my friends loved it and could often be found there. One such friend was

Kurt Mann. Kurt was a good-looking and talented actor that I'd seen in "The Jewel Box Review", an all-male drag show. Kurt's Phyllis Diller stand-up routine always brought the house down. We met him at Big Spender and Lem and I bonded with him immediately. After he left "The Jewel Box Review", Bill offered Kurt a position writing ads and promotional copy for The Big Top.

True to Bill's vision, the Big Top was an immediate success, and he soon found himself flush with money and thinking about his next move.

IMAGE GALLERY

above left: The Amero brothers in 1941, Lem aged 3 (left) and me aged 2 (right).
above right: Our Dad in the Pacific during WWII, 1944.
below: With our mother Gladys in 1947.

IMAGE GALLERY

above: Lem's High School graduation photo, Gloucester, Mass., 1955.

opposite: ...and me in 1958.

right: At CBS in my only suit.

below: In Lem's apartment on West 85th Street, rent $64 a month!

above and left:
Fun times at a Rockefeller Center photo booth.

below:
Lem and I on the Coney Island Boardwalk shooting *Body of a Female* in 1963.

IMAGE GALLERY

above:
Me, Lem, Roberta and Michael (and a windup Eyemo) in an eerily prophetic photo op for *Body of a Female*, 1963. I'm wearing a New York University student jacket so if we were stopped by cops and asked for a film permit, we could claim it was a student movie. Lem looks bedraggled because we just shot a scene with him fighting Michael on the beach – he was soaking wet and freezing cold as a result.

above and left:
Managing the State Theatre in Boston circa 1964.

opposite top:
Mike Findlay "directing" Roberta in *Body of a Female*, 1963.

opposite bottom:
My "hands on" approach to directing Janet Banzet in *The Corporate Queen*, 1967.

IMAGE GALLERY

above: The 'happy family' of *Diary of a Swinger*.

below: The cast of *The Corporate Queen* – I'm on camera.

IMAGE GALLERY

top:
Before the mice destroyed the set of *Bacchanale*.

above:
Lem holds the slate with the cast and crew of *Pepper*.

right:
Lem in our editing suite on 46th Street.

above: World Theater, New York premiere, 1975.

below: Harry Reems and Darby Lloyd Rains, undressed to kill.

bottom right: Harry's double entendre.

IMAGE GALLERY

above: Lem and I taking a break in the office.

right: Lem on the set of *R.S.V.P.*

below: Me, Patty Sumner and Lem at the East Coast Producers Association Awards dinner in 1980.

above:
The London premiere of *Blonde Ambition*.

left:
The original movie one-sheet.

below:
Audiences loved Kurt Mann's "Club Pitts" drag emcee at the London premiere of *Blonde Ambition*.

IMAGE GALLERY

above: From the left: Fabian Stuart, LaRue Watts, me and Lem at the Critics Adult Film Awards at the Copacabana in New York, March 4, 1982 where LaRue won best art direction for *Blonde Ambition*.

right: Chuck very much at home with our cat, JC.

below: Lem, myself, and Chuck on our way to the Caribbean.

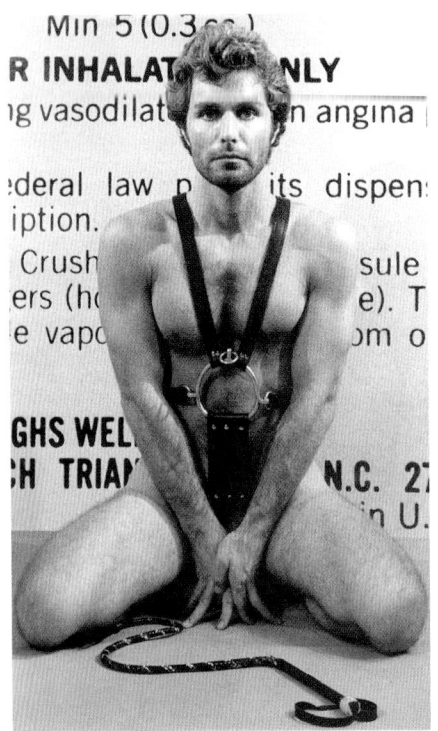

IMAGE GALLERY

Starring: Veronica Hart, Adam Mills, Harry Reems, Allene Simmons, Lynda Wiesmeier
© 1984 Platinum Pictures, Inc.

above:
Hollywood or bust with one of our favorite actresses, Veronica Hart.

opposite:
A Francis Ellie tableau with George Payne (top and left) and Jack Wrangler (right).

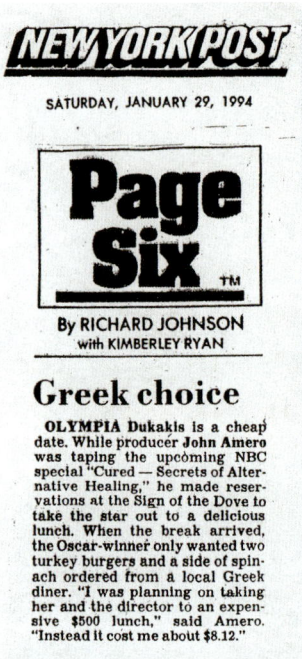

Greek choice

OLYMPIA Dukakis is a cheap date. While producer John Amero was taping the upcoming NBC special "Cured — Secrets of Alternative Healing," he made reservations at the Sign of the Dove to take the star out to a delicious lunch. When the break arrived, the Oscar-winner only wanted two turkey burgers and a side of spinach ordered from a local Greek diner. "I was planning on taking her and the director to an expensive $500 lunch," said Amero. "Instead it cost me about $8.12."

above: Shameless self-promotion... but I loved it!

left: On the NBC primetime *Miracle Cures* set with host Olympia Dukakis.

below: Celebrating years of friendship with Steve and Nancy Gould.

CHAPTER 7

DYNAMITE, PEPPER AND LORD PERRY
(1972-1974)

As 1972 dawned, Lem and I grudgingly decided to give up the lease on our beloved 22nd Street studio. We had made 3 films in our 2 studios – *Diary of a Swinger*, *The Corporate Queen* and *Bacchanale* – but they just didn't pay the rent. And our exploitation competitors like Joe Sarno, Radley Metzger, and even Mike and Roberta never had a studio. So we traded in 22nd Street for an office suite on West 52nd Street between Broadway and 7th Avenue.

While we were facing financial hardship, Lenny and Bernie were raking it in at the Circus Cinema. But while customer demand was strong, film supply was not. Lenny and Bernie could get a three or four week run out of a movie and the prices filmmakers charged were taking a significant cut of their profits. So they approached Lem and I for product, offering us a modest budget to finance our next movie. Always eager to be making films, Lem and I agreed to the deal.

We came up with a story about an Avon-style door-to-door saleswoman but rather than have her sell cosmetics, we had her peddle sex products. The plot focused on the lead character Suzy trying to become the number one salesperson in Manhattan by whatever means necessary. It would be our first venture into comedy, something we'd been wanting to try.

During the casting process, a slightly older woman with fantastic legs and an elaborate wig walked into our office. She introduced herself as Dolly Sharp and was confident, straightforward and theatrical. Lem whispered to me that she was the perfect "talking lady", a burlesque term used to describe a woman who could deliver witty dialogue as well as strip.

As the audition went on, I kept feeling like I'd seen this woman before. It took me a while to put my finger on it but it finally dawned on me – this was the Radio City Music Hall actress, dancer and violinist from "Music Box Mine" that my brother and I had been absolutely fascinated with. Now here she was in our office telling us how she'd appeared in the adult film *Deep Throat* (1972), uttering the best line in the movie: "Do you mind if I smoke, while you're eating?" *Deep Throat* had changed the face of erotic entertainment forever. It had comedy, an attractive cast that could actually act, production value and a plot, albeit a flimsy one. Suddenly, porn was chic and couples flocked to see an adult film together. *Deep Throat* solidified the demand for hardcore sex and ensured that there would be no turning back to softcore.

I didn't let on to Dolly that we knew her from Radio City Music Hall in case this would cause her any embarrassment. Lem and I both felt she was perfect for the part of Suzy and didn't want anything to jeopardize our opportunity to work with her. She was mature, experienced and had a compelling presence, not to mention amazing gams. But unfortunately, Lenny didn't agree with our casting choice and wasn't about to play the role of silent partner. He thought Dolly was too tough, too ballsy and flat out said, "She's too old!" Lenny pushed for another woman to play the part of Suzy, someone Lem and I suspected Lenny was having an affair with. Controlling the purse strings, Lenny got his way and his paramour got the lead. We called her Monica Rivers after Joan Crawford's character in *Berserk* (1967). Fortunately, we were able to keep Dolly for a supporting role though we never stopped believing she would have been much more fun as the lead.

Monica's boss was played by our old friend Artie Giannini. After *Bacchanale* Artie said she was retiring from the adult film business, but she agreed to a non-sex cameo strictly as a favor to us. We also cast a handsome, talented young actor named Jamie Gillis in a small part. Jamie had made quite a name for himself in hardcore loops but was a feature film newcomer. He plays a man who can't perform in bed and buys an "Everhard" product from our traveling saleslady that induces a long-lasting erection. To celebrate his new-found virility, I stole a technique from a Danish film that I'd seen a couple of years earlier. Using 2x4s, we built a platform that ran up in front of Jamie's legs and had Monica balance on it. We shot from an angle so it looked like she was standing atop Jamie's erection.

Filming hardcore scenes like these still felt new to Lem and me. Although *Bacchanale* had hardcore sex in it, the fact that those sex scenes were shot as inserts made them feel somewhat separate from the film. This was the first time we actually set out to make a bona fide hardcore movie and we were still quite shy about it, particularly Lem. We just didn't feel comfortable using the clinical terms I assumed other directors employed. Lem's embarrassment meant he didn't always issue clear sexual directions to the actors. In those instances I'd intervene and issue a veiled metaphor as I could never say "Get into doggy position" or worse still "Start fucking!". Instead I'd offer "Start mumbling in the moss", "How about some muff diving?" or "It's time to take a slow boat to tuna town". And I would always say it from behind my Arriflex where I felt protected.

DYNAMITE, PEPPER AND LORD PERRY (1972-1974)

But while shooting hardcore could be uncomfortable, it was also exciting because it was new and taboo. Working with Dolly was especially fun because once the camera was rolling, she'd start improvising and was a real pro. And what athleticism! At one point, Dolly slipped from the missionary position to anal with the ease and grace of a trained dancer. Of course the producer in me thought, "I hope she's not going to charge us extra for this anal." But being the trouper that Dolly was, she never did. We also thoroughly enjoyed working with Jamie. He was very professional, and I hoped we'd get to work together again soon. Luckily, we would.

The film was also noteworthy because it was the first Amero Brothers production that featured our friend Kurt Mann. We wrote a scene where Suzy gets a call from a theater manager promising to buy all her wares if she visits him at work. When Suzy arrives she finds there's one catch – the manager wants to have sex with her in front of the screen on which patrons are watching a film. While Suzy complies, the theater usher (played by Kurt) and cashier (played by Darcy) perform a tap dance aside the lustful couple. It's a patriotic number set to "Stars and Stripes Forever" and I believe it's safe to say it's a sequence you won't often see in an X-rated film. Kurt went on to appear in every movie we made from then on and worked with other filmmakers as well. I lost track of Darcy but heard that she moved to Chicago and became a schoolteacher.

Like many Amero Brothers productions, the film's title changed. We started out with *Dynamite* and then switched it to *TNT* – both names referring to a scene where our leading lady helps the man in a couple achieve climax through explosive measures. Suzy recommends the couple insert an experimental explosive dildo – in reality a fat candle with a sparkler on the end – into the husband's butt as they have sex to help him finish the act.

The only problem was that Billy Love – the actor who played the husband but who in reality was Dolly Sharp's boyfriend – absolutely refused to insert the prop. Hoping for a creative solution, I assessed Billy's rear and thought Lem's rump looked pretty much the same. So I shot Billy pumping, humping and moaning from every angle and dismissed him. Then I talked my poor, beleaguered brother into doing the inserts. If you watch the film, every time you see a close up of the sparkling candle burning down, it's in fact Lem's uncredited rear you're witnessing.

With the help of Lem's rear, we finished production and reverted to the film title *Dynamite*. Post-production started well until we realized that the movie's running time came in at exactly one hour while our contract with Lenny and Bernie specified a minimum of 70 minutes. There was no money left but Lem and I hatched a brilliant idea. We decided to delve into the Amero Brothers' archives and create a short documentary prelude we called *The History of Erotica*. It started with silent movies, such as the classic stag reel *Eveready Hardon* (1929), and went on to show nudies from the 1950s and '60s, including clips of Artie Giannini and Gigi Darlene. This ten-minute history of erotic films padded out our feature's running time and saved our behinds.

After the film opened at Circus Cinema, we began looking for a national distributor. We screened the movie for theater owner Chelly Wilson who knew exactly what she was looking for – but unfortunately it wasn't *Dynamite*. But Screw magazine positively reviewed *Dynamite* and that was enough to seal a deal with Howie Farber and Arthur Morowitz. Their company Distribpix did a good job on the press book and ad campaign and the film went on to make a nice profit....at least for them.

Upstairs from the Circus Cinema, Bill Perry was focused on his next project. In the early 1970s, men's bathhouses were popping up all over Manhattan and Bill wanted to get in on the action. He found a space above the Trans-Lux West cinema and, using profits from the Big Top, negotiated a long lease for The Broadway Baths.

The business included a gym, pool, steam room, locker room and billiards hall. There were also small overnight rooms covered on top by chicken wire. Bill hoped to rent the rooms to attractive gay men but they wound up being let by exhausted Chinese waiters who crashed there when the restaurants closed in the early hours. When I asked Bill if the bathhouse was profitable he responded, "Are you kidding? I'd own 30 of these if I could!"

Business was also good at the Circus Cinema, but staff turnover continued to cause me problems. One day, I had just sacked another cashier and happened to mention to Roberta that I was looking for help. While Roberta and Mike's film *College Girls* (1974) was playing at the Circus at the time, Roberta was between engagements and asked for the position. The job was straight-forward. We didn't issue tickets so all Roberta had to do was take the admission money and direct customers through a turnstile so we could track the number of entrants. Then every time Roberta collected $300, she would package up the money and drop it into a chute that led straight to my office.

DYNAMITE, PEPPER AND LORD PERRY (1972-1974)

I soon noticed that the money Roberta collected didn't match the volume of patrons the turnstile counted. I went out to furtively observe the ticket booth and see if I could help correct the issue. As I watched, I saw Roberta taking money from customers and directing them to walk through the exit door instead of the turnstile. When I confronted Roberta about it, she responded with her customary giggle and insisted she wasn't doing anything wrong. From my office directly below the ticket booth, I could hear Roberta conversing with the customers and confirmed that she was pocketing some of the cash. Lenny also became aware that money was missing and insisted I fire Roberta. The incident certainly tested our long friendship.

Meanwhile Roberta and Mike were having serious relationship problems. On one of our drinking nights out, Mike confided to me that Roberta wanted to put their daughter up for adoption. Mike had hoped having a child would bring them closer together, but instead it pulled them further apart. It was evident from the start that Roberta had little interest or aptitude for motherhood – I saw this firsthand as I sometimes babysat their little girl. Mike ended up doing everything for the baby and it was clear he was brokenhearted by his wife's haphazard attitude toward motherhood and her desire to give their daughter up. We spent many nights in conversation about his heartache, becoming even closer during this time.

Ultimately, Roberta and Mike decided to separate. Roberta moved into the Camelot on West 45th Street and Mike into the Whitby, also on West 45th Street. Lem was living at the Whitby at the time and Mike took a studio apartment on the same floor as my brother.

It wasn't long after the separation that Roberta began seeing a film distributor named Allan Shackleton. Roberta seemed to have a knack for bringing out the worst in her partners and her relationship with Allan was no exception. She seemed to use sex to influence men and manipulated them intellectually – even smart ones like Allan.

Allan died of a massive heart attack in 1979 while jogging in Central Park with Lorraine Borden. By then, Roberta had already moved on to Walter Sear, a sound engineer who made adult films on the side. And I had distanced myself from Roberta after the Circus Cinema incident and her separation from Mike.

After *Dynamite* (1972), I decided the time was ripe for Lem and I to try our hands at an R-rated feature. Our friend and part-time playwright LaRue Watts had written a script called *The Chess Murders*, a blatant James Bond rip-off with a saucy female lead named Pepper Burns, Agent 00X in the Bond role.

James Bond movies were doing extremely well at the box office so the premise seemed promising, and Lenny Clark was willing to put up $20,000 in funding. This was a ridiculously low budget to make an R-rated film worthy of playing in legitimate theaters, but there had recently been a series of cheap films featuring a bed-hopping private eye and spy named Ginger that had been mildly-successful, so we hoped to emulate these. To help control costs, we cast a number of competent local actors but Lenny insisted on hiring a blond-haired California actress named Diana Wilson to play Pepper.

I impressed upon Lenny that an R-rated movie meant relatively tame sexual scenes but I don't think he got the point. As we were finalizing the script, Lenny began insisting that we include simulated sex in the film – just the type of scenes Lem and I were trying to move away from. Lenny told us that he liked the plot but the film should be more explicit. He would scan the script and say things like, "Shouldn't she finger herself before she kills him in that scene?" But both Lem and I stood firm against his suggestions, believing the plot could stand on its own without the sex.

The story line was fun as well as funny. The plot revolved around a missile orbiting the earth, controlled by keys held by four global diplomats. The evil Madame Chang spends the film seducing these diplomats to take control of the weapon and blackmail the governments of the world.

Madam Chang was played by An Tsan Hu, a striking woman and wonderful Asian actress with extensive credits in Hong Kong. Sadly, in 2004 I read in the New York Times that An Tsan and her husband, publishing executive Lloyd Schiller, were killed by a fire in their Upper East Side apartment. Lloyd could have survived but tragically died while trying to save his wife.

While Lenny's imposed lead Diana Wilson wasn't a great actress by any stretch of the imagination, her character didn't call for Shakespearean tones. She was pleasant, easy to work with and had a spectacular figure.

And true to the Amero Brothers film name-changing tradition, *The Chess Murders* became *Checkmate* and finally *Pepper*, as Lenny Clark felt that *Pepper* was similar to *Ginger*, which would help pull in a larger audience. Since he was the man with the money, it was hard to argue with him.

Despite our personal difficulties, I wanted Roberta as our cinematographer on *Pepper* because she was extremely talented. But not much time had passed since her shenanigans at the Circus Cinema, so we had to downplay her production involvement in our discussions with Lenny. I told him that I would be the DP (director of photography) and Roberta

DYNAMITE, PEPPER AND LORD PERRY (1972-1974)

would act as AC (assistant cameraman). I stipulated to Roberta, "any time Lenny shows up on the set, I'll get behind the camera. Then the minute he leaves, you go back to being DP." Roberta agreed, and she wound up doing a fantastic job on what was a complicated shoot. There were a large number of locations and lots of action sequences, including a helicopter-flying stunt, a big shoot-out in Central Park involving nuns, and runaway horse carriages.

Even with our ducks all in a row, *Pepper* was still a gamble. Lem and I had negotiated a deal with Lenny whereby we'd get a series of flat payments and then a piece of the action after the film recouped its expenses. But those expenses were considerable and it didn't take long before Lenny fell behind on payments to us. It got to the point where Lenny was avoiding us, having his secretary tell us he was out of town whenever we'd visit his office to collect our money. I'd plant myself in his reception area for hours on end to flush Lenny out. But one year after *Pepper* (1973) was released, we were still waiting on the rest of our payments and the first royalty check. It was infuriating because I'd see in Variety that the film was playing around the country in drive-ins and various 'multiples' – what we'd call multiplexes today. Variety even carried the headline "Pepper Hot, 15 Gs in Detroit Debut" at one point.

To make matters worse, unbeknownst to us Lenny had decided to insert some softcore sex scenes into *Pepper* in an attempt to yield a greater profit. He approached exploitation director Ron Sullivan, who would soon become known as Henri Pachard, to film these inserted scenes. It was much later that we learned the truth when Lem and I were asked about a pool table scene in *Pepper* that we never shot.

In the 1980s, Lenny ended up selling the cassette rights of *Pepper* to Vestron Video. When this happened I thought there might be a chance we'd finally see some of the money owed to us, but I was wrong. It was clear that if we wanted to make any significant profit we were going to have to return to making X-rated movies.

Bob Sumner and Sam Lake leased the World Theater from distributor Jean Goldwurm and producer Felix Bilgrey. Jean and Felix were keen to distance themselves from pornography whereas Bob and Sam were eager to capitalize on it.

Bob had officially joined forces with Sam in 1972 on the heels of selling him *The Sidewalk Cowboy* (1970). They formed Mature Pictures in 1973 and became a formidable duo in the adult film business. Sam was laser-focused on making the maximum money off the most modest investment possible. Though only 26, Bob had become a good promoter, showman and publicity seeker with a fine appreciation for film. Bob also had a good commercial sense as he demonstrated soon after taking over the World Theater. Having booked *Deep Throat*, Bob quickly noticed the film's growing success and cleverly lowered ticket prices to $3 when everyone else was charging $5. Audiences came to the World in droves. When Judge Joel E. Tyler ruled *Deep Throat* obscene and ordered it pulled from theaters, it was Bob who ran the memorable marquee, "Judge Cuts Throat, World Mourns."

Bob saw no reason why adult films shouldn't be held to a higher standard of quality and taken "above ground". His motto was, "Don't hide, make it more acceptable. Build a new, recognized industry." Somehow, Bob convinced Sam to stop producing low-budget, cheap-looking films and represent a better class of director such as Armand Weston and Radley Metzger (aka Henry Paris).

Despite their professional union, Bob and Sam would fight frequently, especially over money. Sam thought Bob was tremendously wasteful, especially when Bob suggested filming in Europe – unheard of at the time. But while Sam initially resisted, Bob successfully elevated the quality bar and was the driving force behind opening up foreign distribution markets, bringing in additional revenue. Ultimately Sam was willing to be swayed as long as the films they made were profitable. And Mature Pictures subsequently became the company everyone wanted to work with.

One day, I got a call from Bob. He was in a fix because the World Theater manager was sick and Bob was having trouble finding someone to cover for him. Bob asked if I would step in to open the theater and work until five o'clock when the night manager came on duty. Since Bob was such a good friend, I agreed. Besides I always enjoyed working at the World. The last time I helped out there had been at the New York premiere of *Behind the Green Door* (1972). It had been a klieg light affair where I presented the star, Marilyn Chambers, with a large bunch of roses as she got out of her limousine.

I headed over to 49th Street and opened up the theater which was showing *High Rise* (1973), a film by director Danny Steinmann. After ensuring the theater was set up and ready to go, I headed across the street for a beer at a bar called the Blarney Stone. The bar had a perfect view of the World so I could monitor things from my bar stool. I also gave the bar's pay phone number to the box office cashier – a sweet, little white-haired lady – telling her I'd be directly across the street and instructing her to call me if she needed anything.

As I sat drinking my beer, I noticed an ominous black car pull up in front of the World and a few men get out and walk over to the box office.

DYNAMITE, PEPPER AND LORD PERRY (1972-1974)

A moment later, the bar pay phone rang. I picked up the receiver and heard the box office cashier with a quiver in her voice say, "Mr. Amero, there are several men here saying that if I don't get the theater manager they are going to take me to prison. I've told them I'm not sure where you are." In all good conscience, I couldn't let this little old lady go to jail even though I knew that as soon as I headed back to the theater I would be the one to get arrested.

I hung up and immediately called Bob to let him know what was happening. No fool when it came to publicity, Bob called all the local newspapers and television stations to tell them what was going on. When he arrived at the World, so did reporters from papers like the Daily News and the New York Post. Bob and I were photographed being taken from the theater in handcuffs. We were hauled off to the notorious Tombs, a jail downtown officially called the Manhattan Detention Complex. It was a massive monolith taking up the entire city block of White Street, between Lafayette and Centre Streets. The Tombs infamous history dates back to the 1930s, so everybody who was anybody in New York City crime ended up there. Now here I was, getting fingerprinted, then waiting in line for a mug shot to be taken, When I asked the photographer if he had a comb, he replied "Look buddy, these ain't gonna be 8x10 glossies."

Bob and I were placed in a filthy, bare holding cell with about 35 other prisoners, a number of whom were shackled to chairs by ankle restraints. Bob and I stood out like sore thumbs among what I assumed were more dangerous criminals. We tried to blend in but Bob was 5'4", a full foot shorter than I was, so we looked like Mutt and Jeff. We were soon approached by a number of cellmates asking what we were in for. I tentatively muttered that we'd been nabbed for exhibiting X-rated films. All of a sudden, we were the most popular guys in holding. Bob and I wound up passing the hours waiting for our lawyer entertaining the other prisoners with adult movie war stories. Our audience was in awe, saying "You met Marilyn Chambers…?! Do you know Linda Lovelace?…That's so cool, man. Good luck." Their response temporarily turned the grim reality of being in the Tombs into something almost fun.

After several hours, in addition to being anxious, Bob and I were starving. Finally, some simple bologna sandwiches were handed to all of us through the bars. Bob took one look and said, "I'm not eating that crap!" so I asked if I could have his ration. A few hours later, Bob was offering me cigarettes, money, drugs and just about everything else for that sad bologna sandwich.

Thankfully, we made night court later that evening. Sam Lake arranged for Seymour Detsky from the law firm Kassner and Detsky to meet us in court. Seymour Detsky and Herb Kassner were the go-to lawyers for all of us in the burgeoning adult film business so they were accustomed to this type of call. Seymour had our case postponed and we were dismissed without bail pending a hearing. Over the next weeks I was adamant that I wouldn't even accept a misdemeanor. So, Bob and I had to keep going back to court until the case was eventually thrown out.

This result wasn't unusual. At this stage the authorities were regularly busting theaters on obscenity charges, but they didn't know what to do once they'd made their arrests. The moment the authorities shut down a theater, a bunch of lawyers would descend upon them protesting their clients' innocence. The notion of what was and was not obscene was still being determined in the courts, so every case seemed to be a small landmark in its own right. If taken to court, our attorneys had to prove that the movies we showed were "within the bounds of normal behavior" and therefore, not obscene.

Theater owners were the ones on the front lines who took on the immediate risk. They dreaded arrests because lawyers' fees were hefty, and they lost income if they had to shut down the theater for a day or two. As the police always confiscated the print in question, exhibitors often had nothing to show even if they were permitted to remain open. And if they didn't get the print back, costs were even steeper. The money they put into advertising a film that was expected to run for a month or more could go down the drain. Plus finding another feature to show on short notice was impractical as you had to start again with a new advertising campaign.

Fortunately, Bob always hid a second print of any film he showed at the World and *High Rise* was no exception. Before we were taken down to the Tombs, Bob somehow retrieved the back-up print from its hiding place inside a Coca-Cola vending machine and got it to the projectionist. Customers didn't even have to leave the premises as we were being dragged away. It was business as usual at the World.

With arrests rampant, our nightly get togethers at Big Spender took on a new dimension. So many of our group managed theaters that we only relaxed when everyone arrived at the bar and we could be sure that no one was missing.

In response to this uncertain climate, a group of us formed the East Coast Producers Association. The Association was a collection of New York-based exhibitors and producers that included Chelly Wilson of Chellee Films, Arthur Morowitz of Distribpix, Ava Leighton of Audubon, Bob Sumner of Mature Pictures, and Bunny Atlas from Bunnco. Our meetings were like a

DYNAMITE, PEPPER AND LORD PERRY (1972-1974)

support group. The aim was to share legal advice and common experiences to better deal with the issues we faced. Bob and my legal representation from the World incident – Kassner and Detsky – would occasionally attend to advise us all.

Despite the risks, the adult business was booming. Seeing all the money Bob and Sam were earning at the World Theater, many of the best X-rated filmmakers in New York City were approaching them for distribution deals. Over at the Circus Cinema, owners Lenny and Bernie were also thriving even though they sometimes struggled to get the quality of movies that the World was showing. And Bill Perry was doing well too showing 16mm gay films at The Big Top, getting most of his product from Norm Arno, a West Coast distributor. Norm handled both straight and gay movies, and spent extended periods in New York selling his California-made films to East Coast theaters. His New York business was strengthened by his partnership with Mickey Zaffarano, a member of the Bonanno organized crime family.

It was heady days for those willing to take the adult gamble.

After the production of *Pepper*, I was once again looking for work. Due to my recent problems with Lenny, I wasn't comfortable going back to my fallback job managing the Circus Cinema. Bill Perry mentioned that Norm Arno needed a manager for his New York City company, Lord Perry, since Bill was about to leave the position. I told Bill I was interested and Norm flew in from California with the express purpose of meeting me.

Norm and I got along great so he offered me the job. I began working for him at his offices in the Equity Building on 46th Street, just down the block from the Circus Cinema. Norm and Mickey Zaffarano were pleased with the location because it had two official addresses – 165 West 46th Street and 1560 Broadway. They felt the two addresses might confuse the authorities if they ever faced legal trouble.

While I liked Norm, he was not one of the great beauties of our time. Unfortunately, he reminded me of a troll – he was short, balding and had chronic psoriasis. He would scratch his scalp from the time he arrived in the office until the moment he left. Every part of Norm's desk was covered with tiny flecks of his dead skin.

But while Norm may not have been much in the looks department he was a big deal in the adult business. He'd founded a studio and distribution company called VCX in Hollywood. It could be described as a family business since Norm employed family members like his cousin Rudy Sutton, whose son David runs VCX nowadays. The company started by selling 8mm loops, but moved on to bigger budget productions. VCX later earned its reputation as "home of the classics" by distributing notable adult films like *The Devil in Miss Jones* (1973), *SexWorld* (1978) and *Debbie Does Dallas* (1978).

Norm loved going to the Derby Steakhouse and we'd often dine there together. He was extremely generous and would buy me wildly colorful floral pattern silk shirts with wide lapels from a shop on Broadway. So much for trying to keep a low profile – these outfits could compete with the signage on Broadway. A khaki pant New Englander, I called it my gangster wear. At Christmas time he insisted I give generous holiday bonuses to the staff and myself. Despite the flaking skin and garish shirts, I liked working for Norm.

In contrast to Norm, Mickey Zaffarano was 6'4", well-groomed and a snappy dresser. Despite his reserved manner and lack of humor, I liked Mickey and we always got along well. Our good working relationship included numerous conversations about his lengthy stretches behind bars at Leavenworth Penitentiary. Despite his intimidating demeanor, I grew more confident interacting with him over time. I once cheekily asked if he ever had a bitch in jail. He looked surprised, then amused, and muttered "I did alright, kid" with a half-smile. I decided not to push my luck and left it at that.

Lord Perry distributed 16mm loops on a large scale, with a healthy dose of loan sharking on the side. In the beginning, we were shipping standard 10-minute loops, both straight and gay. About a fifth of Lord Perry's inventory was gay but Norm and Mickey would never use that term. Instead they would ask, "How's the action on the boy/boy films?" It's not that they were squeamish about gay sex, it's just that it was all strictly business. Sometimes a "boy/boy" film would accidentally end up in a suitcase with "boy/girl" product. When this happened, theater owners were not happy as there was definitely no crossover among their audiences.

Distribution extended well beyond New York and California to cities like Boston, Washington, Philadelphia, Baltimore and Atlanta. This cross-country network introduced a new level of potential danger as shipping materials considered obscene across state lines was illegal. To mitigate the risk, we avoided the mail system. Instead we employed trusted friends and colleagues to deliver the product personally. I saw it as an opportunity to help many of my unemployed actor friends pick up extra cash. I always told them what they'd be carrying and explained the risk, so there was no deception involved. They'd need to take a suitcase of 16mm porn loops to the airport, fly to a city, bring the materials to a theater, collect cash and fly back to drop off the money at the Lord Perry offices. I gave them tips on what to

DYNAMITE, PEPPER AND LORD PERRY (1972-1974)

do and what not to do to avoid getting caught and explained that if they were busted we would supply them with a lawyer. Admittedly, it was a gamble but Lord Perry paid well and it was all cash, so for many it was worth the risk. Luckily, over the course of hundreds of transactions under my watch, there were relatively few problems. Once an overstuffed suitcase literally exploded open at the Dallas airport. Our courier described old Texan ladies picking up 16mm gay porn loops and handing them to him saying, "Here, young man, you've dropped your movies."

We went through suitcases at a fast rate as transporting heavy film reels took its toll. I soon realized that Samsonite lasted the longest and spent a small fortune every week on new bags. The guy who owned the nearby luggage store couldn't understand what I was doing with all the suitcases I purchased but he didn't ask questions. There was a certain thrill involved in orchestrating this illegal activity; I felt like a desperado.

My main work duties were dispensing payments to the film labs and the airlines, and setting up film deliveries across the country. Most of the loops were shot on the West Coast and transported directly to me by couriers. To avoid unnecessary risk, we stored the films in a separate room three floors above our offices and hung travel posters on the walls to obscure what we really were doing. We hired a young man to sit in the room and edit and repair films when they arrived. In addition to loops we began to add some hour-long, plotted films. But the story lines were never too complicated – even these feature films were 80% sex and only 20% story. Most theaters would book a two-hour show, so we'd deliver just that – two hours of wall-to-wall sex edited together from loops.

We needed a receptionist/secretary, so I hired Kurt Mann. Kurt had a knack for dealing with the "gentlemen" who called from Chicago or Los Angeles to discuss film deals. Since their business activities weren't above board, they never used their real names in case the phones were tapped. They'd just identify themselves with, "It's me" and somehow Kurt usually could figure out who it was. I, on the other hand, had a terrible time of it, and once in desperation shouted, "But who, Joan Crawford? You all sound the same!" To make matters worse, no one was ever explicit as to what they wanted, so Kurt and I quickly became used to sentences like "Have you got the stuff?", "Did you do the first thing?", and "What about the second thing?"

When Mickey and Norm weren't in town, Kurt and I had fun pretending we were in a James Cagney gangster movie. Kurt would sit filing his nails while thugs who looked straight out of Central Casting waltzed in and out of the office. Many of them went by code names like "Big Red" or "Hymie the Beard." Another regular visitor to our offices was the burlesque stripper-turned-actress, Chesty Morgan, notable for her 73-inch bust. She'd often stop by to chat with Kurt, who would subsequently parade around the office squeezing his pecs together to create cleavage of his own.

A typical day at Lord Perry was chaotic. Theaters would call constantly requesting product. We would offer tempting deals like, "We'll give you the best product if you stick with us for at least eight weeks." Once in a while, a theater would actually buy prints from us instead of lease them. If we had prints that were well-worn and headed for the scrapheap, we'd sell them for a couple of hundred bucks to some third-run theater.

Occasionally we'd get a call from a new theater asking, "If you can get me a complete two-hour show by Wednesday, I'll pay top dollar." When these calls came in, red flags immediately went up and the requests were escalated directly to Norm or Mickey. Strangers often wouldn't return prints to us, and a stolen print could represent a loss of several thousand dollars. When this theft occurred, Mickey and Norm would cryptically say, "We'll take care of it" and the prints would magically return to us shortly after.

There was an awful lot of cash floating around the office. We stopped taking checks for a time because we'd been burned on a few deals. But we began accepting them again as the sums were often too large to take in cash. Business was booming.

I was so naive. I didn't question where Mickey or Norm got the money to run their huge operation. Then one day walking to work, I picked up the New York Times and saw a picture of Mickey on the front page. He was being charged with transportation of stolen securities. While I knew Mickey was Mob connected I told myself "Well, the past is the past, and I'm sure he's not that bad or the police would have come and arrested him by now."

But more and more, I felt Mickey and Norm were hanging out with a rougher crowd and that their dealings were becoming more corrupt. I couldn't ignore the fact that the operation was getting more dangerous when firearms started popping up around the office. I'd jokingly warn them, "What you can do in Texas and California, you can't do here in New York City." I tried to make light of it but couldn't help but wonder what caused them to carry guns wherever they went.

The straw that broke the camel's back was when Mickey asked me to fly to Boston and meet a man in the parking lot of Logan Airport. The guy had no name of course. "He'll recognize you," Mickey assured me. "All you need to know is that he'll be in a green Cadillac. Take a bag of money from him and

DYNAMITE, PEPPER AND LORD PERRY (1972-1974)

fly back." At that moment I told myself that I should start looking for a way out but said I'd do the Boston job even though I had a bad feeling about it.

At the time, I was quite nervous about flying so I got to LaGuardia airport early and fortified myself with a few drinks. A little over an hour later when I landed in Boston I still felt the warmth of the alcohol in my system as I exited the terminal. The parking lot was freezing cold and totally deserted except for a green Cadillac with the motor running. It seemed a cliché straight out of a film noir.

I walked over and knocked on the door. "Get in," the driver said. I complied and as I sank into the passenger seat he handed me a large brown paper bag filled with crumpled bills. It turns out they'd come from the X-rated movie theaters in Boston's Combat Zone where I'd worked some years before.

The green Caddy man said to me, "Are you going to count it?"

I responded, "Are you kidding?"

He in turn said, "Well you're gonna' have to sign for it." I found this administrative request amusing but said to myself, "I'm not signing my own name."

He pulled out a ratty piece of paper and shoved it at me along with a pen. I scribbled "Bette Davis" on the paper, got out of the car with the bag, and walked straight to the men's room in the airport terminal. I slipped into a stall and transferred the money into a black attaché case I'd brought. I exited and immediately found the closest bar, to down yet another drink as I wondered what I'd gotten myself into.

When they finally called my Eastern Shuttle flight, I was reasonably drunk and very ready to head home. I boarded and found my seat, clutching the attaché case on my lap. A stewardess approached me and said, "Sir, you've got to put that under your seat." Reluctantly I did, fully realizing the dire consequences that losing it would mean. It was a bumpy ascent so as we were still climbing when I made another check with my foot. The case was gone! The Fasten Seat Belt sign was lit but I leapt up from my seat, got down on all fours and started crawling down the aisle in search of the case. I finally spotted it four rows back between a woman's legs and started clawing for it desperately. The flight attendant was shouting at me to return to my seat but I yelled "Not before I get that briefcase". I finally wrenched it back and returned to my seat. Clearly, I was not cut out to be a bag man.

Over the next few weeks, I overheard conversations in the office about people getting "whacked" or "hit". To make matters worse I was the only one who signed the company checks. Mickey and Norm always avoided this responsibility like the plague. If we ever got busted, it would probably be me the authorities would nail.

My nerves were frayed. I had begun to drink more heavily to deal with the stress. This led Chuck to drink more as well and our relationship was suffering as a result. I resolved to leave Mickey and Norm's employment as soon as possible. The only problem was that Mickey and Norm were both imposing characters and the last thing I wanted to do was upset them. I needed an excuse to exit gracefully.

One day a tall, blonde Swedish man walked into the Lord Perry's office. His name was Kjell Nielsson and he owned a number of theaters in Stockholm that showed 16mm hardcore films. He was desperate for product and word on the street had led him to Norm and Mickey.

I found Kjell immediately likable. He had a classic sing-song Swedish accent that added color to memorable statements he made such as, "Jesus Christ, I do not know how I will survive if I do not get some pussy on the screen." We chatted for a while about his needs and then he said these magic words: "I only work in the cash. I do not see any reason why you and I could not go out for a drink, and then we could make the deal, ya? I'm sure your boss would not mind…or maybe your boss does not even need to know."

I welcomed Kjell's offer with open arms and told him, "You've come to the right place." We took our discussion to the Rum House at the Edison Hotel and drank and drank. I stuck with beer but Kjell started on vodka and never seemed to stop. He told me all about his life: his operation in Stockholm, his lovely home by a lake, his wonderful wife, and his huge Great Dane Frassa that he loved like a child. In between cocktails, Kjell said, "You will come over and you will visit and you will love this dog. But in the meantime, I must have a product for my theaters. I am losing money because I cannot get product. You can help me, ya?"

I could. Kjell wanted to buy in quantity and Lord Perry had a ton of product. It was just a matter of settling on a price, and it didn't take long for us to do that. I sold him a couple of thousand dollars' worth of our secondary materials – not top-of-the-line product but it fit his needs. Kjell planned to pack up the product and travel back with it to Sweden. He insisted that I draw up phony invoices to undervalue the films because while he could legally bring pornographic material into Sweden, the import taxes were exorbitant.

I told Norm and Mickey about the deal even though Kjell had suggested I might not want to. Based on their recent behavior, I didn't want to risk going behind their backs. They felt I might have been able to get more money than I did, but ultimately said, "John, it's up to you. Get the best you can off this second-tier material. Just don't undersell the good stuff." It wasn't long until Kjell called me from Sweden. He was happy with our transaction and was ready to come back for more in two weeks.

We met again at what would become our regular, the Rum House. In his wide-smiling way, Kjell proposed, "Do you think that maybe we come to another arrangement where you give me a good deal and I make it worth your while?" He knew I had the authority to negotiate prices on Norm and Mickey's behalf. With the door wide open, I decided to take the risk. I quoted him a lower-than-usual price per film and said, "You know in this country, we believe in tipping."

And so began a lucrative friendship between Kjell and myself. For every $3,000 deal that we made, I was able to pocket $1,000 for the next Amero Brothers production. Norm and Mickey did question why the profits from the transactions with Kjell were lower than usual but I told them that Kjell was a tough negotiator. And at the end of the day, with Kjell purchasing so much product, Norm and Mickey were just happy to see money regularly moving into their accounts. I would call them at their West Coast base every couple of weeks and say, "You've got to ship me some more stuff from the lab because supplies are getting low." If they questioned why, I'd respond, "The film is coming back from our clients so chewed up I can't use it. I've re-edited this stuff to death." In reality, I was now selling Kjell our top tier films at a deeply discounted price in return for "tips." Norm and Mickey had no clue about the technical aspect of the business, so it was easy to pull the wool over their eyes.

I knew it wasn't safe to let this arrangement go on for long. I kept telling myself, "I have to stop playing Russian Roulette and get out of this safely while I still can." But in the meantime, I finally got to watch my bank balance grow.

Kjell was a pleasure to work with, very appreciative and fun to spend time with. He would take Lem and me out to dinner every time he was in New York. In return we showed him the Manhattan sights and took him to Broadway shows. He started hanging out with our regular crowd at Big Spender where everyone liked him. One time he brought his wife over with him and she was a delight too. He was fascinated with real estate, and wanted to invest in property in Florida as he was convinced he could make a killing there.

On the downside, Kjell was a Scientologist and I had to listen to his endless religious rants. He also was heavily into Ponzi schemes, which were getting huge in Sweden at that time. But this was a small price to pay for such great company, and such a solid professional relationship.

I knew Kjell was keen for any lucrative business idea, so I suggested that he could earn more with better product than Norm and Mickey's dreck. Kjell was mildly interested but wary; "I'm not made of money," he'd say. But I shared how theaters like the World were making significant profits by playing bigger budget 35mm adult features for several months at a time. Eventually I convinced him to try the same model back in Europe.

Then the lightbulb went off. I'd found a way out of working for Norm and Mickey. I told Kjell I knew just the people to make great quality films for him: the Amero Brothers.

CHAPTER 8

EVERY INCH A LADY
(1975)

Lem and I showed Kjell several of our movies and he was impressed enough to offer us a deal for a new film. But before I could accept, I had to tell Mickey and Norm that I could no longer manage their New York operations. I was nervous as they were both intimidating characters, especially when you gave them news they didn't want to hear. But I got lucky – Mickey was alone in the office and in a good mood when I told him. He was disappointed to see me go but gave me his blessing to go back to making films.

Lem and I soon found an office in the same building as Norm and Mickey and set up shop. Our first order of business was to get together with Kjell to work out the details of our proposed film. It would be the third hardcore film Lem and I made, but it was Kjell's first and he was eager to make a big splash. He was a more generous backer then we were used to, putting up $25,000. He also agreed to pay our office rent if we let him share the space when he was in New York. And Kjell gave us free rein in terms of the film's content, stressing only that the Swedish censors wouldn't tolerate any combination of sex and graphic violence. This wasn't an issue for an Amero Brothers production.

Lem and I turned our attention to writing the screenplay. We decided to make a thinly disguised version of our earlier film *The Corporate Queen* (1969), only this time in color and with a bigger budget. We titled the film *Every Inch a Lady* and Kjell approved the script. Soon after he returned to Sweden, leaving us to shoot our feature unimpeded by an over-zealous producer.

Our bigger budget meant we could employ the best of the new crop of New York adult film stars. We began casting with the part of Crystal Laverne, our female lead who works her way up from streetwalker to high-end madam, and it didn't take us long to choose the actress Darby Lloyd Rains. Attractive and talented, Darby had made several adult films, including Gerard Damiano's *Memories Within Miss Aggie* (1974) which had been a big hit. She was perfect for our lead and we fell in love with her as soon as we met her.

For the role of Chino, Crystal's romantic and business partner, Lem and I returned to Harry Reems. Herb Streicher, as he was known when we first met him, had shot several sex scenes for our film *Bacchanale*. He'd been relatively unknown at that point, but by now he was a big name in the industry and across the country thanks to his role in *Deep Throat* (1972). We knew he would draw big crowds, but Harry was aware of the value of his name too and drove a hard bargain. He demanded top dollar and equal billing with Darby in any advertising related to the film. We weighed our options, and decided that even though he would cost us more, his name value would probably be worth it. Besides, Harry was a consummate professional and a pleasure to work with.

For the second female lead we hired Andrea True, a cute blonde who would become famous the following year with her hit single "More, More, More." In *Every Inch a Lady*, she's almost unrecognizable as Darby's frumpy man-hating secretary Edna, clad in a pants suit, thick glasses and a short dark wig. Like Harry, Andrea demanded equal billing to the other stars so we promised her a full-page ad in Variety.

We cast two other well-known adult film staples, Kim Pope and David Savage. Kim in particular had a good reputation and a proven track record, having worked with directors like Gerard Damiano and Chuck Vincent. David Savage was handsome, muscular and a solid actor. Rounding out our cast were various Amero Brothers regulars, such as Kurt Mann who played Darby's assistant and man Friday.

We gave Darby, Harry, and Andrea complete scripts before we started shooting, practically unheard of in those days of adult films. We also scheduled rehearsal time so they could get a feel for the story. There was a fair amount of dialogue and we knew that if they learned their lines it would help us save time and money in the long run. Harry in particular was a dream; he could look at a page of dialogue and deliver it in one take every time.

Roberta Findlay served as our cinematographer, though we had our usual stylistic clashes. She wanted to shoot the film in black-and-white, filled with moody shadows and an Ingmar Bergman tone; I wanted a brightly colored, Hollywood musical feel. Fortunately, Roberta was a good sport about delivering the upbeat look I wanted.

Once again LaRue Watts and Fabian Stuart designed our sets and costumes, this time enjoying the increased budget we had available. In one scene, Darby wore a long, elegant red dress accented with a red feather boa, channeling a Gibson Girl feminine ideal. Her red, sparkly platform heels were our sexy homage to Dorothy's ruby slippers from *The Wizard of Oz* (1939). Darby wasn't accustomed to so much attention being paid to her clothes, but loved every minute of it.

EVERY INCH A LADY (1975)

We even had enough money to hire a professional hair stylist and makeup artist for the film. Tiv Davenport was a war veteran, former model and cabaret performer who had worked on Broadway, styling Carol Channing for the show "Hello, Dolly!". We met him at the Big Spender and had no trouble convincing him to work on our X-rated movie. Tiv even appears briefly onscreen as a tailor in the opening scene. A new addition to our Amero troupe was Richie Weigle who was seeing Roberta at the time. He helped her out with just about everything on the shoot and did a small cameo with Harry Reems in Central Park.

After years of working in low budget, black and white film production, we were excited to finally be making a film with a slicker, more professional look. We splurged on 35mm Eastman Kodak color stock, knowing we could only afford it if we used it as efficiently as possible. I'd read that Hollywood productions typically shot at a 7:1 ratio, meaning they shot an average of seven takes for every one they used. We knew we couldn't afford this much waste so Lem and I carefully planned to shoot as many scenes as possible in a single take. Lem's skills were key to our success. He always kept a solid sense of how he'd edit the film in mind as we shot, essential for keeping film use to a minimum.

We began shooting *Every Inch a Lady* in the hot, sweaty summer of 1975. To establish the film's location, we opened with a sweeping aerial shot of the East River that was actually left-over footage from the *Pepper* shoot. It's a fantastic view of New York City and a snapshot of history as many of the buildings are no longer standing.

We shot scenes out on the city streets, and included New York landmarks such as Washington Square Park and the then-standing World Trade Center. And no New York exploitation film of the time would be complete without the obligatory montage of Times Square attractions. The iconic theater marquees were fabulous, as were the shots of the Brill Building, Bond's, and the Flame Steaks restaurant with its notorious ad for $1.79 dinners. I loved the New York feel of these exteriors and it was fun to shoot guerrilla style, even though people occasionally recognized Harry Reems, which slowed things down. It always amazed me that we never had any problem from the authorities when shooting on the city streets.

Finding interior locations was more problematic. Even though hardcore films were slightly more acceptable than they were a couple of years ago, nobody knew whether shooting an X-rated scene was actually legal, so we had to be cautious about who we approached. We never spelled out that we were filming actual sex, instead just saying that the film would have a little nudity.

Rather than advertise for locations and put ourselves at risk, Lem and I relied on referrals from friends. That's how we came to shoot many of the key scenes for *Every Inch a Lady* in a spectacular Gramercy Park penthouse apartment. The man who owned the place was a friend of a friend who was very intrigued by the idea of shooting an explicit sex film in his own home.

The space was typical of the weird and wonderful decor you came across in the 1970s. It was decorated with modern cubist furniture and built in a faux Tudor style complete with stained-glass accents, coats of armor on the windows, a vaulted ceiling in the huge living room. The bedroom on the other hand was very small, which made shooting sex scenes in there difficult. And we needed to include a lot of explicit sex – at least six or seven hardcore sequences – to make the distributors happy.

Having filmed the luxury scenes in an opulent location, we needed a small threadbare apartment from which Crystal starts her ascent to riches. Sure enough, we found ourselves back at my apartment on Cornelia Street. First we used the street itself for a flashback scene. In the sequence Darby is wandering through the West Village and steps over a derelict, played by yours truly. Continuing the Hitchcock-like directorial cameos, Lem appears in the background of that scene, entering my building as Darby strolls by.

When we moved inside the apartment to shoot, I had to pay some neighbors to let me run electrical cables into their apartments to avoid blowing fuses. Then we had to move most of the furniture into the bedroom to shoot in the living room. Next we had to move everything into the living room so we could shoot a sex scene in the bedroom. In the bedroom we filmed a three-way sex scene with Darby, Harry and Jamie Gillis. Despite the fact that Lem and I could be prudish, we often looked to push the envelope. So we had Jamie insert a string of beads into Harry's rear, then pull them out at the climax for comic effect. The scene was actually simulated because Harry refused to have the beads inserted.

The only person who was unhappy in all this was Chuck. He would arrive home to find all our furniture moved or, worse still, to find a note on the door telling him to come back later as we were in the middle of a scene. At the end of the day, he would just look at me and say, "You really owe me big time now, and you can burn those sheets!"

EVERY INCH A LADY (1975)

The day after filming in my apartment we moved uptown to take exterior shots of Lincoln Center. The footage was meant to set the context for a scene in which Darby employs a seasoned call girl to accompany a gentleman to the opera. For the role of the escort we were lucky to find Erica Eaton. Erica hailed from Sheepshead Bay in Brooklyn, and had the accent to match. She was enthusiastic about the part and was perfect for it. Tiv elaborately styled her hair, and Erica claimed he sprayed her mane so much that it didn't move for days afterwards.

After the opera Erica takes her client, played by Marc "10 ½" Stevens, to bed. Marc was an actor who appeared in both straight and gay adult films, wrote several books about the business, and was one of the real characters on the 1970s scene. Similar to Harry Reems, Marc was one of the first performers to develop a name for himself so people, even outside of porn, often knew who he was. Marc may have been a stalwart of the business, acting for all the big New York filmmakers, but his vanity and frequent performance issues meant he wasn't always the easiest person to work with.

We shot Marc and Erica's sex scene at our friend Les Hamill's apartment on 54th Street. We did nothing in the way of set dressing as the apartment already had a distinct mid-1970s feel. The sequence begins with Marc asking Erica to read to him from a dirty book as it's the only way his character can get off. They then end up having sex in every conceivable position. The scene is hilarious thanks to Erica's thick Brooklyn accent and Lem's quick cutting as they go through the Kama Sutra.

However agile Marc and Erica were, they could not compete with another actor we found. His name was Vito K. Aras but he went by the nom de porn "Dr. Infinity" owing to his unique talent for auto-fellatio. He took his skill very seriously, believing that if a man ingested his own semen it would increase his life force and make him a better person. He was on his own private crusade, sharing his philosophy of "self-love" with whomever he could. Dr. Infinity saw *Every Inch a Lady* as a vehicle to promote his way of thinking. When the film was finished, he added his scene to a show reel he kept of himself performing his special skill in trees, on famous estates he broke into, even among a herd of buffalo.

Roberta was terrified of Dr. Infinity, convinced he was a serial killer. We filmed his auto-fellatio scene late one night, and Roberta kept saying, "He's got a knife, I know it. He's going to kill us all!" But somehow, we survived, and the worst aspect of the shoot was that Dr. Infinity couldn't complete the act. We wound up faking his money shot using a hastily improvised Coco Lopez piña colada mix.

For years after we finished making *Every Inch a Lady* I'd bump into Dr. Infinity around New York. He was always looking for opportunities to gain publicity for his unique theories. When city officials tried to tear down Radio City Music Hall in 1978, he spent months standing out in the freezing cold chanting "Save the Music Hall!" while handing out Dr. Infinity fliers. He then decided he needed to take his message to Europe. To raise money for air fare, he answered an ad in the New York Times for a nanny. The ad turned out to be placed by John Lennon and Yoko Ono. Somehow Vito's application was successful and he started work taking care of their son Sean. But the job only lasted a few months because Vito thought it would be a good idea to show Polaroids of his act to Sean, and was summarily fired. He eventually did make it to Europe where he married a gypsy fortune teller and settled in Barcelona. He continued to perform his special feat for many years, first with a circus on a revolving turntable, then as part of a live sex show. Despite his continued focus on maintaining his life force, Vito recently passed away in Spain.

The last scenes of the nine-day shoot for *Every Inch a Lady* focused on our two leads and the climax of the film. At the end of the story Darby discovers Harry and Andrea's betrayal so she opens up the oven gas jets – another scene shot back in my apartment – and takes her explosive revenge. We wanted to pull out all the stops for the film's finale. So we had Harry ejaculate directly onto a piece of Plexiglas in front of the camera before we blew up a little model of the Gramercy Park building to simulate Darby's revenge. Sure, the explosion wound up blowing all the fuses in our office but we were convinced it was worth it.

The film closes as Darby is driven away by her chauffeur, played by our old friend Ron Scardera. In homage to the MGM movies that ended with "Made in Hollywood, USA", we closed with the words "Made in Manhattan, USA" on screen.

As always with post-production, editing the film took much longer than shooting it. But luckily Lem loved the editing process and was great at it. Once we finally had our finished cut, it was time to work on the audio. We'd shot many of the scenes MOS, so much of the sound had to be added, including the sex scene noises. Fortunately, we had a secret weapon when it came to recording these specialized sounds, and that was our friend, costume man, set dresser, and sex noise maker extraordinaire, LaRue Watts. Clad in short pants and with Vaseline between his knees, LaRue would drag a box of sex toys into the sound booth and get to work. Any slapping you hear is actually LaRue's greased knees hitting together. Sucking sounds were achieved with his thumb in his mouth. And any moans and groans, whether made by a man or woman, were all LaRue. Sometimes he'd get confused and ask, "Wait, am I supposed to be Harry or Darby now?" But his synchronization was always spot on and Lem and I were extremely grateful for his unique talent.

We paid almost as much attention to the music we used in *Every Inch a Lady* as we did to the dialogue. Lem and I spent significant time carefully matching melodies to the scenes. We both loved film scores so there were none of the funky guitar tracks so prevalent in porn films of the era. We were weaned on the likes of Elmer Bernstein and Franz Waxman, and would have had original music for all of our films if we could have afforded it. But since we couldn't, we shamelessly lifted music from anyone and everyone we admired. I used to kid my brother saying, "I'm taking $10 from petty cash to buy the entire film score."

I particularly liked a sex scene with Darby and Harry we set to a Max Steiner composition lifted from *A Summer Place* (1959). I still marvel at how good Harry and Darby look together in that scene, and how their chemistry came through to that music. Movie buffs might also recognize John Barry's composition "Café Martinique" borrowed from the James Bond film *Thunderball* (1965).

For sound mixing we used Magno Sound, a reputable mainstream company. We had dialogue, music, and sound effects all running at the same time so the balance and synchronization of these tracks was critically important. Sound mixing was a pricey part of the budget but there was no getting around it, and it made a huge difference to the finished product.

Magno had six sound mixers working for them at the time, but only one was willing to work with us on an adult film. This particular mixer had done many of Woody Allen's films, and got a kick out of working on our movie for a change. He treated our film just as seriously as the bigger budget productions he worked on, so the fee was money well spent.

Overall the film cost in excess of $40,000, well over the $25,000 budget we'd agreed to at the beginning. Fortunately, Kjell was not overly concerned, and loved the film itself. He had a great sense of humor so especially enjoyed the movie's comedic nature.

When our screening print was ready, Kjell asked us to put together marketing materials for *Every Inch a Lady* (1975). And while he would handle European distribution he wanted us to approach U.S. distributors.

We wanted a catchy tag line to grab distributor attention so, never passing up an opportunity to pay tribute to the movies we loved, decided to play off Clark Gable and Greer Garson's 1945 film *Adventure*. We updated "Gable's back and Garson's got him!" to "*Every Inch a Lady*: Reems is back and Rains has got him!" and led with it on all our promotional materials.

Lem and I wanted to announce the film in a big way and so we took out a full-page ad in Variety, unheard of for an X-rated film. We'd promised Andrea True that she would feature in the ad campaign, but instead we went with a picture of Darby in a feather boa. Andrea threatened to sue us in response, so we reluctantly ran a second ad in Variety featuring her.

Seemingly inspired by Andrea, Harry threatened us with legal action shortly after. This time we called his bluff, telling him he could sue us if he wanted. He never did. It was a tempest in a teacup, and the situation was resolved quickly and amicably.

On a more serious note, Felix Bilgrey – our old contact at Times Film – also threatened to sue us. While we'd maintained a good relationship with him since we'd made *The Corporate Queen* in the late 1960s, he saw that *Every Inch a Lady* was a thinly disguised remake of our earlier film. He sent us a cease and desist order together with a letter saying we'd stolen the plot of *The Corporate Queen* and accusing us of producing an unauthorized remake.

He was right of course, but after all our efforts we weren't in the mood to start paying him off. I wrote one of my indignant letters to him, refuting the accusation and suggesting that a serious company like Times Film would not welcome the publicity of being associated with a hardcore sex film. I indicated that we would be willing to fight fire with fire, and would not hesitate to share details of the case with the press. We never heard from Felix or Times Film again.

We screened *Every Inch a Lady* for the usual suspects and wound up going with Sam Lake and Bobby Sumner of Mature Pictures as they made us the best offer. They agreed to a 60:40 split in our favor, and an advance of $50,000.

An ad campaign was quickly developed and we opened at the World Theater in record time. It was an extravagant premiere complete with a klieg light and a red carpet, and all of the film's stars turned out dressed to the nines. Since the World Theater had a stage, we decided to open the proceedings with a fashion show featuring the original lingerie from the film. Erica Eaton was emcee for the evening and narrated the show in a hilarious way with her unmistakably thick Brooklyn accent. She'd had far

EVERY INCH A LADY (1975)

too much to drink prior to arriving and teetered on the edge of the stage her entire performance while the audience held their breath.

The promotion worked and the theater was packed. We invited everyone involved in the film as well as our friends and fellow filmmakers. We'd recently met adult film director Chuck Vincent at the Big Spender, and he came along with his partner Billy. Chuck was starting to make a name for himself on the New York porn scene with successes such as *Mrs. Barrington* (1974) and *Farewell Scarlet* (1975). He was of Maltese descent, short in stature and wore thick glasses, but what he may have lacked in physical presence he made up for in character. He was a dynamic, fearless person – outgoing, friendly and loud. And he was always wheeling and dealing, constantly pitching ideas to anyone who would listen. We didn't know him well as he didn't hang out at Big Spender and our social lives revolved around the bar, but he was entertaining to have around.

We also had critics in attendance from all the major men's publications like Playboy and Penthouse. Even mainstream papers like Variety – which was still reviewing X-rated films at the time – covered the premiere. It was all great publicity.

After the opening in New York, Kjell insisted that Lem and I fly to Stockholm to launch *Every Inch a Lady* in Europe. Kjell put us all up in a luxury hotel and was a gracious host. It was a festive, party atmosphere and a wonderful experience to be treated so well. By coincidence, the actor Eric Edwards was in town filming a movie, and Kim Pope was also there to get married with Chuck Vincent giving her away. We all attended her wedding, and she agreed to make a personal appearance at the theater screening the film, showing up in her wedding dress.

We thought the world of Kim and always loved seeing her. She was sweet, fun, and talented, but sadly we couldn't say the same for her new husband. They seemed a strange combination; she was gentle, cultured and social while he was thuggish and possessive. To make matters worse there were rumors that he was abusive with her. Some of the wedding guests with adjoining hotel rooms to Kim's reported loud shouting and crying until the early hours. I never saw Kim again after meeting her in Stockholm, but was pleased to hear news of her thirty five years later. She was alive and well and mercifully long parted from her ex-husband who it transpired had been murdered while in prison.

The most notable absentee from the Stockholm trip was my partner Chuck. His interest in the film world was still negligible and I thought that he'd feel out of place. Looking back I'm surprised and disappointed that

I didn't encourage him to accompany me on trips like this more often. We had a close, loving relationship, but it didn't extend to the films I made. Lem still came first in that respect.

Kjell, Sam, and Bobby all did well financially with *Every Inch a Lady*. Kjell made a healthy profit showing the film in his theaters and selling it across the rest of Europe, and Mature Pictures continued to distribute it widely across America for many years. But while our partners made good money, Lem and I didn't wind up with much. We'd taken a small salary from the budget to keep ourselves afloat, but our percentage of the film was slow to materialize.

Nevertheless, we were happy with our efforts, and Kjell was so pleased with his return that he was eager to invest in another film. So it wasn't long until we turned our attention to the next Amero Brothers' production, *Blonde Ambition*.

CHAPTER 9

BLONDE AMBITION
(1977-1981)

Kjell was willing to spend $30,000 on our next film thanks to our successful foreign sales of *Every Inch a Lady*. This would be our highest budget project ever and we wanted to take full advantage of it. So in 1976 we began pre-production for an homage to the flamboyant musicals we grew up on, like *Singin' in the Rain* (1952) and *How to Marry a Millionaire* (1953).

We came up with a basic plot that we thought befitting of the genre, and called it *White Tie and Tails*. It was a breezy comedy focused on two hapless sisters with a vaudeville act who dream of making it big in New York and marrying millionaires. In pursuit of their goal they become embroiled in all manner of crazy adventures, such as a porn remake of *Gone with the Wind* and a harebrained scheme to recover a priceless brooch by posing as drag queens in a Greenwich Village gay bar.

With the story set, we commissioned our friend LaRue Watts to write the screenplay. LaRue had been a playwright for years, and had always expressed an interest in writing a script for us. It wasn't long before he came back with a fantastic draft – re-titled *Blonde Ambition* – full of comedy, music, dancing and, of course, hardcore sex. It was more like a mainstream film than anything we'd done before in that it had plenty of dialogue and a large number of locations. We felt the story was so strong that we'd be able to cut a high-quality R-rated version in addition to the hardcore release we'd promised Kjell.

Lem and I always seemed to work with a perfect unspoken understanding between us. As I laid out how I saw the film unfolding, I could see Lem editing in his head. But I managed to surprise him when I suggested we travel to London to cast the two female leads, Candy and Sugar Kane. I told him we could also film exteriors there, which would lend an air of international class to our production and bring it even closer to our vision of a mainstream musical. And as an Anglophile, I was looking forward to filming in England.

Lem liked the idea so we caught a flight and checked into London's Pastoria Hotel.

We only intended to stay a few days but wound up in London for over two weeks. It happened that Chuck Vincent was in town to explore film ideas with the English film producer Harry Alan Towers. Knowing Chuck's inclination towards promiscuity, I immediately told him that I'd read about the London cruising scene. I warned him to avoid the public restrooms in Piccadilly Circus and instead try Leicester Square, which was considered a much safer option. Chuck laughed off the advice saying he was in London for business and would have no time for extra-curricular activities.

A few days later I was with Chuck when two London Bobbies turned up. Apparently, Chuck had been arrested for soliciting in the Piccadilly men's room. As the Bobbies took Chuck away, he said, "John, you told me that Piccadilly was safe, and to avoid Leicester Square!" He'd gotten my advice backwards. Fortunately, he was released a few hours later after paying a fine.

Back to the business of film, we hired a car, a driver, and an Arriflex camera and spent the first few days driving around the outskirts of London shooting the countryside for B-roll footage. We were then ready to find our leading ladies. Harry Alan Towers had given Chuck the name of an agent who was supposedly well-connected, so we told the agent what we wanted and he started to send women over for auditions. We didn't feel it was appropriate to hold these auditions in our hotel room, so we used the hotel lobby and bar instead.

We soon realized how difficult it was to find women who could sing, dance, act, and were also willing to perform sex on camera. Finally, we narrowed it down to two actresses.

Suzy Mandel had been in a number of British softcore sex comedies in the 1970s and had appeared many times on the popular Benny Hill TV show. She was lovely and interested in our film and the opportunity to come to New York, but she didn't want to perform any actual sex. Lem and I liked her so much that we didn't want to lose her. We asked how she'd feel if we used someone that looked like her to do inserts for the sex scenes. Suzy was fine with this approach so we put the following clause in her contract:

> "The Player shall not perform any immoral act and, specifically, shall not be required to engage in any actual sexual acts although she may be required to do simulated sex acts other than simulated oral sex acts; but Player shall be required to appear on camera nude or semi-nude and play her role in such a state. The Producer shall have the right to use a double for the Player in any scene of explicit or simulated sex act or any scene of nudity or semi-nudity."

BLONDE AMBITION (1977-1981)

We had sister number one, Sugar Kane.

For the role of Candy Kane, we met with another British actress who like Suzy had performed in a number of 1970s British softcore films. But unlike Suzy, Heather Deeley had recently acted in a rare British hardcore feature called *Diversions* (1976) so we knew she wouldn't be averse to performing sex on camera. She was a very attractive girl and her dark features would contrast well with Suzy's blonde hair.

We were ready to sign her up but just as we were about to leave for New York, a jealous boyfriend emerged angrily forbidding her from taking part in our movie. At first Heather stood up for herself, but it was clear that she was becoming more and more upset. The drama showed no signs of letting up and we were running out of time, so in the end we walked away.

We lost another British actress along the way as well. The agent had arranged for us to meet Diana Dors, a British blonde bombshell in the style of Marilyn Monroe who was popular due to her starring appearances in a series of British sex-film-comedies. We liked her and thought about casting her as a London aristocrat we named Lady Sybil Buckingham. Diana expressed interest in taking part in the film but soon started making demands. First it was to stay at the Plaza Hotel which we were willing to concede to. Then other requests followed, seemingly made by her agent who started to smell money. In the end it was more trouble than we wanted, so sadly we let Diana Dors go.

We returned to New York, one sister short.

Back home we had our eye on Gloria Leonard for the role of Candy Kane. Gloria was a talented and feisty actress who lived a few buildings down from us on Cornelia Street, but it turned out she was booked up. So in desperation we placed an ad in the trade newspaper Backstage, and it wasn't long before we met Dory Devon. Dory had appeared in a number of Broadway and off-Broadway productions and was a seasoned actress as well as a terrific dancer. Luckily for us, she'd recently started doing a few adult films using different pseudonyms so sex clearly wasn't an issue. Dory had a lovely personality, and was a great addition to our cast as Candy Kane.

Another actress we cast was Genie Josephs. Genie was a student at the local Jesuit seminary raising money to fund her studies by doing X rated films. In one of the more bizarre scenes in *Blonde Ambition*, she plays a wife who lives with her husband in a home built on ice. We filmed it at an indoor ice skating rink on 58th Street normally used to train young children. For the shoot we draped the large room in fabric and brought in a number of props, including a fireplace and a grand piano, to give it a homey feel. We even had the actors simulate a sexual romp on the ice, no small feat as it was freezing-cold and the performers were wearing ice skates.

We also came across a wonderful comedic character actress who took the nom-de-porn "Molly Malone" in tribute to an actress from the early days of silent film. Just like her namesake, Molly was a late bloomer in the film industry and didn't start acting until she was in her 50s. We cast her in the "Diana Dors" role of Lady Sybil Buckingham. It wasn't a sex role but Molly nevertheless made it clear that she didn't want to be on set when any explicit sex scenes were shot.

As usual it was easier to find male talent. We called upon the best of the New York City porn actors, including Jamie Gillis, R. Bolla (Robert Kerman), George Payne and Eric Edwards. All had extensive training and legitimate roles in their credits in addition to X-rated film experience.

We did hire one relative newcomer named Dennis Posa. Dennis had been acting consistently in theater over the years. A Long Island native with dreams of stardom, he was a handsome and talented actor as well as a solid sex performer. As he had ambitions to perform in mainstream films and didn't want his adult film appearances to ruin his chances, he acted in porn under the name Wade Nichols, or Wade Parker in *Blonde Ambition*. With help from Jacques Morali, music producer of acts like the Village People, he later went on to release a disco album titled "Like an Eagle" (1979) under the name Dennis Parker. Unlike many of his fellow adult film performers, Dennis was successful in breaking through to the mainstream, and from 1979 through 1984, he had a recurring role on the popular television soap opera *The Edge of Night*. Sadly, Dennis passed away from AIDS in 1985.

Kurt Mann, our stalwart among the non-sex performing actors, plays George Payne's roommate who is the reigning diva at the "Club Pitts", a Village drag bar. Kurt's close friend Bob Meehan, a fixture at the Big Spender whom we all knew, also appears in a non-sex role. A travel agent with an acerbic tongue, we knew Bob would be great. He appears under the nom-de-porn Adam DeHaven in tribute to Gloria DeHaven. Bob went on to appear in other films we made as well as movies by Larry Revene, Chuck Vincent and many others. Also appearing in a non-sex role was our friend Patty Finnegan. Patty does a great *Gone with the Wind* (1939) parody of Prissy under the name Patricia Dale.

BLONDE AMBITION (1977-1981)

And as usual we roped in our good friends for cameo roles, now including Roberta's latest boyfriend Richie Weigle. Richie worked as a sound mixer for Ross-Gaffney, a small film rental and production house in New York. Richie was a genuinely nice guy who happened to date some of the more colorful women in the industry including Roberta and later Erica Eaton. Erica returned for a small part in the film, and we even found a role for Kjell as a sketchy producer named Ben Dover.

For the first time, our budget allowed us to hire two people on camera. We brought on the tried-and-true Roberta Findlay as our principal cinematographer and then employed Larry Revene to support her. Larry was an experienced cinematographer who had worked on industrials and documentaries since the 1960s. He'd also been at the forefront of the sex film industry when he shot 8mm loops with a director named Bob Wolfe in the early 1970s. He was easy-going and fun to work with so we found him all kinds of additional tasks on the film, including several non-sex acting roles. One of these was as a drummer in the opening scene of the film, a nod to Larry's early days as a drummer in New York jazz bands.

The area we needed most help with was the choreography required by the script. It was here that we really struck gold; we'd met and become friends with the Broadway dancer and choreographer Mary Ann Niles, first wife of Bob Fosse. She was a renowned Broadway gypsy with countless shows to her credit, and luckily a regular at the Big Spender.

Having Mary Ann on board was a marriage made in heaven. Not only did she create some fantastic dance routines, but she also convinced a group of Broadway dancers to perform in the movie as well. Worried about the impact a pornographic film might have on her Broadway career, Mary Ann insisted that we use another name for her. So when it came time to craft the credits, choreographer Rosetta Stone was born.

We had only contracted with Suzy Mandel for seven days of shooting so we had to work fast. During her time in New York, we paid for her to stay at the Wellington Hotel with her boyfriend and future husband, the British film financier Stanley Margolis. Stanley had ties with Tigon British Film Productions, the company that had released some of Suzy's best-known films. Margolis would later co-produce the 1993 film *True Romance*. Suzy was in the process of permanently moving from London to Los Angeles in the hope of making it big in Hollywood, so we were a stop along the way.

Things didn't start well as Suzy hated the Wellington, the hotel we'd chosen for her. Stanley quickly intervened and moved her into the Waldorf Astoria, and we ended up splitting the costs. Suzy also wasn't pleased when we sent a friend with a pick-up truck to transport her to the set. But she let it go and wound up being co-operative and fun to work with.

For locations, in addition to the footage we'd shot in England we had been busy scouting New York. We wound up shooting inside two now-defunct locations – the ballroom of the Diplomat Hotel on 48th Street and Broadway and inside the punk rock club CBGBs on the Bowery. CBGBs had only been open for three years but was already hugely popular thanks to bands like Ramones, Blondie, and Talking Heads. It was considered the cutting edge of the music scene, which was ironic as we used it to represent an old watering hole in Wyoming. The club's owner Hilly Kristal was happy for us to film there but gave us strict instructions to put everything back exactly as we found it after we'd finished. When we turned up we found the club to be so filthy that we had to clean it extensively in order to make it presentable for our scene. Taking Hilly's instructions literally. we scattered all the garbage we'd collected back onto the floors and tables after we were done.

We spent one day in Queens shooting a scene at JFK International Airport. We convinced the airport administration that we were shooting a G-rated comedy and asked to lease a training jet for a scene between Dory Devon and Eric Edwards. Before officials would approve our request, they wanted to see the script so we wound up writing some phony dialogue to win their trust. They approved but unfortunately were excited to see a film being made so they lingered around while we were shooting. We didn't dare shoot any actual sex on board, so we wound up dressing our office to match the airplane for the explicit shots.

The exteriors we'd shot in London didn't turn out as well as we'd hoped so we filmed some establishing shots at the Phipps Estate in Old Westbury Gardens out on Long Island. It's a beautiful turn-of-the-century English mansion on the National Register of Historic Places. It was open to the public, but we didn't want to risk asking – and being turned down – for permission to film, so Larry and I carried in large knapsacks filled with camera equipment and each paid $5 admission to capture some great footage.

When we weren't on location, we were mostly at Manhattan Studios on the Upper East Side. We shot our most ambitious scene there, recreating the antebellum south when the Kane sisters get involved in a pornographic remake of *Gone with the Wind*. The sequence centers on the southern belles being ravaged by Confederate soldiers against a hand-painted backdrop of an elaborate southern estate.

The scene was not an easy feat to pull off. We prepared the props and rented costumes in advance, but even though we started dressing the set at dawn we were unable to start shooting until mid-afternoon. We needed to set up the sound stage, dress and style the cast and prepare the "peacocks" who walk the grounds. Our peacocks were actually humble chickens with feathers taped on, chosen deliberately to accentuate the cheap nature of the production. But the birds weren't great at taking direction so we brought them back to Larry Revene's studio on West 14th Street and shot some inserts later.

Key to this elaborate set piece was Jamie Gillis who played the flamboyant, gay director. We originally asked Harry Reems but as usual Harry wanted more money than we could afford. Jamie turned out to be an inspired choice. He played the part with camp humor, shouting sexual commands to his cast with the most deadpan delivery.

One of the most challenging aspects of the scene was making it appear as if all the plundering Confederate soldiers climaxed at the same time. We thought that synchronized cum shots would be a nice touch for such a high-concept sequence, but pulling it off was another story. With a handheld camera, Roberta weaved among our couples as they performed but even with her talents, there was no way we were going to get six men ejaculating simultaneously. But thanks to Lem's editing the scene appears smoother than the best Busby Berkeley synchronized extravaganza.

Once we were done filming the core story, we needed to shoot our required hardcore sex inserts. Suzy Mandel was very conscientious about tracking her appearance to try and make the transition to her body double as unnoticeable as possible. She believed it would be painfully obvious that it was not her performing in the explicit scenes. Little did she know that the Amero brothers would work their editing magic.

Certain male actors had to stick around to be in both the simulated sex scenes with Suzy as well as in the actual sex scenes with Suzy's double. The first actor we used was a young, good-looking newcomer named David Morris. David played Suzy's main love interest and was very accommodating as we attempted to match up his shots.

Another of the actors doing double duty was George Payne. George had started out in a couple of gay films, but said he was much more comfortable with straight sex. His scene with Suzy was shot in November when his skin was New York winter white. I told George, "I'm going to call you back in a few months for inserts so just make sure you stay the same color." Unfortunately, George's vanity got the best of him and when we called him back, his skin was a deep golden brown. I was annoyed with his disregard for my request and convinced it would wreak havoc in the editing room. But his chemistry with Suzy was so palpable I hoped it would distract the viewing audience from George's obvious tan lines.

Shooting the inserts was time-consuming as we needed to recreate many of the original sets, but thanks to the reasonable physical similarity of Suzy's body double and Lem's skillful editing, we were pleased with the outcome. Most people did in fact think it was Suzy having sex all the way through the film. I even fielded a suspicious call from Suzy's beau, Stanley, after the film came out. He skeptically commented, "Gee, you definitely made it look as if she was really doin' it there…"

The process of filming inserts wasn't our only problem. Post-production was grinding to a halt because Kjell was having financial troubles and was slow to send the completion funds to us. After a while, the flow of money stalled completely. Kjell had over-extended himself by a considerable margin. In addition to his network of cinemas and his film production companies in Sweden, Kjell had bought extensive land in Florida with the aim of creating a tourism hub for wealthy, elderly Swedish clientele. He'd bought a large run-down hotel in Clearwater with the expectation of turning it into a five-star luxury establishment. In reality it was in a terrible location and the first customers who stayed there took out lawsuits against him. And he'd financed the whole venture with money from loan sharks who were charging him exorbitant interest rates and starting to threaten him. To make matters worse he was being pursued by the Swedish government for tax irregularities.

To be fair, Kjell had always been a gentleman with us, and in truth there wasn't much we could do. Kjell wasn't willing to give up the large sum he'd invested in the film so all we could do was wait.

Unlike other movies we'd made that took a matter of weeks or months to finish, *Blonde Ambition* wound up taking years to complete. We had started gathering our ideas in 1976 and shot the majority of the film in 1977, but the movie didn't premiere until 1980 and wasn't officially released

BLONDE AMBITION (1977-1981)

until 1981. When it was finally shown to audiences, we played up the delay to make light of it. Our invitations read, "Every ten years the Amero Brothers finish a film; you are fortunate to be living in such a decade."

The editing took forever and Lem clearly needed a break. One sweltering day in August 1980 I noticed a line outside the Winter Garden Theater on 50th Street. The musical "42nd Street" had just opened and was getting rave reviews. I thought I'd surprise Lem and Chuck by getting tickets, so I joined the line. I soon became aware of a woman whose voice sounded familiar as did her speech impediment which made it difficult for her to pronounce her R's. Finally she turned around and said, "It's vewy hot, isn't it?" I couldn't believe I was face-to-face with Gloria Grahame. I had loved Ms. Grahame ever since she'd played the elephant girl in *The Greatest Show on Earth* (1952) directed by C.B. DeMille.

Finally, Ms. Grahame made it to the box office window and requested two tickets. Then began a comedy of errors where she couldn't remember which date and was hemming and hawing about the seats on offer. She was finally ready to pay but found she was $5 short. Feeling the frustration swelling among the people behind me I said, "Ms. Grahame **please** let me give you the 5 dollars…" Gloria answered "Well, I'll take the money only if you let me 'wite' you a check." I replied "No, really, it's OK, it's only 5 dollars." At which point the ticket seller lost it and shouted "Take the check, don't take the check, I don't give a rat's ass, just get off my line!" When she handed me the check I said, "You know, Miss Grahame, I'll never cash this." She just blew me a kiss and walked off.

I couldn't wait to tell Lem about my encounter. I found him at the Big Spender with Kurt Mann and Armand Weston, a fellow director of both X and R-rated films. When I began to tell my story, Armand interrupted me saying, "I don't believe this! I'm using Gloria in my R-rated horror film, *The Nesting*, and she's due on set next Thursday. Since you're a fan, would you like to drive her up to Irvington where we're shooting?" It was Kismet – I would now have a chance to properly chat with one of my favorite bad girls of cinema.

The following Thursday I drove to Ms. Grahame's apartment at Manhattan Plaza on West 43rd Street to pick her up. The doorman rang up and said she'd be right down. Thirty minutes later, Ms. Grahame emerged from the elevator in dark sunglasses and with her hair in curlers. I greeted her saying, "Hi Ms. Grahame, we meet again." She lowered her sunglasses and said "We do?" After refreshing her memory, we get under way but it didn't take me long after leaving the city to realize we're lost.

Sweating from nerves I rolled down my window only to have a strong gust of wind suck my map right out of the car. Somehow we made it to the set three hours late but thankfully Armand was three hours behind so it all worked out.

Some people today say they can't believe anyone ever thought sex films could lead to the mainstream. But seeing a great actress like Gloria Grahame working with sometime-adult director Armand Weston made even skeptics like me take pause.

When we finally completed post-production on *Blonde Ambition* in 1980, our first priority was to repay Kjell for backing the film. We felt partly responsible for Kjell's financial difficulties so wanted him to be the first to reap the benefits of the movie. But most distributors were only willing to pay filmmakers from the profits they made exhibiting the films so it was difficult to get much money upfront.

There were only two companies we thought might consider paying in advance for a higher quality film. One was Audubon Films run by Ava Leighton and Radley Metzger; the other was Mature Pictures, run by Sam Lake and our old friend Bob Sumner. We arranged for two showings at the MGM screening room on 6th Avenue and 55th Street, the classiest place in town to show a film. The screenings had their desired effect and we got offers from both Audubon Films and Mature Pictures. After some negotiation, we wound up going with Sam and Bobby because they were willing to give us an advance that would cover Kjell's investment and beyond.

We produced three versions of *Blonde Ambition* to maximize the number of markets Sam and Bobby could reach; one hardcore, one softcore, and a stripped-down R-rated cut. In later years the R-rated version played on the Playboy channel and became a midnight cult hit at the 8th Street Playhouse in New York. Kurt Mann showed up for many of these midnight screenings. Wearing the same drag outfit that he wore in the film, he would hold court in the lobby, signing autographs and taking photos with fans.

Lem and I were involved in the promotion of *Blonde Ambition*, helping to develop the posters and ads. I came up with the overall tagline which I remain proud of to this day: "If you liked *Deep Throat* and *Singin' in the Rain*, you're gonna' LOVE *Blonde Ambition*."

There was an unwelcome last-minute surprise when the posters came back from the printer listing Bobby as Executive Producer. I stormed over to his office demanding that he remove his name. Bobby tried to placate

BLONDE AMBITION (1977-1981)

me by saying it wasn't a big deal, but I remained steadfast. Lem, Kjell and I hadn't put our blood, sweat and tears into the film just to have someone waltz in at the end and claim credit. It was typical of Bobby; he was always trying to claim a little extra credit for himself. We didn't let it affect our friendship, but it certainly made me wary of doing business with him.

The official premiere of *Blonde Ambition* took place at Bobby's World Theater in Times Square. It then went on to play in many cities, including London's Prince Charles Theater and in Kjell's hometown of Stockholm.

Overall, we had a strong turnout for the film and reviews were mostly positive. The only negative comments concerned the lack of eroticism, and therein lies the rub. Lem and I wanted to make films but our hearts weren't in hardcore. Story and production were more important to us than sex. *Blonde Ambition* wound up being one of the last straight adult films Lem and I made together.

THE FRANCIS ELLIE FILMS
(1976-1988)

Bill Perry's Broadway Baths continued to do extremely well, as did his gay movie house the Big Top Theater. But Bill struggled to secure a steady supply of films that could keep up with the demand for new product. He wanted to show full-length features leased from San Francisco filmmakers, but complained that their high prices made it so he could barely eke out a profit from the films. Instead he typically showed a series of loops grouped into an hour-long sequence.

One night when we were out having a drink, Bill asked me if Lem and I would be interested in making a gay feature for him. He proposed a $10,000 flat fee for a 16 mm film, explaining that he estimated we could make a feature for six or seven grand, then keep the remaining money as our profit. To be honest, I was taken aback and even a little shocked by the idea. Despite being gay and an adult filmmaker, I'd never considered making a gay feature. I told Bill I'd talk to Lem and get back to him.

When I pitched the idea to my brother, he had a similar reaction, except more pronounced. In short, he just wasn't interested. He was busy, and happy, editing our straight movies and working on other people's films in between. He said he'd be willing to help me out if I really needed him but he didn't want to get too involved.

I was mildly intrigued by Bill's proposal, but knew I wouldn't be able to make it by myself. So I gingerly approached the only other person I thought could assist me; my old partner-in-crime Mike Findlay. As I'd worked with Lem on *Every Inch a Lady* and *Blonde Ambition*, Mike and I had remained close and still got together socially on a regular basis. He'd suffered badly in the aftermath of his split from Roberta and had cut back on his film work. Legally, he was still married to Roberta but since she'd started dating Allan Shackleton, I'd encouraged Mike to divorce her since there was no likelihood of them reuniting. To deal with the pain, he was regularly taking Valium - which we jokingly referred to as "brain candy" or "attitude adjuster" tablets - and washing it down with copious quantities of beer. But despite Mike's struggles he remained good company and I valued our friendship.

Talking to him about Bill's offer was always going to be a difficult conversation. For a start, despite our close friendship, we'd still never

CHAPTER 10

discussed my being gay. Furthermore, Mike continued to lead a strangely sheltered existence, full of sexual hang-ups despite his adult film career. He certainly hadn't been exposed to any aspects of gay life.

My strategy was to take him out for drinks and see if I could convince him to make this film with me. After numerous beers, I laid out my proposal, with an added emphasis on the monetary component to pique his interest.

Mike didn't jump at the idea, but he didn't say no immediately either, and this was as good as I could have expected. The big stumbling block for him was clearly going to be shooting the sex scenes. I wasn't surprised as I knew he was conflicted about shooting straight hardcore sex. He'd always seem to get an initial vicarious thrill but would then be overcome by guilt. The idea of filming gay sex clearly bothered him even more.

I followed up carefully: "Bill Perry is offering me $10,000 for a 16mm, 60 to 70 minute, color, gay feature, complete with soundtrack and trailer. He thinks we can make it for $7,000 and pocket $3,000 as profit. But I figure we can do it for $3,000 and make a $7,000 profit, wrapping the whole thing in two to three weeks." I could almost see Mike doing the math, adding and subtracting. For good measure I repeated, "We'd make a few thousand dollars apiece in a couple of weeks. It'll be a challenge but who knows, it might be fun." Mike finally agreed.

With Mike on board, I had to figure out the plot of the film we were going to make. Bill was easy-going and wasn't particular about what he wanted - his only request was to "make it more interesting, enjoyable and erotic than the stuff I've been getting." I was confident that wouldn't be a problem as I'd seen several films at the Big Top and was thoroughly underwhelmed.

In an attempt to alleviate some of the discomfort I anticipated Mike would feel, I decided we should make a comedy. I wrote a story about a man from Naples, Italy named David who visits his American uncle Mike who runs a travel agency with his partner Angelo. The film follows David and his pet chicken Giuseppe as they fumble around New York getting involved in an array of sexual exploits. I called it *Michael, Angelo and David*, drew up the script and shot list, then turned my mind to casting.

As usual we placed an ad in Backstage and waited. The response turned out to be pretty good but we attracted some strange characters. One of the first actors I interviewed arrived wearing a camel hair coat and ascot, sporting a phony Rex Harrison British accent. He had a bona fide portfolio of tasteful head shots and modeling stills, and was extremely polite and formal. "I've heard so much about you," he gushed upon meeting me. He asked to see the script, and said his manager would want to review it, as well as a copy of the contract. I wanted to say, "My friend, this is a fuck film and we don't deal with managers or agents," but I bit my tongue and gave him our standard release. I thought that was the last I'd hear from him but the next day his agent called to inform me Rex would like $1,500 a day for his services. Needless to say, Rex didn't get the part.

For the role of David, we returned to David Savage, an actor we'd used in *Every Inch a Lady*. He was boyishly attractive, easygoing and I knew he was dependable. I liked him and had no problem giving him one of the lead parts. For the role of Mike, I cast an unknown actor named Brian Haines whom I'd met recently. We got to chatting in a bar one night, and I told him I was a filmmaker. To my surprise he told me, "I'm dying to be in a gay film" so I invited him back to our offices for an interview.

I found the process of interviewing Brian, or any newcomer for that matter, rather uncomfortable. I was aware of all the stories of the casting couch, and at first was anxious not to come across as predatory. Half the time I tried to convince the actor not to take the role as I didn't want him to feel pressured in any way or have second thoughts when we started filming. In Brian's case, he didn't have a portfolio so I asked him to disrobe which felt pretty sleazy. Luckily Brian didn't pick up on my uneasiness and happily stripped. In fact he was so gung-ho and confident that I took the risk and offered him the part.

Apart from David Savage, the only other known actor we cast was Marc "10 ½" Stevens, who we'd also met on the set of *Every Inch a Lady*. Fortunately, I didn't need to audition Marc. By now, he was ubiquitous and never slow to recommend himself to anyone. Marc was a veteran by sex film standards, and the size of his ego matched the size of his penis. He had an opinion on everything, from camera angles to costumes to script improvements. I wasn't in the mood to have a high maintenance person on set for such a low budget film but in the end we decided he was worth it.

For our crew, I commandeered my old pals LaRue Watts and Fabian Stuart. Both being gay, they didn't have a problem with what we'd be shooting, but were appalled when I told them their budget would be close to nothing. "You must beg, borrow and steal everything and anything you can," I instructed them. "The budget is very, very tiny, and there will be no profit whatsoever if you go over it." Despite the constraints they were happy to sign on, and I was glad to have their "Sparkling Sets and Costumes" once again add some panache to the project.

THE FRANCIS ELLIE FILMS (1976-1988)

Mike and I decided to co-direct the film under a single pseudonym because neither of us wanted to use our real names. I was keen to create an identity separate from the Amero Brothers brand, and Mike... well, he just didn't want anyone to know he was making a gay film.

All the other gay director's pseudonyms of the day were super macho like Rock Hard and Beef Johnson. We decided to buck the trend and use Mike's middle name, Francis, and my middle name, Ellsworth, and give the director's credit to "Francis Ellie". It was a bizarre sounding name that we had used once before on *Body of a Female*, although at the time we never expected we'd be using it again.

As co-directors, Mike and I were strange bedfellows: I found the whole enterprise amusing and vaguely ridiculous, whereas Mike treated the project with deadly seriousness. We worked well together however, and I was very happy to have him on board. Most of all I liked making films with him again like in the early days.

As we readied for production I realized I hadn't fully taken into account that, unlike on a straight film, we now had two or more penises to worry about in every sex scene. And we didn't have the medicinal options that exist today to help actors achieve and maintain an erection. We somehow had to manage this performance risk as, with our miniscule budget, we couldn't afford any delays. To help the shoot run as smoothly as possible, I outlined all the sex scenes in advance, including who was top and who was bottom. I also decided it would be helpful if our actors got to know each other before we started filming, just enough to relieve any stress but without spoiling the freshness of their encounters. So I put them in touch with each other a few days before the shoot hoping this would help avoid issues in front of the camera.

While money was tight, I didn't want to skimp on equipment and film so we rented an Arriflex 16mm camera and bought Eastman stock. Like most filmmakers of the time, we picked the equipment up late on Friday afternoon. As most of the rental houses were union-run, they were closed Sundays so we could shoot all weekend and, as long as we returned the camera before 10am Monday, we'd only be charged for one day. At some point, the unions realized what we independent filmmakers were doing. After that, union guys would sometimes turn up unexpectedly and threatened us, so we had to be careful.

From the get-go, *Michael, Angelo and David* was a difficult shoot. Because we were filming in the middle of February shooting outdoors for any length of time was not an option due to the freezing temperatures.

But I was determined not to have endless indoor scenes so we pushed ourselves. To depict David's arrival in New York, we shot the Leonardo da Vinci ocean liner coming up the icy Hudson River at dawn. We immediately followed that by filming exteriors of David walking through the gray snow-laden streets of Manhattan. We worked as quickly as we possibly could but it was still a painfully cold experience.

As usual we shot in my apartment on Cornelia Street. By now it was a real challenge for LaRue and Fabian to make the place look different from all the other times we used it in films, but somehow they worked their magic. As always Chuck was banished from the apartment during filming, unlike our cat JC who made uncredited appearances on several occasions.

As we approached the first sex scene, I took Mike aside and said, "Listen, you've shot loads of sex films and they're all the same. This is just a variation on the theme". But the trouble was that Mike always took sex very seriously. For both him and Roberta, filming the act had always been a down, dirty, and solemn activity, whereas for Lem and me, it was a fun, even lighthearted experience.

Things started out well with Mike and he was holding his own - until we got to an intense sex scene between Marc and David. I came up with the idea of staging a Hitchcock-style POV shot that would show Marc lowering himself onto a prone and fully erect David. I envisioned the camera shooting the action from the perspective of David's groin.

I mentioned the idea of a POV shot to Mike and, before I could explain the details, he said, "Great! I love POV shots!" I got him into position, lying down on the floor pointing his camera upwards, and then instructed Marc to slowly squat down towards the lens. I warned Marc to do it carefully to avoid sitting on Mike and his camera.

It slowly dawned on Mike what he'd let himself in for as Marc's spread buttocks descended towards the wide-angle lens. And despite my instructions, Marc couldn't help himself and sat straight down on the camera, jamming the eyepiece into Mike's face. I immediately called "Cut!" fearing Mike was about to lose it.

The look on Mike's face said it all. He choked back a Valium and tried to compose himself. Seeing how visibly shaken he was, I called for lunch and took Mike around the corner to Emilio's where I bought him a shot of liquid courage. Fortunately, the combination of drugs and alcohol did the trick and Mike was able to resume work.

The only scene that remained left to shoot was the closing sequence where Marc's character declares his love for David and decides to return

THE FRANCIS ELLIE FILMS (1976-1988)

to Italy with him on the Leonardo da Vinci ocean liner. In those days, you could pay fifty cents to the Seaman's Fund and go aboard the ship before it set sail, so Mike and I hid ourselves on the dock with our camera and told David and Marc exactly what to do when they boarded the ship. The script called for Marc to approach David on the outside deck of the ship, throw his arms around David's neck and kiss him passionately. As Mike and I waited for the action to begin, Marc started chatting up the ship's Italian crew, seemingly forgetting that he was supposed to be shooting a scene for a gay film. It turned out that some of the crew had recognized Marc from his appearances in straight porn films that showed in the 42nd Street grindhouses.

When we finally caught Marc's attention and gestured for him to hurry, he invited the crew to watch the scene from inside the ship, drawing notice to what was supposed to be a private moment in the film. We were wasting precious time, so in the end I shouted, "Marc, you gotta kiss David for the fade out and hold it until I yell, 'Cut'". I was hugely frustrated with him, so I made him hold an uncomfortably positioned kiss for far longer than was necessary. The ship's crew reacted in horror as their macho sex film hero was locked in an embrace with a man. It was time for Marc to make a very swift exit, much to Mike and my secret delight.

We shot *Michael, Angelo and David* in two days, hardcore scenes and all. I wasn't terribly happy as I found the finished product rather sappy and unerotic, but when I showed it to Bill he was elated. He kept repeating that he'd got a better quality film for significantly less than he usually paid.

To start the publicity ball rolling, Bill threw an elaborate opening night party for the film at the Big Top Theater and invited the gay press. *Michael, Angelo and David* got some decent reviews and audiences seemed to love it. But the success of the film didn't make me feel much better about it. That said, thanks to our frugality Mike and I did make the profit we hoped for. The income made it possible for Chuck and I to go on a two-week trip to Italy. Mike on the other hand used his money to start inventing a new 3D camera he called "Super Depth".

Like me, Mike was a 3D movie fan and we'd spend hours talking about it. The films had been particularly popular in the early 1950s when, thanks to a booming postwar economy, more consumers and theater owners were receptive to new technology. Since then however, they'd fallen out of popularity for mostly technical reasons. For a start, 3D films were shot with 2 cameras and in theaters, two projectors were required to run together in perfect synchronization to show the film.

Mike wanted to simplify the process to cut costs and make it more reliable. He thought up a system that used just one camera and one projector. Costs would be cut in half, and there would be no risk of a film shown out of sync.

Mike developed a prototype and found a film company in Taiwan interested in using it to make a 3D kung fu film titled *13 Nuns*. He flew over to Taiwan to oversee use of his new equipment, and was upbeat about how well it worked. When the film was released in the states I went to see it at the Rivoli in New York and was impressed. The film itself wasn't great but the 3D effects worked to dramatic effect. It seemed Mike was really on to something.

Because Bill owned *Michael, Angelo and David* (1976) outright through his company, PM Productions, he actively worked to distribute it across the country. PM was named after (Bill) Perry and Manny, the latter being Manuel Vasquez, Bill's professional and personal partner. Manny was a great friend to us and worked throughout Bill's organization, at both the bathhouse and the Big Top Theater.

Bill made an excellent return on his investment in our film, so I shouldn't have been surprised when he asked Mike and me if we wanted to make another Francis Ellie film. It hadn't been a terrible experience, and we liked the money and the freedom that Bill gave us, so we decided to try again. This time we set ourselves the goal of making a more polished film with the same budget.

To make a better-looking movie I knew we'd need more attractive actors. George Payne had been in *Blonde Ambition* and was both a good actor and pleasant to work with, so I had no hesitation approaching him again.

With a strong male lead secured, I decided we should make an old-fashioned Hollywood romance with a gay twist. I wrote a script about an affair between a construction worker, played by George, and a married man, played by adult newcomer Lew Seager. I titled the film *Kiss Today Goodbye*, lifted from the song "What I Did for Love" from the Broadway musical "A Chorus Line".

For the role of the wife, we secured the services of our old friend Erica Eaton, with whom we'd worked on *Every Inch a Lady*. Erica loved chewing up the scenery so I made her character a real shrew, and predictably Erica played the part well.

To our surprise, Erica had become a ubiquitous figure on the adult film scene at this point. She was organizing publicity, throwing parties, staging premieres and writing film reviews for various men's magazines. She was as

THE FRANCIS ELLIE FILMS (1976-1988)

entertaining as she was earthy, often unintentionally. I once saw her in a bar after a gay porn film screening, and asked her what she thought of the movie. With a straight face, she replied: "It was wonderful; I thought the fist-fucking scene was in very good taste."

We assembled our usual suspects including Kurt Mann, who recorded a solemn voice over for the film, David Savage, and LaRue and Fabian working their magical "Sparkling Sets and Costumes" yet again.

Even though *Kiss Today Goodbye* was a more complicated shoot than *Michael, Angelo and David*, I was adamant that we complete filming in two days. This time we were graced by warmer weather so we were able to shoot more exteriors. The film starts and ends in front of the Plaza Hotel; one reviewer commented that this book-ending of the movie symbolized the existential notion that nothing really changes in life, but in reality it was because we could shoot the scenes quickly back-to-back.

For the opening credits of the film, I created a classic Hollywood sequence similar to the style used in films produced by Ross Hunter. I wanted to show a hand turning the pages of an album across folded satin, so I tested Chuck's patience by getting him to be our hand model.

Once again, Bill Perry declared himself impressed with our efforts and threw another opening night gala at the Big Top to premiere the film, inviting George Payne to make a personal appearance. George was the center of attention and truly in his element, signing autographs and graciously accepting the adulation of the crowd. Bill was so pleased with George's popularity that he asked him back to appear between subsequent showings of the film, where George would perform short melodrama spoofs that were popular at the time thanks to TV shows like *Mary Hartman, Mary Hartman*.

Bill also hit upon the idea of holding a male beauty contest to capitalize on George's popularity. Bill asked Erica Eaton, Lem and me to act as judges. It wasn't the type of event that Lem and I normally enjoyed, and predictably Lem flat out refused to attend. I on the other hand was closer to Bill and felt indebted to him, so, with the help of some liquid courage, I agreed to take part. George was more reluctant, only agreeing to appear if he was paid and guaranteed to win. The event proved to be a great success and The Big Top's beauty pageants became an annual affair after that, with George "agreeing" to take top prize most years.

By now Mike and I had convinced Bill that we should be his production team for all low-budget new films. I was determined that the superior quality of *Kiss Today Goodbye* (1976) would persuade Bill to increase the amount he would pay us. Furthermore, the two films we'd made had been hugely profitable for him. Armed with these arguments, I went to see Bill, only to be told that he wouldn't budge from $10,000 per movie. Nonetheless, Mike and I made two more movies for Bill in 1977, *Point Me Toward Tomorrow* and *Christopher Street Blues*.

For *Christopher Street Blues* I asked a gifted pianist named Dan Lanning to create an original song. Dan had composed music for Broadway and Off-Broadway musicals so I wasn't sure how he'd respond to the idea of writing for a down-and-dirty gay porn film. But I needn't have worried as he was excited by the idea of creating something different. I thought also calling the song *Christopher Street Blues* was a good idea, and pitched Bill the idea of selling 45 rpm records of the song wherever our film would be shown. Soundtracks were popular with mainstream movies but I'd never heard of anyone doing this for an adult film, straight or gay. Bill was intrigued and gave me the go-ahead provided we could come up with a B-side for the single. The title song Dan composed turned out great, so I gave him free rein to create whatever he wanted for the flip side. I was surprised when he penned a track with the catchy title "Piss on Me".

We gathered some musicians and I explained the nature of the ribald song so they wouldn't be surprised when they heard the lyrics. I booked the least expensive recording studio I could find and prepped the musicians to lay down the tracks as quickly as possible since we were paying by the hour.

When we arrived at the studio, a famous gospel group was waiting to record after us. Unfortunately, the sound guys forgot to turn off the external speakers once we started recording. The waiting gospel group was treated to the lyrics of "Piss on Me", with the subtle chorus "Buy me another beer and I'll show you a good time…if you know what I mean". I only discovered what happened when we were leaving, and somehow managed to utter the words, "Don't worry, we were just warming up the studio for you" as we walked out. I'm not sure if they prayed for us, but the record went on to sell pretty well.

Working with Mike on the Francis Ellie films, I sensed a real improvement in his state of mind and felt he'd started to return to his former self. He was clearly enthusiastic about his new 3D camera and had convinced his old film distributor Stan Borden to back the idea. Mike was so confident in its promise that he decided to take the camera to the 1977 Cannes Film Festival to see if he could generate further interest.

Lem and I were excited for Mike, and it was encouraging to see him optimistic and energized by his new venture. We were keen to give him a

THE FRANCIS ELLIE FILMS (1976-1988)

good send-off on his trip to Cannes. So late afternoon on May 16 1977, Lem and I went to the top of the Pan Am Building near Grand Central to see Mike off. He'd paid $25 to take the 10-minute helicopter ride to JFK airport. Mike was terrified of flying, so traveling to the airport this way was a bold move for him. I took it as a sign of his new-found confidence overcoming some of his phobias and perhaps enjoying himself at last.

We all met at the Pan Am Building's Copter Club. We enjoyed a few drinks and discussed the exciting experience that lay ahead in Cannes. As it came time for Mike to leave, Lem and I asked the staff if we could accompany him to the flight deck but were told that for safety reasons, only passengers were allowed up top. Lem and I hugged Mike goodbye, wished him a great trip and left him at the elevators.

As we exited to the street from the Pan Am building, Lem and I looked up to see if we could catch Mike taking off. We were surprised to find several helicopters hovering near the top of the building. We waited a few minutes to see if Mike's helicopter would ascend but when it didn't we decided to set off to meet a friend.

When we arrived at our friend's apartment we found him glued to his television set. There was a breaking news story about an accident at the Pan Am Building. The landing gear of a helicopter waiting to take off for JFK had malfunctioned, turning the craft on its side and breaking off a rotor blade. That blade had slashed four of 21 waiting passengers, killing three of them instantly. The blade fell over the side of the building, falling to the ground along with a shower of glass from breaking windows. It ultimately came to rest on the street below killing one more person, a woman walking on Madison and 43rd Street.

I silently prayed that Mike wasn't one of those killed and held my breath for what seemed like an eternity. My worst fear was confirmed when the name Mike Findlay was displayed on screen, listed as one of the deceased. He'd been struck in the chest by the spinning rotor and died almost immediately.

We were all in shock. I felt incredibly numb as I tried to take in the fact that one of my dearest friends was dead. Mike had been like a brother to me, and his importance in my life is impossible to overstate. We'd shared innumerable hours talking happily about films. We'd made our first film together and continued to make movies with each other over the years. We'd experienced life's ups and downs together, and creating Francis Ellie had brought us even closer. The gangly, awkward and lovely young man I'd met in the shipping department of ABC was now gone before he was even 40 years old.

Mike's funeral was a heart-wrenching affair. His brother organized the service which took place at a Catholic church on the Upper East Side. It was well-attended though there was a noticeable split between one side of the church where his understandably devastated parents and relatives sat, and the other side where Mike's film friends such as Bobby Sumner, Chuck Vincent, Lorraine Borden, and Lem and myself sat. As is Catholic tradition, it was an open casket ceremony and it was surreal to see our friend made up and carefully arranged.

Roberta also attended the funeral. She told us that she deliberately left her strong prescription eye glasses at home as that was the only way she could approach the open casket without breaking down. Our conversation was cordial enough but I had started to feel bitter towards Roberta. She'd been very hostile to Mike ever since they'd broken up and this had caused him much anguish, so I wasn't able to muster any great amount of sympathy for her grief.

But perhaps I was just in deep pain over Mike's passing. Lem and I didn't go to the cemetery the day of the funeral because we were too distraught. It was a heavy loss. We both felt immense sadness for many years after, and I still think about Mike to this day.

CHAPTER 11

THE END OF AN ERA
(1978-1982)

After Mike's death, I tried to focus on the positive things in my life. I had Lem, and my relationship with Chuck was as strong as ever. And my good friend Steve Gould had surprised us all and married his girlfriend Nancy Keller. Nancy was a Broadway singer and actress Steve had started dating a couple of years ago. She's become a regular among our social group and a particularly close friend of mine. Being hopeless romantics and travel addicts, Steve and Nancy had secretly planned to tie the knot in Casablanca, and we were all thrilled for them.

But I was soon reminded of the pain of losing Mike when Bill Perry approached me to make another hardcore gay film. My immediate reaction was that I just wasn't interested, not without my creative brother-in-arms. But the more I thought about it, the more I wondered if making another Francis Ellie film could be a sort of tribute to Mike's memory, carrying on the spirit of what he and I had created together and excelled at: low budget films that made money.

I asked Lem to reconsider partnering with me. I told him, "I've got this down pat. I'll write, produce, direct and cast, but I need help with the editing and scoring." Both the last two tasks were critical, but to me they spelled agony. Perhaps sensing that I needed his assistance more than ever now that Mike was gone, Lem agreed to cut and score the film. And the obvious choice to shoot the movie was Larry Revene, who had already worked on gay features.

I got down to writing a script and penned the story of two gay sailors on leave in Manhattan. I called the film *Navy Blue* and it was basically a gay version of *On the Town*, a 1949 Gene Kelly and Frank Sinatra musical that I loved. The need for two strong male leads gave me the opportunity to do something I'd had in mind for a while: I was determined to cast George Payne and Jack Wrangler, two popular stars of gay cinema that had never made a picture together. Signing up George wouldn't be an issue due to our friendship with him, but I'd never worked with Jack Wrangler.

Jack was an all-around entertainer having done Broadway, summer stock and television, and at the same time making a name for himself appearing in a cabaret act at the Bijou Theater downtown. The theater would show one of his films and then Jack would come out to sing and do stand-up comedy.

The general public perhaps knew Jack best for living with Margaret Whiting, a nightclub singer who had been famous in the 1940s and 1950s. Margaret and Jack's relationship caused quite a stir. For a start Jack was known to be gay while Margaret was heterosexual and eighteen years his senior. But their relationship helped give Jack crossover appeal and made him an object of fascination with both the gay and mainstream press.

I arranged a meeting with him and showed him the script I'd written for *Navy Blue*. I had named his character Jack Whiting in honor of Jack and Margaret, hoping it would sweeten the deal. He loved the idea, particularly as he thought the story was better than the standard gay porn film. While he was interested in the role, he wanted much more than we were willing to pay, and much more than we were paying George Payne. But I was keen to have him so I approached Bill Perry requesting that he increase the budget, reasoning that with two big stars, the movie was all but guaranteed to be the biggest hit yet for him. Bill was a businessman however and held firm to the standard $10,000 agreement, refusing to provide a penny more.

In the end I decided the chance to get both Jack and George was too good to miss, so I bit the bullet and agreed to Jack's elevated price. I knew it would place even more pressure on my profit margin so I went back to the script to find ways to cut costs. I reduced the shoot from three to two days and committed to producing the final cut within a month. I explained the logistics to Larry and Lem, and we prepared to dive in.

Fortunately the experience of working with Jack was worth the extra money. He was by far the most theatrical person I ever dealt with in films, both in terms of talent and attitude. He was funny, exuberant and loved performing, especially the dialogue scenes. He'd arrive on set well dressed and in full makeup, carrying himself as if paparazzi could show up at any moment. Before any sex scene he'd carefully shave his body and apply full-body make-up. He couldn't have been more different from George, who was quiet, serious and a little intimidated by Jack's showy bravado. There was definitely a competitive tension between them.

I held casting sessions for the other actors. I hired Giuseppe Welch, an attractive fair-haired Italian actor, on recommendation of the actress Genie Josephs. Giuseppe would go on to become a regular in the remaining Francis Ellie films. We also cast another of our regulars, Bob Meehan, for a small non-sex role. We were ready to begin filming.

THE END OF AN ERA (1978-1982)

As we moved from pre-production to shooting I wasn't sure how I'd feel working without Mike, but the 18-hour days left me little time for grief. We shot the film over a weekend in December 1978, when the city was dressed up for the holidays. I always loved the Christmas window displays, and wanted to include a fantasy sequence set in one. So back in our offices LaRue and Fabian designed a set to match one of my favorite windows at Saks Fifth Avenue, sort of an homage to my first employer in the city.

Despite cost pressures I was also keen to stage a sequence that would get people talking, so I decided we should film a sex scene in a helicopter as it flies over Manhattan. Only years later did I realize the strangeness of this choice given that Mike had just died in a helicopter accident. All I can say is that at the time I just didn't put the two together. I'm not sure if it was a strange and morbid coincidence, or whether something was at work in my subconscious.

I knew nothing about helicopters so to prepare for the scene, I scoped out the 34th Street Heliport to get a sense of how we could do it. I watched several flights land and take off and peeked inside; four seats in back and one next to the pilot. Obviously, we couldn't let the pilot see what was going on so filming would be tricky. The only way I imagined it could work was if I sat next to the pilot and distracted him while Larry shot the action in the back.

On the day of the shoot, we hid Larry's camera in a canvas bag and waited until no other passengers were in line. When our chance arrived, we climbed on board. As planned, I took the seat up front with the pilot. Jack and Giuseppe Welch, dressed as sailors, and Larry climbed in the back.

I immediately began gabbing away to the pilot hoping that Larry could concentrate on the shoot. I glanced back and saw Larry capturing some footage of the city skyline for cutaways as Jack and Giuseppe prepared themselves for the BJ. It was freezing cold in the helicopter so I was afraid Jack wouldn't be able to manage an erection but fortunately he didn't seem to experience any problems. The bigger issue was that we soon discovered Giuseppe was terrified of flying. At one point, we hit an air pocket and the helicopter dropped about 20 feet. Giuseppe let out a low scream and the expression on his face was one of pure horror. I just kept talking to the pilot, pointing out landmarks and shouting silly questions to prevent him from turning around. Before long the pilot informed us we'd be landing shortly. It had been a quick flight so I was surprised to see Jack and Giuseppe all zipped up and ready to disembark. Fortunately Larry had captured all the necessary footage.

As we deplaned I kept thinking that Mike would have loved that we didn't actually rent the helicopter, which would have cost thousands. Instead, as "tourists", the total cost was $50 for 4 tickets.

The last scene we shot was the most anticipated: the long-awaited tryst between George and Jack. Jack gave a phenomenal performance, and George did his best but still seemed intimidated by Jack. Lem decided that the right music for the scene was Ravel's "Bolero", soon to become iconic when Blake Edwards used it the following year in his film *10* (1979) with Bo Derek and Dudley Moore.

We completed post-production in record time and proudly took the film to show it to Bill Perry. Much to my surprise he wasn't overly pleased with the finished product. It turned out he was put off by an explicit heterosexual encounter I'd included between George and Genie Josephs. He was extremely upset, especially as we'd dedicated almost 7 minutes to the coupling. He kept repeating, "The audience is going to hate this! Absolutely hate it!" I insisted he was over-reacting but it was clear I couldn't change his mind. But the film was cut and ready to go, so Bill eventually decided he would have to show it without alteration.

Navy Blue premiered at the Big Top Cinema on August 1, 1979 and it turned out Bill's fears were justified. During a close-up of Genie Josephs' privates, a horrified queen in the theater yelled, "It's the gash! It's the gash!"

But despite "the gash", *Navy Blue* was extremely successful. We made a big play of Jack and George together for the first time in the marketing for the film, and everyone was in awe of the helicopter scene. After a lengthy New York run, the film went on to play in San Francisco, Los Angeles, Miami and Chicago, making *Navy Blue* one of the top-grossing Francis Ellie films.

On the last day of shooting, Jack invited Lem and me to Margaret Whiting's annual Christmas party at their upscale Manhattan apartment. We'd heard of their extravagant gatherings, with stories of surreal sights and show business luminaries, so we had high hopes. And we weren't disappointed. When we arrived we were greeted at the front door by Jack and his pet rabbit. The apartment was bathed in a golden glow that all actresses of a certain age seemed to adore, and Margaret rushed to greet us warmly and accompany us to the bar where a handsome attendant served us.

Rosemary Clooney arrived soon after to a flurry of cheers from those gathered. Naturally, there was a baby grand piano in the living room and it wasn't long before Miss Clooney was persuaded to sing "White Christmas" from the movie of the same name she'd starred in. It was all too strange, too dreamlike, too perfect – and I loved every minute. I couldn't help going over to Margaret and saying, "thank you so much for inviting us. This is really

THE END OF AN ERA (1978-1982)

just like an MGM musical." But rather than the gracious demeanor I'd been greeted with earlier, Margaret, looking distracted, replied, "Yeah, Rosemary's singing "White Christmas" and Jack's in the bedroom blowing the bartender... So Merry Christmas". Lem and I looked at each other. Party's over!

By this time in my movie-making career, I was growing weary of adopting plots from our favorite films, or worse still, recycling previous Amero Brothers plots. So when Bill Perry requested yet another Francis Ellie movie, I resolved to make something completely different. I wrote *The Jockstrap Strangler*, the story of a disturbed gay man who arrives in New York and commits a series of bizarre murders, killing his victims at the moment of sexual climax. Due to the new direction I was taking, I took the script to Bill for approval before moving further into pre-production. Apart from our *Navy Blue* argument over a straight sex scene, Bill had always been happy to give me complete creative control. But this was about to change.

First of all he hated the title, so we changed it to *Killing Me Softly*. He was even more dismayed with the tone of the script, expressing grave misgivings that I was showing gay men in a bad light when the homosexual community was under constant siege. I tried to convince him that the plot line was so ridiculous nobody could possibly take it seriously, but it was clear Bill wasn't going to accept the script as written. So I re-worked the film's tone to make it more tongue-in-cheek, and added a happy ending. Bill agreed it was an improvement and finally gave me the green light.

George Payne was the natural choice to play a deranged killer but I figured that I'd used him enough in recent films, so I contacted Jack Wrangler hoping he'd lower his rate sufficiently to be affordable. Jack expressed interest and I managed to negotiate a price for a single day of his time. But it wasn't going to be enough time to give him the lead role. I had to hire someone affordable, so LaRue recommended a friend named Stanley Richards.

I called Stanley the next day and asked whether he'd be interested in taking the lead role. When he said he would I made it clear that he would be required to have sex on camera four times in two days. He replied, "John, I'm so horny, I could fuck a toad."

Rather than hire him sight unseen, I brought him into our office to meet Lem and I. In truth, we found him a bit strange looking, but he had a certain charm, a great sense of humor, an athletic build and an adorable twang. When I told him he'd be playing a bad guy and would be required to have sex with Jack Wrangler, he was overjoyed.

Despite his confidence, hiring a complete novice for a lead role in a hardcore sex film was a huge risk. But with Bill Perry calling constantly to ask about our progress, we had to take the plunge.

Fortunately we needn't have worried about Stanley's capabilities on any front. Not only was he able to perform in the sex scenes but he also had an acting intensity that was perfect for the role. He was so believable as the killer that at times I had to ask him to hold back for fear that he was showing up some of the other performers. Jack was the only one to match Stanley's acting, and he loved that Stanley treated him like an Academy Award-winning Hollywood star.

Having filmed a sex scene in a helicopter, I wanted to do something even more daring and outrageous this time. I'd long harbored the idea of filming a sex scene in the middle of the Brooklyn Bridge. Larry and the actors looked at me incredulously when I suggested it, but I outlined how I thought we could do it and they decided to give it a shot. Larry's last comment was "John, you're going to defile every tourist attraction in New York!"

Besides the fact that we didn't have a filming permit for the location, it was illegal to shoot any sort of sex in public so we surreptitiously set out early one Sunday morning. We posted two lookouts at either end of the bridge while Larry, myself and two actors proceeded to the span's apex to shoot our explicit encounter. Unfortunately our lookouts weren't entirely successful, allowing a cyclist to slip through and pedal his way straight past the action. We held our breath anticipating an outraged reaction, but he just cycled by without a glance. We left his unexpected cameo in the film, hoping it would get a laugh.

Killing Me Softly also includes footage of the West Side Piers, later torn down in 1991 because the piers were literally rotting and collapsing into the Hudson River. In their heyday the piers had seen some of the finest ocean liners. But by the time we filmed there, the cruising was of a different sort, the piers now a common venue for sexual activity between men. I thought it would be visually and narratively engaging to shoot a sequence of Stanley looking for prey among the piers but they were closed off to the public. So we did what everyone else did – we broke in. We shot some atmospheric interiors but it was too risky to stage the strangling scene that I'd scripted, so we finished filming back at our office.

While I promised Bill a happy ending to the film, I decided to defy him and have the murderer and his beloved partner, Jack Wrangler, escape the police's clutches through an act of joint suicide. They mix champagne cocktails with poison and drink to their love. To make this final scene even more climactic, I had Jack strangle Stanley as they both reach orgasm and

THE END OF AN ERA (1978-1982)

finally die in each other's arms. We scored the scene with "Love and Death" from Wagner's "Tristan and Isolde". We shot the scene in such an over-the-top manner that no one could possibly take it seriously. Indeed one reviewer wrote, "Theirs was a love that transcended all reason" which I thought was an appropriate summary.

While I hadn't kept my promise to Bill, he ended up liking the film. In fact he was so excited about it he took out ads announcing its impending release at the Big Top. Unfortunately one of singer Roberta Flack's management team saw the ad for *Killing Me Softly* and Bill quickly received a cease and desist letter from Atlantic Records. Unable to afford a costly legal battle, we wound up changing the official title to *Killing Me Gently*, though people continued to refer to the film by its original name.

Despite this legal snag and the film's bizarre ending, *Killing Me Gently* (1979) did well for Bill. In fact, it wound up being the most popular and highest grossing of all our Francis Ellie films. A few people found the murder scenes off-putting with one critic described them as being "in questionable taste". This made us laugh as the whole film was in questionable taste. It was a cheaply made hardcore gay film after all.

In February 1980, I opened the pages of the morning newspaper to read that my old boss, Mickey Zaffarano, had died of a heart attack at age 59. He'd had a troubled existence since I'd left his employ and I'd often read about him in the crime pages of the New York tabloids. In addition to being accused of planning a murder in 1975, Mickey had become a key link between organized crime and the pornographic film industry. He apparently died in a New York stairwell, fleeing cops trying to serve him with an arrest warrant.

I'd enjoyed knowing Mickey – he'd always treated me kindly and with respect so I was sad to hear of his passing. And working for Mickey had been an adventure and then some.

Mike Findlay's passing still weighed heavily on me, but I was fortunate to have the support of good friends. Lem and I were close with Bobby and Patty Sumner, even as Bobby continued to aggressively pursue power in the New York sex film scene. Bobby was still working with Sam Lake at Mature Pictures distributing exploitation and hardcore films, now including on videotape under the company name Quality-X-Pix. Then Sam suffered a heart attack and Bobby made a move to try to take over the company. Against all odds Sam recovered and fired Bobby. But Sam's recovery was short-lived, and he died in August 1982.

Bobby was now out of a job and over his head. Bob and Patty had married in 1981 and had a great apartment on 5th Avenue in the Village. But what no one knew at the time was that Bobby was heavily in debt, a secret he kept even from Patty. Desperate for money, Bob took a temporary job in Key West managing a restaurant, leaving Patty with mountainous debt. Bob never returned and in 1997 was struck by a car in Key West and died. It was a sad end for a complex and conflicted individual. But Patty soldiered on and we remain close to this day.

The last Francis Ellie film I made was based on a tryst I'd had a couple of years earlier with a guy I met at one of New York's oldest gay bars. I titled the movie *Boots & Saddles* (1982) because the bar had a Western motif.

The true story is that one night I sat atop a ranch fence post in the bar, wearing a new pair of hand-tooled leather cowboy boots that I bought and loved. I was nursing a drink and surveying the scene when a young man approached me. He was blonde and not unattractive, so we struck up a conversation. He had a certain charm and at closing time, he invited me back to his apartment on Perry Street at the corner of West 4th. As we walked out of the bar, my date asked, "By the way, are you Jewish?" I was caught off guard by his question and reflexively answered, "No, why?" He shrugged it off and said, "No reason" so off we went to his ground floor studio apartment.

When we arrived, he unlocked the door but didn't switch on any lights as someone normally would do. The only source of illumination was a light over a very detailed painted portrait of Adolf Hitler that hung at the end of his entrance hall. I thought to myself, "This does not portend well" but having consumed more than my fair share of beer, my hormones bested my reason and I followed him to the sofa. I soon realized he wanted me to get rough with him, which wasn't my thing. In a state of semi-undress, I halfheartedly tried to give him what he wanted but my heart wasn't in it, and I clearly wasn't meeting his needs. He began yelling at me, screaming that I wasn't hitting him hard enough. He became so loud that a female voice from an adjoining apartment shouted, "Shut up in there, you faggots, or I'm calling the cops." My wrestling partner yelled back, "They should have burned you, Jew bitch, with all the rest of them."

Horrified, I decided to leave but because it was so dark in the apartment, there was no way for me to find my boots. As I scrambled to find them, the neo Nazi began striking me with anything he could get his hands on. I responded by punching him as hard as I could. As he regained his wits and prepared to come at me again, I decided to forget my beloved boots and get

THE END OF AN ERA (1978-1982)

out of the apartment as fast as I could. The neo-Nazi blocked the passageway to the front door, but as his apartment was on the ground floor I made a hasty exit out the living room window. I hurried home in my socks, a sadder but wiser man.

Several years later, I was back at Boots & Saddles when a man started chatting me up. There was something familiar about him but I couldn't put my finger on where I'd seen him before. He told me he lived at the corner of Perry Street and West 4th which gave me pause, but I still couldn't place him. Our conversation was entertaining so I decided to go home with him when the bar closed. When we got to the building, he headed straight for the same apartment from a few years ago. It finally dawned on me that he was the Nazi. Before I could gather my wits, the door was open and I was inside his apartment. And amazingly there at the end of the hallway just past the portrait of Hitler stood my boots. My mind immediately switched away from the prospect of a sexual encounter: This time I was going to get my boots back.

We began kissing but when he tried to lead me further into his apartment, I told him I was too drunk, thinking I'd just grab my boots and run. Rather than take no for an answer, he lunged at me and hit me across the face. This time however, the outcome was going to be different. I hit him back, knocked over a bookcase to block his path, grabbed my boots, and dashed for the door slamming it behind me. Luckily that was the last I ever saw of the West Village Nazi. It had been a horrifying experience to say the least, and it taught me the perils of being unfaithful to Chuck. And it left me with a great idea for a film.

Boots & Saddles is the story of three old friends who meet periodically at a local bar. One of the friends meets someone he doesn't realize is a Nazi and his friends have to come to the rescue. I of course wanted to use Jack Wrangler again so when he said he wanted to play one of the heroic rescuers I let him have his way. I told him, "You're going to beat the shit out of the Nazi, then set fire to his apartment and drag the victim to safety." Jack loved the idea and entered into the spirit with great enthusiasm. Chuck was decidedly less excited and made it clear I was not to set fire to any part of our apartment. So we went over to Larry Revene's studio on 14th Street where he'd just finished shooting an apartment scene for a straight sex film. We took advantage of the existing set, simply adding a portrait of Hitler and a large swastika flag.

Boots & Saddles (1982) didn't live up to my expectations, but as usual Bill Perry was more than satisfied. He wanted me to continue making films but by this point the idea of making more Francis Ellie movies had started to lose its appeal. The series had been good to me, allowing me to work regularly and spend valuable time with Mike Findlay before he died. But what I really wanted was to make films closer to those Lem and I had made.

It was time to put Francis Ellie to rest.

With the Ellie films behind me, I wanted to re-focus on my relationship with Chuck. We'd been together for 20 years and outside of two brief, meaningless encounters, I remained faithful to him and very much in love. And despite being unhappy with the work, Chuck had kept his job at the Post Office in order to supplement my meager and infrequent income. There was nothing stimulating about handling other peoples' mail all day but he never complained. He even soldiered through health issues caused by his diabetes and asthma that were getting progressively worse.

I decided to arrange a 20th anniversary party to celebrate our relationship. We invited all our friends to what turned out to be a very happy occasion, and we both seemed to be heading in a better direction.

Unfortunately that momentum would be short lived.

CHAPTER 12

THE PLAYBOY YEARS
(1984-1989)

Lem and I were thinking about our next step when I got a call from Chuck Vincent at Platinum Pictures. Chuck had just made a deal with the Playboy Channel to make two R-rated features in Hollywood and asked if Lem and I would be interested in taking part. We were excited by the prospect of working on more mainstream fare. Additionally, I thought I might be able to persuade Chuck to suggest a script LaRue had written with the Playboy Channel in mind. It's the story of a party at the Hollywood mansion of a popular writer. The author invites the people who inspired his latest book and the festivities quickly turn into an evening of bed-hopping.

I told Chuck we could pitch a three-picture deal to Playboy where we retained the theatrical rights to the film based on our script. Chuck liked the idea so he submitted the proposal to Playboy and they approved it. With that, LaRue's *R.S.V.P.* (1984) became part of the package. We didn't wind up working on the other two features but *R.S.V.P.* became our baby, with me producing and Lem directing.

Lem and I celebrated the deal at the Big Spender, then I headed home to share the news with Chuck. He was happy about the opportunity for me and Lem, but I could tell he was crestfallen. Our annual Christmas separation, when Lem and I went to Gloucester and Chuck would go to Steve and Nancy's, was bad enough. This would be the longest we'd ever been apart. I tried to console him by stating that at least for the period he wouldn't be kicked out of our apartment by a film crew and our bedroom would remain actor-free, but Chuck wasn't comforted. So I left for L.A. with familiar feelings of guilt about our relationship.

Lem and I approached our work on the West Coast with some trepidation. This was to be our first Screen Actors Guild (SAG) production and I had received a manual from SAG that must have been 200 pages long. But my spirits were lifted when I realized that as a representative of a SAG-sanctioned movie, I could phone any agent in Hollywood and they would at least take my call.

The budget for *R.S.V.P.* was $50,000. The money needed to cover 3 weeks pre-production, 10 days of shooting in Hollywood and whatever post-production time was required. We booked six rooms at the Sunset Plaza Hotel on Sunset Boulevard to serve as our temporary home and office. But we soon realized that we couldn't have legitimate actors coming to a hotel to audition, so we rented office space on Highland Boulevard for casting.

I sat in an inner office, and my casting director just outside to pre-screen the actors as they came in. At one point I heard the casting director speaking with a woman who said her name was Marie Windsor. My ears immediately perked up as I knew a Marie Windsor who was a film noir actress with MGM and Columbia Studios in the 1940s and '50s. Much to my horror, the casting director – who was about 23 years old and didn't have a clue who she was – dismissively asked "have you got an 8 by 10?" I ran out to take over, terribly excited to meet a noir legend. She looked wonderful but I found it so depressing that a woman who used to act for major studios and co-starred with Clark Gable and John Garfield was now auditioning for a small-time production like ours. I explained to her that even though the film had an R rating, there would be some nudity involved for other roles. Ultimately, and perhaps thankfully, she decided to pass. I would have hated to see Marie Windsor work on something she wasn't comfortable with.

We wound up casting a relatively unknown actor named Adam Mills as the handsome male lead. For the female lead we cast Katt Shea, an actress with a handful of films to her name. Both wound up being good choices, delivering solid performances and handling themselves professionally on the set. For some of the other roles, we cast players from the X-rated world who we knew had strong acting chops. Harry Reems, Veronica Hart and Georgina Spelvin all participated. They had experience with legitimate productions and would fit comfortably into a more mainstream movie. Playboy insisted we hire one centerfold for the production so we wound up casting Lynda Wiesmeier, who thankfully was a delight to work with.

For the crew, we stuck with some of our old favorites whom we flew out with us. Larry Revene acted as cinematographer and of course LaRue and Fabian designed the sets and costumes. We also hired Chris Covino whom we'd worked with on *Blonde Ambition* to serve as Assistant Director. Unfortunately, we had to let Chris go halfway through production. It is critical that the AD keep detailed notes to match scenes and provide for continuity, but Chris did not. He was constantly exhausted and could barely stay standing on set; he even missed one day of shooting completely. I finally pulled Chris aside and he admitted that he didn't have the energy to finish out the shoot. I was sad to replace him, as aside from being talented he was a good friend. It was only later that I found out why Chris was unable to fulfill his duties.

THE PLAYBOY YEARS (1984-1989)

The logistics of shooting *R.S.V.P.* weren't simple. We had to follow SAG rules for locations and any film-related amenities. Things like where and how we were going to feed the cast and crew became a big deal. With the X-rated films we could say to the actors, "here's 10 bucks, go buy your own lunch". With SAG the entire production had to be catered.

Despite the increase in administrative overhead, I loved being part of a Hollywood production, including choosing the locations. We wanted to film in an old-style Hollywood mansion and at first, I thought I found one in Encino. The owner seemed nice and even traded ideas with me about how to configure the space to meet my needs. But just as I was about to sign the contract, the woman made an off-hand comment about putting portable toilets out by the swimming pool. When I asked her why she said, "You don't think I'm going to let your crew use my toilets do you?" I took it as a sign and walked away.

Luckily, we quickly found a beautiful 1920s mansion in the Hollywood Hills that F. Scott Fitzgerald had owned and Ringo Starr had rented. It had eight bedrooms, a wonderful swimming pool and great vistas, so we decided to shoot the majority of the picture there. The only issue was that some of the walls and windows were bare which took away from the rich look of the place. So one night when LaRue, Fabian and I were having a drink back at our hotel, I looked at the drapes and was inspired. Early the next morning we snuck into several rooms and borrowed the curtains for our shoot. We had become friendly with the hotel manager so I figured I'd explain the situation to her after we returned the drapes. Unfortunately, in the intervening hours it turned out we left several chambermaids fearing for their jobs.

We shot for 10 days and things went relatively smoothly. The only thing out of the ordinary was that Lem looked particularly haggard to me. It reminded me of a time six months earlier when Lem said he was feeling run down. After several days without improvement, he finally went to a doctor who told him he had some kind of virus. I asked Lem what type of virus and he replied, "I'm not sure. The doctor just told me I should go home and get some rest. But when I left I noticed something strange. As I walked out of his office the doctor tore up my file. What do you think that means? Why would he do that?" We both found it odd but let it go.

As I watched Lem one day on set, he sat down several times, something I had never seen him do when working. He even directed an entire scene seated, which struck me as very strange. And he just looked gaunt and exhausted. I wondered if he would make it through to the end of the shoot, but somehow he did and we finished production. We celebrated the wrap with a big party at the mansion where we filmed. The talented stage and screen actor Charles Durning showed up, as did Aldo Ray who had soared to Hollywood popularity in the 1950s. We even invited our hotel manager to make up for borrowing the drapes without prior notice.

Playboy wound up sending Platinum Pictures' three films to the Cannes Film Festival, but only *R.S.V.P.* was reviewed in Variety and the feedback was favorable. All in all, I loved making the film and was energized to return to New York and to my partner Chuck.

When I got back east, Chuck Vincent called almost immediately asking me to cast two new R-rated features he was working on, both staring the adult film star Tracey Adams. *Wimps* (1986) was a college love story based on *Cyrano de Bergerac*, and *Student Affairs* (1987) was a teen movie filmed on location at a New Jersey school. I found it highly amusing to cast actors in their 20s and 30s to play high school students.

But I wasn't laughing for long. After completing this new work for Chuck, a pall began to spread. Lem seemed to be feeling better since he was back in New York and was editing *R.S.V.P.* But mild symptoms still persisted so I encouraged him to see a doctor. This time he returned from his appointment with a name for what was causing him to feel so run down. The doctor said that Lem tested positive for what was known as the human immunodeficiency virus; HIV.

Nobody had a real understanding of this new disease but we did know that it was spreading. Our friend Chris Covino told us he had the virus, which explained why he had been unable to handle his assistant director duties on the *R.S.V.P.* shoot. Then Chuck Vincent's partner Billy Slobodian tested positive. Billy had been with Chuck for many years and was also his right-hand-man at Platinum Pictures.

Not long after Billy was diagnosed, Chuck also found out he was HIV positive, though he tried to keep it under wraps. He decided to auction off his studio and move to Key West. Before he could do either, he wound up in the hospital. He tried to keep that quiet as well, but one day when I was visiting a friend with HIV in the hospital, I passed a room and saw Chuck propped up in bed. He was clearly shocked to see me, so I nonchalantly strolled in and said hello. We chatted for a bit but I never asked anything about why he was there and he didn't offer any information. After I left neither of us ever mentioned the encounter.

Chuck was a good friend. He had also been a source of income for Lem and me, hiring us to help with his films. When it came to *R.S.V.P.*, in

THE PLAYBOY YEARS (1984-1989)

addition to the modest salaries we were paid for the work we had negotiated a percentage of the film. But when Chuck got sick and was selling off his holdings, he sold his movies to a distributor named Anant Singh at Golden Harvest Films. Chuck wasn't legally allowed to do this as we and others owned a piece of these pictures, but he was desperate to move on so he proceeded with the sale anyway. He fled to Key West, buying a lovely bungalow and moving in with his close friend Marco. But not long after heading south, Chuck's health took a turn for the worse and he passed away.

We were so naïve then. I had no idea that the doctor had torn up Lem's file because there was a terrible stigma attached to what was thought of as "the gay disease". Now there was no hiding that this illness had a name and was spreading through New York's gay community. We all understood that the disease didn't have a cure or effective treatment, but for a short while I fooled myself into thinking that like most other viruses, HIV was something Lem could live with. We had both survived polio as kids, and we were tough.

But the death of so many friends was a wake-up call for me. I began to realize that most likely Lem wasn't going to make it through the disease. Aside from the fact that I found this emotionally devastating, the realization also forced me to think about my professional future. All my plans at that point included Lem and the projects that we would produce together. While I had worked on films without him, the idea of never collaborating with him again left me dumbstruck.

But Lem didn't want to talk about his health. If I tried to bring it up he would turn the discussion to what we'd do for our next film project. He wanted to distract me – and himself – by focusing on work and thinking about our next feature. And we had a wonderful group of friends to divert Lem's attention. We'd meet up with LaRue, Fabian, Kurt, Bobby and Patty several times a week at the Big Spender to discuss what was going on in the business. We'd compare notes on who if anyone had been arrested, since the city was cracking down on adult films again at that time. When it got late I'd run back downtown to Chuck, feeling grateful that we were in a monogamous relationship and guilty that I wasn't spending more time with him.

I would hear stories of friends still having unprotected sex and that would upset me. I wasn't angry so much as offended that people could behave so irresponsibly when it was clear by that point that HIV was primarily contracted through intercourse. I knew Lem wasn't dating any more. When he went to the bar he was only looking for friendship. In truth Lem had never gone to bars to look for sex; he had always been interested in finding love. It worried me sometimes as I thought some hustler might sense Lem's romantic vulnerability and take advantage of him. But now those concerns were in the past.

Lem and I had made some money making *R.S.V.P.*, but without any significant work immediately ahead of us, we decided we could no longer afford our office space. The overhead was just too much and while we had a couple of R-rated script ideas, they weren't enough to justify the expense, so we gave up our lease.

Our friend Bunny Atlas – a tough but kind character who ran the adult film distribution company Bunnco – had extra room in her office in the Paramount Building. She had already leased some unused space to producer Jack Bravman, but still had more to let. So she offered to lease us a room at a very reasonable rate.

I had first met Bunny when all the local distributors and producers banded together to create the East Coast Producers Association. The group met monthly to discuss related legal activity taking place around the country. Lem and I were members as were Chuck Vincent, Radley Metzger and Joe Sarno. Even theater owners like Chelly Wilson joined though they didn't always attend the meetings. We paid membership fees but it was worth it as the money lost through confiscated prints was much more significant.

Among the group, Bunny was unusual. A married, middle-aged Jewish lady with children, she was a woman in a sea of men. She teased her dyed black hair and piled it high on her head into what Lem and I called a "Hadassah dip". She was a den mother to us all, warm and wonderful, but tough when she needed to be. It wasn't unusual to catch her yelling at a theater owner over the phone, saying "I told you there were six come shots in that film and there ARE six come shots so what are you complaining about?!" She started by distributing low quality product, but then began to meet young, aspiring filmmakers and produce films of her own, so the quality improved.

When Lem and I were trying to figure out what to do for our next project, Bunny had an idea. She had struck up a conversation in her local Queens supermarket with a handsome young gay man she initially mistook for a woman. The man had been kicked out of Cuba by Castro, fled to Miami and now was in New York trying to earn enough money for sex reassignment surgery. Bunny thought that Lem and I could make a film about this young man who lived as a woman and went by the name Pamela.

THE PLAYBOY YEARS (1984-1989)

She felt the film would do well due to the novelty of a seemingly beautiful young woman with male genitalia and that participation could earn Pamela the surgery she so desperately wanted. Lem and I were both skeptical, in large part because Bunny said that Pamela's English was heavily accented and quite limited. But Bunny said, "Don't say no until you meet her".

Pamela was indeed beautiful with a lovely figure and was charming as well. Lem and I were softening to Bunny's suggestion, but we couldn't imagine how we'd find an actor to play opposite Pamela in the film. Bunny encouraged us to work on a script and said she'd take on finding someone to play the love interest.

Pamela loved the fashion industry, so I devised a plot where she'd play an up-and-coming model with a big secret. A competitor at a fashion magazine learns the truth and attempts to blackmail our star. I thought with this plot we could have the supporting cast handle most of the dialogue and avoid having Pamela speak any more than she had to. We shared the script with Bunny and she loved it, but Pamela had reservations. In the shocking revelation scene, we wanted to have Pamela show her penis and get an erection. To do that, Pamela would have to discontinue her hormone pills a few months prior to when we shot, something a person intending to transition is not supposed to do. Pamela weighed her options and finally reluctantly agreed, reasoning the film was her best option to get money for her operation.

With our leading lady in place, we quickly hired Sharon Kane – by then a mainstay player in the adult industry – to play a fashion magazine executive. But casting the male lead didn't happen as fast. As I feared it was difficult to find an actor who was willing to perform opposite Pamela. But true to her word, Bunny came through suggesting an adult actor named Joey Santini. Bunny's exact words were, "he'll fuck anything", and he certainly had no problem performing with Pamela.

In addition to our male lead, we had difficulty finding a film crew. The ever-trustworthy Larry Revene was working on another project. Outside of LaRue and Fabian's Sparkling Sets and Costumes, most of our other regulars were also engaged with prior commitments so we wound up with a largely new team. Working with a new group made me nervous, and unfortunately my trepidations were justified. The crew brought a judgmental air to the set that was palpable. They didn't do or say anything that was outright derogatory but they carried themselves like the production was beneath them. And every day at lunch they drank, so getting things going again in the afternoon was an effort.

The shoot lasted four long, difficult days. There were a number of exteriors such as on the "Intrepid" Aircraft Carrier. Interiors were mostly shot at Bunny's offices, though we did shoot a fashion montage in a beautiful loft.

The crew may have been challenging but the cast worked out beautifully. The men preformed reliably, Pamela looked fantastic and gave it her best and Sharon Kane was an absolute pro as always. Sharon delivered her lines well and went above and beyond, working hard to get Pamela aroused. Sharon really rose to the occasion and critically, though briefly, so did Pamela.

As an added bonus, love blossomed on the set. We cast an actor who went by the name of Johnny Nineteen for a role in the film. Johnny had been in a few R-rated movies mainly playing cops and had several X-rated credits to his name. After his first day on set, I noticed that he was planning on leaving with Pamela who had let me know earlier that day that she had taken a shine to Johnny. I pulled Pamela aside and asked if she had told Johnny that she wasn't anatomically female yet. Pamela responded, "he'll find out tonight." I was sure with that kind of surprise there was a good chance we wouldn't see Johnny back on set the next day, but he came back and performed beautifully. Sometimes love really can conquer all.

After production wrapped, it took Lem and me about a month to edit the film. One day as we were nearing the finish, Pamela stopped by our offices. She was wearing a little schoolgirl outfit and a big smile on her face. She called Bunny in and said, "I want to show you. I must show you. I'm all done." With that, she sat down on one of our swiveling editing stools and proceeded to lift up her skirt. Lem had his back turned but Bunny and I were presented with the results of Pamela's sex reassignment surgery. To be frank, it was not a thing of beauty. The area was hairless and swollen and full of suture and stitch marks. But Pamela was thrilled and so I exclaimed, "Oh, that's wonderful and I'm so happy for you." I turned to my brother and said, "Lem, you've got to see this. It's just spectacular." Lem turned around and there are no words to describe the look on his face. Holding it together, he replied "Wow, that's really something".

Bunny released *A Passage Thru Pamela* (1985) shortly after we completed editing. For those who didn't want to be credited, I used names from *The Young and the Restless*, a soap opera I followed at the time. The film did fairly well, and wound up winning an award for most unusual sex scene. In some ways producing an adult film after having worked on an R-rated SAG feature in Hollywood felt like a step backwards, but I didn't linger on those reservations because I didn't have the luxury. We needed the money. And besides, these projects were fun to work on.

THE PLAYBOY YEARS (1984-1989)

Soon after *A Passage Thru Pamela* wrapped, Jack Bravman approached me with some work. We hadn't stayed in close touch since I helped him on a few disastrous shoots in the late 1960s but now that we worked in the same building, we were back in contact. He asked if we'd help with production responsibilities on two films he was planning, *Sex Styles of the Rich and Famous* (1986) and *Lady Madonna* (1986). Based on past experience I didn't jump at the idea but he really put on the hard sell. He said, "When I show you the location, you're going to love it. It's a million-dollar loft and we can make it look like 10 different places." I was skeptical so I asked him to let Lem and me visit the loft first.

A few days later, we met Jack at the loft and it was in fact spectacular. It was located near Gramercy Park and featured a great Jacuzzi, a private veranda, a gym, a garden and a large number of rooms, each decorated in a different style. As Jack showed us around he mentioned something about a drug dealer owning the apartment, but assured us this wouldn't be a problem. He quickly continued, describing the scenes he had in mind. "So, Jane Fonda will give Sylvester Stallone a BJ in the Jacuzzi…" I immediately cut him off, and gave Jack a quick lesson in libel. Outside of the loft, none of the other aspects of this project were appealing, but I found myself agreeing to work on the film. Lem took longer to convince but I pushed him, saying "Look, it will be one horrible day. We'll start at 6am and just go until we drop."

Not long after, we found ourselves pulling up to the Gramercy loft building at dawn with all our equipment. We found Jack and the actors he had cast all standing outside, looking unsure of what to do. When I asked why they weren't upstairs, Jack said he had buzzed the apartment several times but there was no response. Anxious not to lose any time, I sent one of the PAs up the fire escape in back to wake up the owner but there was nobody home. Growing impatient, I suggested we break in but we soon found that the apartment was too well secured.

Jack was in an absolute panic by this point because it was Bunny Atlas' money behind the film. He said, "She's going to kill me. She's going to cut my balls off. We have to shoot this movie." The mention of Bunny's name immediately reminded me of the six-room work suite she had. I asked Jack if he had keys to Bunny's office and he said yes. So I told everyone to grab some equipment and pile back in the truck. Jack wasn't thrilled about the idea since in part he got Bunny to invest on the basis of shooting in this incredible loft. But I said, "We either shoot everything at Bunny's, or we lose the money altogether."

When we got to the office, LaRue and Fabian immediately got to work. It was a mad scramble, but somehow we pulled it off and wound up shooting everything in Bunny's offices. The only surprise left came later in the afternoon when we were trying to film one of the sex scenes. Jack had hired a couple he knew, their relationship leading us to expect they'd have no trouble performing with each other. But here we were and the boyfriend could not get an erection. He tried and tried but after a number of failed attempts, I called cut and suggested the couple go away to see if they could inspire each other in private. A short while later, we went to see how things were going. We walked in to find the girlfriend striking matches from a book, throwing them at her boyfriend's penis and yelling, "Get it up you faggot." Lem looked at me beseechingly and said, "John, I'm sorry, but don't we have to draw the line somewhere?!" I responded, "Give them a chance. He just might get it up." And he did.

We thought this was the most horrendous shoot we'd been on. But worse was yet to come.

Jack's film *Lady Madonna* was up next. He promised that this shoot would be drama free. He said we'd shoot in his apartment and take two days maximum. Jack was excited that his beloved pet parrot could be in the movie. I jokingly asked, "Is this for a non-sex role?" I was hopeful that the beautifully plumed, colorful bird could add some pizazz to Jack's dreary one-bedroom apartment.

The day Lem and I showed up at Jack's for the shoot, we could hear the parrot squawking through the door as we waited to be let in. When we entered, we were faced with an almost completely denuded bird. Jack had been away for a week, leaving his pet behind. In his absence, the bird had fallen into depression and plucked every feather out of its body except for the few on the very top of his head that he was unable to get to. This spelled the end of his film debut.

The one thing Jack's apartment had going for it was a brick fireplace, so I wanted to shoot the key love scene – a fantasy sequence – in front of it. The crew and I moved all the lights and props into place to film the scene and then went out for a quick lunch break. We came back to find that Jack had moved all the props and lights to the other side of the apartment facing a filthy blank wall. When I asked him why, he responded, "We're too far behind schedule to mess around with fancy angles. Just shoot the sex scene in the corner, right there." I overheard one of the unpaid crew members saying sarcastically that he admired Jack's "innate sense

THE PLAYBOY YEARS (1984-1989)

of blocking". I was close to losing it, but luckily LaRue and Fabian's laughter calmed me down.

After an incredibly long day of production at Jack's, we made our way over to an after-hours club to shoot the last scene of the film. We had been at it since 6am and now at 4am the following day, we were desperate to wrap things up. As we set up the shot, I noticed a spot at the end of the bar, and decided to sit there and write out checks for the crew and cast. I told Jack, "Don't let the actors screw their way down the bar to where I'm working." But as I should have expected, just a few checks in I could see the actors fucking their way towards me. At my wit's end, I stood my ground. Shortly thereafter, some dirty feet entered my peripheral vision, heading towards the checkbook. Jack didn't stop filming so I assumed he was shooting close ups of the actors' upper bodies. In the released film though, you can clearly see my disembodied elbow moving back and forth in the frame as I wrote the checks. It was another classic lesson in film making from Jack Bravman.

As 1985 drew to a close, Lem and I headed to Gloucester for Christmas as we did every year. Chuck spent the holidays with Steve and Nancy, which had become a tradition for them. He knew that as long as our grandmother was alive this would be the arrangement.

Despite her initial shock when she first learned that we made exploitation films, our grandmother was always supportive of Lem and me. Perhaps she would have felt differently if she had known that our films came to feature hardcore and gay sex, but I believe she never found out. Like so many other things in life, we just didn't discuss our careers with family. Being a staunch Republican, our grandmother was mostly concerned that our movies made money. Once we assured her that they did, she seemed satisfied, but instructed us not to tell anyone.

That 1985 Christmas in Gloucester would be the last we would spend with our grandmother as she passed away a few months later. While she had lived a full life for 92 years, her passing was still very traumatic for me. She had been the first and constant stabilizing force in my life. When I was young and my mother was in and out of hospitals for her mental health issues and my father essentially moved on and out of my life, my grandmother was always there.

The following Christmas was one of the most emotional times I went through. I was finally in New York with Chuck, my love and life partner. But my grandmother was gone, and any feelings of being anchored by family history went with her.

Between film projects Trans-Lux and Crown Cinemas called me quite often to manage press screenings for new features. Over the years I'd gotten to meet famous directors and stars like Tom Cruise, Bette Midler and Audrey Hepburn among others. Most of the time it all went splendidly. But one of the screenings that did not go well and was eerily prophetic was Oliver Stone's 1986 film *Platoon*.

As a rule, I'd learned to avoid the director at premieres as much as possible as they were usually stressed out and unpleasant if approached. Oliver Stone was no exception. I had to ask him when to start letting people in and if there was a VIP list. His snapped back, "Nobody, and I mean NOBODY gets in until seven and there is no VIP list. No Exceptions! Is that clear?" and stormed away.

The theater's glass doors were locked and people started lining up. Then a man pushed through the crowd and started knocking loudly on the doors. It turned out to be Donald Trump. He started shouting through the glass, and I made the big mistake of opening the door a crack to ask him to join the line. He shoved his foot in the door and a pushing battle ensued. I explained the director's order not to let anyone in but he just kept pushing on the door. When I told him to get his foot out of the door, he used the line I've heard countless times: "Do you know who I am"? I replied, "I don't care who you are, you're not coming in until seven, now get your foot out of the door!" Trump threatened me with the usual bully taunts about how he'll get me fired. At this moment Oliver Stone appeared and calmly said, "Oh, you can let him in". Trump pushed past me and snarled, "I told you so!" As they both walked away together, I said to my ushers, "You're looking at a couple of class acts guys, class acts."

Lem and I avoided discussing the details of his disease until he started taking a combination of experimental drugs. I tried to support Lem throughout his doctor appointments, but felt there was not much I could do. HIV and AIDS were much more in the news now, especially after Rock Hudson was diagnosed with the disease. Like everyone else I was starting to understand the desperation of the situation, and felt helpless. I offered to write a letter home telling our family about his illness, and he agreed.

That letter was the hardest thing I ever had to write in my life. I tried to make the message as upbeat as possible, letting the family know that Lem was in good shape and had a wonderful support system. We always felt our family knew we were gay, but it was never discussed. This, of course, was confirmation. The family received the letter as well as a conservative

THE PLAYBOY YEARS (1984-1989)

New England clan could. Which means they employed a stiff-upper-lip attitude and we barely spoke about it again.

In 1988, Bill Perry gave up the Big Top cinema and the bathhouse across the street. With the threat of AIDS hanging over the gay community, attendance was down and it just wasn't worth it any more.

Bill moved full time into distribution of gay features. He leased an entire floor in Tribeca with fantastic views of the Hudson River. He had a small group of employees and offered both Lem and I employment alongside them. I had the feeling that what Bill really wanted was for us to shoot a new movie for him, despite the fact that I told him I had no desire to make another gay X-rated film. But while his intentions may not have been forthright the prospect of steady work was appealing, especially to Lem whose declining health left a low-key editing job about all he could handle. I also thought the job might help lift Lem's spirits, since editing was what he loved.

We took the job, cutting Bill's existing feature films to re-package them as fresh products. Lem produced a large number of "Best of" compilations for actors such as Jack Wrangler and George Payne. Relatively quickly, he gained an incredible memory for scenes in Bill's film library and would knit them together with voice-over to tell a new story. I would then come up with titillating titles such as *Golden Boys of the SS* and we would develop advertising campaigns together.

I handled foreign sales, trying to find new markets for these re-edited movies. The work was laid back as anticipated but after about six months, it was getting tedious. Then, as I anticipated, Bill started pushing Lem and me to make a new film. Bill had the video equipment and studio space; he just needed the production talent. Lem and I were so bored by that point, we said yes to Bill's offer.

The plot we landed on features a young man who falls in love with a burglar who robs him. The twist we added was that unbeknownst to our leading man, the burglar is a UPS worker he had known in the past. We had our leading man work at a mail order gay distribution business so we could conveniently shoot in Bill's office without having to change anything. For our UPS man we were able to get our hands on a real company uniform and then covertly shot around a delivery hub in lower Manhattan. We called the film *Big Mack*.

We figured we would approach the rest of the production in our usual fashion, but Bill insisted we shoot on video to save money. I wasn't looking forward to shooting on video, in part because the equipment Bill had was primitive. But we decided to go ahead, determined we could shoot the film in three days. I would be DP and Lem would again direct. And for what would turn out to be our last collaboration, LaRue and Fabian would manage the costumes and set design.

The film had six actors in total and I cast them all. The lead was a beefy guy who was a bit obnoxious, but he was good looking so I hired him. On the first morning of production, this actor met his scene partner for the first time. His partner was attractive, but our leading man hesitated and said he wanted to go out for coffee before we started to film. After waiting 30 minutes or so, we realized he wasn't coming back.

We were down to a cast of five and I had to come up with a backup plan fast. I pulled aside the actor cast to play the UPS employee and congratulated him on his promotion to male lead. I convinced him this was going to make his career and he was naïve enough to believe me. I asked one of our second choices to step in as the sixth actor so I wouldn't have to adjust the script.

After our bumpy start we finally got going. To make up time, we shot for almost 24 hours straight. The production as a whole was pretty horrendous but somehow we got through it. When Lem began editing I would often catch him commenting under his breath, "Oh this isn't going to be good," but surprisingly he wasn't referring to the way the film was produced. His observations centered around the ugly, flat look shooting on video created and once I saw the movie, I couldn't agree more. I missed shooting on film and I missed Larry's cinematographic skills. But one person who wasn't disappointed was Bill. To him the film was another finished product he could now sell. After that experience, I swore I would never shoot anything like this for Bill again. Luckily, Bill decided to relocate his offices to cheaper space in New Jersey, providing Lem and I the opportunity to gracefully back out of working with him.

Bill didn't last long in New Jersey. He sold his company and moved down to Hollywood, Florida with his long-time partner Joe. They started a new gay film distribution business down south but a year into this new venture, Bill was arrested for interstate shipment of obscene materials. Like everyone we knew, we thought Bill would get off easy as cases like this were being thrown out of court all the time. But Bill must have had the worst lawyer in the world because about $100,000 in fees later, he was convicted and sent to prison for 5 years. I corresponded with Bill while he was incarcerated and he eventually told me that it was my film, *Navy Blue* that was the cause of his arrest. Even though it wasn't my fault, I felt terrible.

THE PLAYBOY YEARS (1984-1989)

While he was in prison, Bill's partner Joe passed away from AIDS. Soon after that Bill wound up being released early, but just as he was settling into retirement, he developed lung cancer and eventually passed away as well. We had made eleven films together and had known each other much longer, so I lost yet another friend as well as a business partner.

Around this time, I got a call from a neighbor and good friend named Colette Connor. Colette started her career as a film reviewer, then went on to work with Chuck Vincent and was also in a few of our films in non-sex roles. She had a new job in programming for Paul Klein, an ex-network executive. She and her assistant, Tom Russ, were swamped with work and she kindly thought of me for help.

Paul had had a successful career with NBC, coming up with the concept of the top 10 list for David Letterman during his tenure. He then went on to form the Playboy Channel for Hugh Hefner. Now he had his own company called Home Dish Satellite Networks creating programming for satellite dish owners across the United States. Home Dish was actually composed of three networks. The first was Stardust Theater, which showed first run Hollywood features. The second was the R-rated channel Tuxedo Network that showed Playboy-like softcore programming. The third, called American Exxxtasy, was the real moneymaker. It showed hardcore pornography available at a steep cost, and basically supported the other two Home Dish networks through its earnings.

Colette and Tom were creating programming guides for all three networks and needed another set of hands. The idea of a stable 9-to-5 job appealed to me so I accepted the offer. I wasn't sure about the work but I thought the job would keep me from obsessing about Lem. To my surprise, I soon found myself really enjoying the role.

To produce the programming guides, we wrote reviews of all the films and had layout support from our in-house art department. One moment I'd be reviewing a Tom Hanks feature for the Stardust network, the next an R-rated version of *Blonde Ambition* for the Tuxedo Network, then a hardcore feature for American Exxxtasy. The adult films we carried were explicit, but they never pushed the boundaries too far. Paul Klein dictated that there could be no violence – especially nothing like rape or sadism. We were fairly conventional but there was such demand for pornography that Paul's conservatism didn't dampen sales one bit.

I began traveling with Colette to cable conventions all over the country to sell programming for Stardust Theater and Tuxedo Network (we never peddled American Exxxtasy in public forums). Paul's operation wasn't small time. He spent over $40,000 on our booth design and set up next to big time players like Ted Turner, HBO and Cinemax. He had three floors on Park Avenue South, and employed about sixty staff members.

It was interesting for me to travel to all these new places I had never been like Las Vegas, San Diego and Chicago. But on the home front, the traveling was putting further strain on my relationship with Chuck. Being left alone again was yet another disappointment for him.

But Paul appreciated the work I was doing. And I got a big kick out of the fact that he knew of me before I was even hired. He said he was well versed in the work of the Amero brothers and was potentially interested in producing non-sex films with us in the future. Specifically, his interest was in reality-based projects. It all sounded quite promising to me.

CHAPTER 13

A TIME OF GRIEF
(1989-1990)

By January 1989, Lem had entered the hospital full time. In the beginning he was at St. Vincent's in Greenwich Village, which was a wonderful facility. But because he lived in midtown and wanted to be closer to home, Lem insisted on moving to St. Clare's, which was notorious for sub-standard care. I couldn't stop him from transferring hospitals but I was at least able to get him a private room.

I would go visit Lem every day after work. Each time I'd walk in determined not to break down in front of him and I think he felt the same way. It seems ridiculous now but we tried to preserve any sense of normality we could even considering the circumstances. We'd talk about what film projects we'd take on when he got out and what was happening with friends. When I'd arrive at the hospital, I would stop at the nurses' station and address them very loudly as I knew Lem could hear me from his room when I did. Normally he would prop himself up in bed once he heard my voice and be reading or watching television when I came in.

One day I got off the elevator to find the hall extremely quiet. There was nobody at the nurses' desk to talk to so I proceeded straight to Lem. As I turned to enter his room, I stopped dead in my tracks. There was my brother sitting in a chair with his head in his hands and a look of absolute despair on his face. It took my breath away. Luckily, he didn't see me so I quickly retreated and found my way to a linen closet before I broke out crying. I buried my face in a bunch of towels to muffle my sobs. When I finally was able to compose myself, I walked back into the hall and pretended to talk to the nurses even though nobody was there. I slowly returned to Lem's room and this time found him as I always did, sitting in bed. Somehow I kept it together and made it through the visit, but in truth it was the darkest moment of my life.

My interactions with Lem changed when he began suffering from AIDS-related dementia. I let everyone at work know about my brother's condition and asked that he be put through immediately if he called. He'd dial the company switchboard and tell the operators he was phoning from London or California and that they should get his brother because his hotel room was unacceptable. These operators were incredibly kind to me when they patched through these unorthodox calls.

Lem's personality altered as his dementia progressed. Normally gentle and kind, Lem could now at times be cruel and judgmental. He took to berating other patients, telling me who was drug addicted or a "total psycho". But he was also often amusing and quite imaginative, creating elaborate fantasies.

Lem loved ocean liners as did I, and occasionally he'd say "let's walk the deck." We'd stroll the hospital halls pretending we were on board the Normandie, a beautiful French ocean liner from the 1930s. We'd imagine that people like Marlene Dietrich and the director Erich von Stroheim were on board and that we might bump into them at any moment. We might comment on the fact that we were disappointed in the pâté de foie gras served at dinner that night or that we were due to arrive in Venice the next day. We were creating scenarios for films that would never be made.

When we'd return to Lem's room, he was always convinced that he was finally going home. He would try to get dressed and pack his belongings so that he could leave with me. Sometimes he would even disconnect his IV. With the nurses help I would finally convince Lem to get back into bed but the staff pleaded with me to take Lem's clothing out of the hospital. He would check every day to make sure that clothing was in his closet as it gave him hope he might go home one day. I hated to remove the clothing but I finally did. I told him I was just taking the clothes to be cleaned and that I would bring them back, hoping he would forget after a day or so. But Lem never forgot, asking me every time I'd visit when his clothes would be returned.

Lem languished in the hospital for over six months but the end, thank God, was swift. In the summer of 1989 Lem was moved to the intensive care unit. About two weeks into his stay there I got a call in the middle of the night saying Lem had gone into cardiac arrest but that they had revived him and put him on a respirator. I was totally distraught not just due to the news but because it went completely against Lem's wishes. Before he entered the hospital my brother had made clear that he did not want any extraordinary measures taken to prolong his life. We took extra care to sign all the right legal papers and ensure I had medical power of attorney so that his wishes would be respected. Instead the doctors had gone against his legally sanctioned orders.

A TIME OF GRIEF (1989-1990)

I rushed to the hospital with copies of all the paperwork I believed they already had. The staff immediately admitted their mistake and were extremely apologetic but said they couldn't legally take him off the respirator without a court order. I was in total despair at that point knowing that Lem was languishing while I would have to find an attorney and jump through what I assumed would be legal hoops. I went home and began my search for a lawyer but in the end I didn't have to search long. The following morning of August 5, 1989 I got another call from the hospital letting me know that Lem had passed away.

My first feelings were of relief, knowing Lem would no longer be suffering in a state he was so opposed to. But relief was quickly followed by total emotional devastation. Chuck came home straight away and my good friends Steve and Nancy quickly joined us, all trying to help me bear my overwhelming grief.

Lem wanted to be cremated and I complied with his wishes. I organized a memorial service at our favorite screening room at 1600 Broadway. To honor Lem, I treated the occasion like a screening of one of our films. I invited all of his friends and showed a video tribute. LaRue and Fabian spoke before the video, sharing a heartfelt eulogy. I also wrote a piece read by friend Tom Russ sharing my memories, love and gratitude for Lem.

While I tried to make the memorial a celebration, the weeks following it were some of the bleakest of my life. Lem was more than my brother; he was my best friend and most inspiring creative partner. I had many of my best times and produced some of our best films with him. Lem understood where I came from and how far we had come. We were – and always will be – the Amero brothers.

I tried to move forward after Lem's death, but I struggled. Rather than turn to Chuck for solace, I inflicted my grief on him, often lashing out over the loss of my brother.

I badgered Chuck about his health, and in particular about his smoking. I had recently quit, and urged him to do the same. At one point I thought my pleas were working because I didn't see him smoking as often but it turned out he was just hiding his habit from me. He did try hard to quit, even going to hypnosis which was popular at the time, but he was addicted and couldn't stop.

By now, Chuck had to take insulin by injection. He was terrified of needles which didn't help. A side effect of the injections was a diminished sex drive which ate away at Chuck's self-esteem. I tried to reassure him that it didn't matter and that after 20 years our relationship was based on so much more. It was, but sex had always been a way for us to connect – we had strong chemistry and a lot of fun together – so the side effect was difficult for us.

To try to smooth things over in our relationship, we decided to take a trip to London, one of our favorite places in the world. But soon after we arrived I began to notice how fatigued Chuck was by almost any activity. His mood wasn't helped by the fact that due to his worsening diabetes he couldn't have a drink with dinner, while I could.

When we returned to New York, unbeknownst to me Chuck continued drinking as well as smoking. I only found out about the drinking when I came across a bottle of vodka hidden in our apartment. Shortly after, I got a call from the Post Office one day telling me Chuck had collapsed and been taken to the hospital but was subsequently released. When Chuck finally came home a couple of hours later he was extremely evasive, saying that he had fainted and it was nothing. But I wasn't satisfied with such a vague answer and we wound up having a real heart-to-heart. It ended with Chuck promising to take better care of himself and give up drinking for real this time. I wanted to believe him but in truth, I didn't. He was addicted to alcohol and nicotine and I felt powerless to help.

As I feared, Chuck's habits persisted and his health continued to deteriorate. One evening we had plans to go out with friends after I came home from work. I found him lying on the bed ice cold, motionless and unresponsive even after shaking him. I called 911 and feared the worst. The EMTs arrived quickly and were able to revive him. They said he'd had a reaction to the insulin but would be OK.

After they left, Chuck admitted to me that he'd had a couple of drinks that clearly set off the reaction. I was extremely upset and yelled that his drinking was killing him. I vented my anger, asking over and over "What are you doing to our relationship?" After several minutes Chuck looked at me dead on and said, "You shouldn't have left me alone so much."

His comment cut like a knife and stopped me cold. Yes, I was away a lot at conventions and film shoots. But I always thought Chuck understood that this was part of my life. I quickly grew defensive, frustrated that he had suffered in silence for so long. But on some level I always knew Chuck felt left out of parts of my life, and believed that my brother had always come first. It wasn't true, but sometimes it was easier to emotionally engage with my brother. When Lem and I would fight, Lem could hold his own and we'd slog through the conflict. Chuck on the other hand always deferred to me, holding in his feelings. As much as I loved Chuck there was a lot left unsaid and that really frustrated me.

Soon after this incident I came home and could tell Chuck had again been drinking. We argued and I stormed off to bed on my own. At about three in the morning, I woke up to the sounds of the television in the living room. I assumed Chuck had fallen asleep on the couch and went out to get him. But he was nowhere to be found and I immediately became enraged, convinced he had gone to the corner pub.

I threw on some clothes and headed down to the bar, but when I asked the bartender whether he had seen Chuck, he answered no. I walked out onto the street to head towards another bar we used to frequent about two blocks away. As I turned, I saw a parked ambulance in the distance with its lights flashing. In my heart I immediately knew it was for Chuck. I started running and arrived just as they were about to pull away. I pounded on the ambulance window and forced my way into the back. Chuck was in fact inside, lying unconscious on the gurney.

The EMTs let me ride with them to the emergency room at St. Vincent's. When we arrived, they rushed Chuck inside and asked me to remain in the waiting area. I sat down expecting many hours wait ahead of me, but half an hour later the doctor emerged with the worst possible news. Chuck had died.

I was in shock. The hospital staff said it would be a few minutes before I could go in to see him. I called Steve and Nancy who lived nearby and when I hung up the staff brought me into Chuck's room. They explained that he'd had a massive heart attack. I later found out he hadn't been at the pub long, just starting a first drink when the attack came on.

I sat next to his lifeless body and held Chuck's hand, sobbing uncontrollably. I finally wandered out into the dawn and made my way back to our apartment. When I got there, Steve and Nancy were waiting for me. I immediately started wailing, "I killed him, I killed him." They were confused for a moment as they didn't know about Chuck's struggles with alcohol and my attempts to get him to stop. But everything eventually came out in my ravings.

When Lem passed away, as terrible and sad as it was, I had months to brace myself. And as much as I wanted to save him, there was nothing I could do in the face of AIDS. But with Chuck I really believed that if I had just done more, acted differently or somehow been better, Chuck would not be dead. Steve and Nancy were incredibly supportive and tried to convince me that there was nothing more I could have done; that ultimately it was Chuck's choice. But the guilt I felt was immense.

Even though I was not easy on Chuck after Lem's death I couldn't have made it without him. He was my life partner and my emotional anchor, the man who had always been there for me. With both Lem and Chuck now gone, I was at a loss for how to move on.

CHAPTER 14

PRIMETIME
(1991-1994)

To quote Charles Dickens, "It was the best of times, it was the worst of times". I had lost both Lem and Chuck in a period of two years, and I was badly hurting. Thankfully Paul Klein and Colette gave me a great deal of support on my return to work. And cranking out three program guides against sometimes impossible deadlines was exactly what I needed to temporarily forget my pain. Paul's son Adam was a lawyer who fancied himself a screenwriter. He decided to write a TV script on homeopathic medicine having become interested in the topic after his mother, Paul's wife, was diagnosed with cancer. Adam asked Paul to pitch the project to his contacts at NBC and they bought it with a production budget of $800,000. There were two stipulations to the agreement – the show had to be a two-hour documentary program and NBC would have to approve the host who would do one day's work for $40,000 maximum. For the host they suggested Richard Chamberlain, Mary Tyler Moore or Lauren Bacall.

With this green light, *Miracle Cures: Secrets of Alternative Healing* was a go and much to my surprise, Paul asked me to be the producer. This would be a big step up for me. I'd never worked with such a big budget let alone on something airing on network television. I wavered for a moment, but the opportunity was just too tempting to pass up.

Paul brought in his friend Forrest Murray to be supervising producer. Forrest had extensive producer credits and truthfully, I was relieved to have someone to help with the pressure of this production. NBC approved my hiring and I officially signed on for a salary of $30,000.

The first thing Forrest and I needed to do was cast the host. We began with Lauren Bacall, meeting at her apartment in the Dakota where John Lennon had lived until his murder a decade or so earlier. We pitched the idea and she seemed enthusiastic. She had some conditions, but nothing out of the ordinary. She was even willing to let us shoot her in her lovely home library. But after our discussion, Ms. Bacall passed us on to her agent and things fell apart. Even though she had agreed to the offered fee of $40,000, her agent demanded more. We got NBC to raise the fee to $50,000 but that still wasn't good enough for her agent, so we had to walk away. We tried Richard Chamberlain next but while he expressed interest, he had previous commitments and we couldn't make the timing work. Then we tried Mary Tyler Moore, but she only wanted to do it if we focused exclusively on diabetes, which she suffered from.

With NBC's recommendations knocked out, we began to brainstorm alternatives. Colette, whom I had hired as associate producer, suggested Olympia Dukakis and we all thought that was an idea worth pursuing. Before taking the idea to NBC we approached Ms. Dukakis to get a sense of her interest. She was enthusiastic and had no unreasonable requests. We agreed on $40,000 for a one day, ten-hour shoot. With Olympia's recent success in films like *Moonstruck* and *Steel Magnolias* we thought she was a good choice and NBC agreed, giving their approval.

With our host in place, we moved on to hiring the crew. We brought on TV director Cliff Fagin and production manager Ethan Prochnik who had worked with Forrest Murray on *The Cider House Rules*. I then was able to convince NBC that my long time DP, Larry Revene, would be a good choice.

We had to film Olympia Dukakis first as she had a previous commitment. We found a Masterpiece Theater-style library for the ten-hour shoot we had agreed on. The idea was to have Olympia go to the shelves and pick out books dealing with various homeopathic themes as lead-ins to the segments that would follow. I had seen to every detail I could think of so that the 10 hours of filming would go smoothly. When Olympia arrived, I greeted her and started to lay out the day. She quickly interrupted me, saying "Just as long as I'm out of here by 5:30 because I have an appearance at Lincoln Center this evening."

My heart sank. Even if we had gone all 10 hours to our originally anticipated time of 8pm it was going to be tight – now our shoot seemed impossible. I quickly found Cliff and Larry and said "You know all the walking to the bookshelves that I wanted? Forget it. Never let her out of her chair. It'll take too long to shoot." So she stayed seated the entire time and read everything off a teleprompter. Thankfully Olympia's reading was reasonably natural and outside of the time snafu she was very accommodating. By the time the day was over we even bonded a bit owing to the fact that we both had polio when we were children.

With our host footage in place, we were ready to film the dramatizations. There were a total of 10 segments, five contemporary and five from the past ranging from ancient China and Greece to 18th century France. It would be demanding as we had lots of locations to work across.

We began shooting in our Brooklyn studio, the easiest of options as it was a controlled environment. We then moved on to some challenging locations.

In one of the segments Paul's son had written, a woman with a medical problem untreatable by conventional means learns of a homeopathic treatment from her cleaning lady. This seemed a bit boring to me so I changed the location to a cruise ship where her cabin steward recommends the treatment. While I, loving ships, thought this was a wonderful idea, our production manager Ethan Prochnik was less enthusiastic. Finding a cruise line that would let us shoot on board while briefly docked would be challenging. But Ethan rose to the occasion and at 5:00am our bleary-eyed cast and crew boarded the Regent Sea. We had to be off the ship by 5pm and unfortunately everything worked against us that day. We couldn't use the elevators, which meant we lugged equipment up and down the narrow and greasy crew stairways. The pool, which was supposed to be filled, wasn't. Passengers constantly walked into the shots, staring into the camera. And one of the actors – dressed as the Captain of our fictional cruise ship – was so convincing that passengers and crew came up to him for pictures or orders. But somehow we finished that day – and the entire shoot – on time and on budget.

Feeling quite pleased with how production went, I wrote a puff piece for Page Six in the New York Post. Much to my surprise, they printed it verbatim under the headline "Greek Choice":

> **Olympia Dukakis is a cheap date. While producer John Amero was taping the upcoming NBC special *Miracle Cures: Secrets of Alternative Healing* he made reservations at the Sign of the Dove to take the star out to a delicious lunch. When the break arrived, the Oscar-winner only wanted two turkey burgers and a side of spinach ordered from a local Greek diner. 'I was planning on taking her and the director to an expensive $500 lunch' said Amero. 'Instead it cost me about $8.12'.**

When I showed the paper to Colette she smiled, commenting "Shameless self-promotion!" She was right, and I loved it.

All-in-all *Miracle Cures: Secrets of Alternative Healing* took about a year to make. When we were done, Paul and NBC seemed reasonably pleased. None of us expected great success from the show but we all hoped it would hold its own in terms of ratings.

As it turned out, ratings were going to be the least of our problems.

In the Spring of 1990, a conservative Montgomery, Alabama district attorney named Jimmy Evans became outraged at American Exxxtasy.

It turned out one of the station's feature films was taped by someone's son who had figured out the password to his parents' satellite box. He decided to show the taped film to some fellow students, one of them being the DA's son.

It was a case tailor-made for a conservative like Evans who, by the way, was running for re-election. Evans brought charges against Paul Klein, his companies and GTE, the owner of the satellites relaying American Exxxtasy programming to Alabama. Evans also started a media stir by contacting CNN to air his indignation and indictments publicly.

Back in New York, there wasn't much coverage of the events and Paul Klein worked to keep everything quiet. Those of us in the office only found out about the case when a CNN crew showed up asking if Paul Klein had any comments about the lawsuit. After that Colette gingerly approached Paul to find out what was going on, and the truth came out.

During this time we all found it hard to work with the storm clouds forming.

The news networks were camped out in front of our offices and we might be subpoenaed – and even charged – at any point. And we knew that we would all lose our jobs if American Exxxtasy, the money-making channel among Paul's offerings, went bust.

Paul's lawyers had him shut down satellite access in the state of Alabama but the damage was done. The ACLU tried to help Paul, but ultimately he had to pay $150,000 in fines and agree to never again distribute or promote sexually explicit films.

It was the death knell for Paul's business. As we anticipated we all lost our jobs. And without Paul, it looked like my first big time producer credit would likely be my last.

Miracle Cures: Secrets of Alternative Healing aired in early July 1994. A few of us who worked on the show – as well as Steve and Nancy and some other friends – gathered at Colette's place to watch the program. I was curious to see my work on network TV, and wondered what my reaction would be. Even though the script wasn't the best, I felt I had done a decent job as producer. I thought of Lem and felt he would have approved. And I knew Chuck would have been thrilled that no one had been rutting in our bed. But they weren't here, and I missed them. I couldn't share this moment with the two most important people in my life.

As the show progressed I found my mind wandering. Watching on a small TV in a living room – rather than on the big screen in a movie theater – was underwhelming. And as I tried to remember a really exciting or

PRIMETIME (1991-1994)

memorable moment during the shoot, I drew a blank. There were no blow jobs on the Brooklyn Bridge. No night spent in the Tombs. No inspecting Pamela's newly made "lady parts" after surgery. Those things I remembered, and with great nostalgia.

It had taken 30 years to make it from porn to prime time, but it wasn't all I'd hoped for.

With Paul's company defunct, I wondered what I would do next. Fortunately, it wasn't long before I got a call from Private Screenings, a production company run by Ernie Sauer and Gary Connor. They made features for Cinemax and Showtime, and wanted me to be line producer on their upcoming R-rated feature, *Breakfast in Bed* (1990), starring Marilyn Chambers. Ever since I gave Marilyn roses at the *Behind the Green Door* premiere at the World Theater, I thought it would be fun to work with her. And Larry Revene, who was always great to work with, was signed on as DP. So I agreed, considering it short-term work as I figured out my longer-term plans.

We filmed *Breakfast in Bed* in a beautiful mansion on Huntington Bay in Long Island. Marilyn surprised us all when she showed up with her iconic long blonde hair cut very short and dyed red. But outside of this one hiccup the shoot went well and Ernie and Gary asked me to work on their next film, *Affairs of the Heart* (1992), starring Penthouse centerfold Amy Lynn Baxter. After this second film, there was nothing else in the Private Screenings pipeline, which was fine by me. I needed a break and frankly working on those productions made me miss making my own films. I called up the Gotham Cinema to see if they needed help filling in for movie premieres, and thankfully they did.

While sitting in the Gotham lobby one afternoon, my former production manager Ethan Prochnik dropped by. I hadn't seen him since we'd watched the network airing of *Miracle Cures: Secrets of Alternative Healing* so we went to lunch to catch up. I knew he had been writing a script called *Speed and Absinthe* about two idealistic college students who get in over their heads dealing drugs. Ethan had finished the script and was now looking to form a company to produce it. He had a copy of the script and asked me to read it, leading me to think his drop in at the Gotham was no accident. The more he talked the more I felt myself being drawn into his risky venture. Fade out, fade in: three months later we were in business, with me as producer and Ethan as director. We had an office in SoHo and a nameplate on the door; "Raven Sol Productions". Now all we had to do was raise $400,000.

Over a year passed and we raised only $30,000 as Ethan was a first-time director with no completed projects to show potential backers. The only way Ethan would gain any credibility was to actually shoot something so we decided to film and edit two key scenes using some of the money we'd gotten. Luckily Larry Revene agreed to serve as DP on spec so after a few weeks we had 20 minutes of *Speed and Absinthe* to show prospective investors. We rented a screening room at the posh Tribeca Film Center, complete with food and drink and, after short speeches by Ethan and myself, showed the scenes.

The reaction was favorable but ultimately, no money came through.

Both Ethan and I were just about broke by this time. We weren't getting anywhere in New York so Ethan headed to Los Angeles to see if we might have any luck out west. Unfortunately, we didn't. Out of money, time and options Ethan shelved *Speed and Absinthe* and became an independent producer in California.

Back in New York, I was feeling the pinch. I was hoping I could pick up some work back at the Gotham Cinema but after 38 years, the owners decided to close it down for good. I was sad to see the theater go. Unbeknownst to the owners, I'd shot many Amero Brothers scenes there after hours. I'd also met some fascinating people at the cinema like Tom Cruise and Montgomery Clift. It dawned on me that my various and sundry careers in the world of film all seemed to be ending.

I needed some income so I looked through the New York Times help wanted section. I saw an ad for a "NYC tour director for student groups. Part time and must have license". I was interested so I did a bit of research into the license required. I would need to pass a test on New York City landmarks and history and pay a $400 fee. With my knowledge of the city it was an easy test so $400 later I mailed the license and a G-rated version of my resume in and got the job.

Tour director turned out to be a good option for me for many years. I ushered groups of high school drama and chorus students around the city for three or four days at a time. We'd stay at good hotels, eat at nice restaurants and see a Broadway production every night. The pay was decent and I could pick and choose how many groups I wanted to take during the season. It could be grueling to wrangle forty teenagers in "The Big City", but I really enjoyed the work.

During this time I would often travel to Gloucester for the Amero family reunions and became closer with my half-brother Jeff and my sister Joan.

Jeff asked me to be godfather to his daughter, Julia, and I was honored. Joan would visit from her home in Oregon and we would gorge ourselves on fried clams and lobsters. By now the whole Amero family knew about Lem and my work and accepted it without judgment. It seems sometimes you can go home again.

Back in New York, I would often find myself smiling as I walked the students past many of the landmarks Larry Revene had once said the Amero Brothers defiled. One day while I was waiting for the kids I wandered through Times Square. First, I stopped on the corner of 46th and Broadway where The Amero Brothers had our office on the seventh floor of the Equity Building. The building was now covered with brightly lit signage and looked nothing like it used to. I then strolled over to where the Trans-Lux theater used to be on 49th Street – it was now a hotel. Our old bar the Big Spender on West 48th Street was long gone. I started to walk towards 42nd Street and Broadway, where the Globe Theater used to be.

My thoughts drifted back to a night in 1965. Mike Findlay and I had just left McCann's Bar and were heading south when the Globe Theater marquee came into view:

"BODY OF A FEMALE IN ITS EIGHTH BIG WEEK!"

We both had a light buzz and just stood there looking up at our film in lights. Mike turned to me and said quietly, "You know John? I don't think it gets any better than this." And you know what? It never did.

EPILOGUE

Some days I can't believe it's been over 25 years since my last film production, especially as movies and theater remain central to my life. I continued as a student tour director for many years, helping teens interpret the Broadway productions we'd attend and regaling them with stories of stars past and present. I head to the cinema regularly, oftentimes with my partner of the past twenty years. And my old confederate Kurt Mann and I regularly dissect movies, both classic and current, in lengthy emails traded almost daily.

Once I retired, I was able to more frequently indulge my love of travel with friends. London, the city Chuck and I felt like we'd made our own, remains a recurring destination. And I regularly return to Gloucester, Massachusetts. Visiting my hometown keeps me close to memories of Lem, my grandmother, and family that I cherish.

I still live in the same West Village apartment featured in many of my films, another source of happy reminiscences. And many close friends from my movie days remain nearby, including Steve and Nancy Gould and Patty Sumner.

I happily remain a celluloid man in a streaming world.

BOLDLY EXPLORES THE BIZARRE, TWILIGHT WORLD OF ABNORMAL SEXUAL BEHAVIOR!

BODY OF A FEMALE

A Story of
THE WHIP AND THE FLESH!

starring ANNA RIVA • LEM AMERO
ROBERT WEST

A JOS. BRENNER ASSOCIATES RELEASE

A Motion Picture Intended Only For the Adult

JOHN AMERO FILMOGRAPHY

Body of a Female (1964)
Directed and produced by John Amero (as J. Ellsworth) and Michael Findlay (as Julian Marsh)
Written by John Amero and Michael Findlay (as Francis Ellie)
Camera: John Amero (as John Firth), Michael Findlay (as Douglas Fenway)
Editor: Michael Findlay (as Michael Crane)
Cast: Roberta Findlay (as Anna Riva), Lem Amero, Michael Findlay (as Robert West), Gigi Darlene, Jack Ballard (narration)
A Joseph Brenner Associates release

Diary of a Swinger (1967)
Directed and produced by John Amero and Lem Amero
Written by Robert Parker
Camera: John Amero
Editor: Lem Amero

Cast: Rita Bennett (as Joanna Cunningham), Ron Scardera, Darcy Brown, Rose Conti, Biff McGuire
A Box Office International release

The Lusting Hours (1968)
Directed and written by John Amero and Lem Amero
Produced by John Amero (as J. Ellsworth) and Lem Amero (as L. Firth)
Camera: John Amero (as J. Ellsworth)
Editor: John Amero (as J. Ellsworth), Lem Amero (uncredited)
Cast: Roberta Findlay (as Anna Riva), Michael Findlay (as Julian Marsh), Sheila Britt (as Lina Lamont), Ron Scardera (as Don Lockwood), Janet Banzet (as Kay Rice), Steve Gould (as Satch Gould), Chuck Federico, Lem Amero
An American Film Distributing release

The Curse of Her Flesh (1968)
Directed by Michael Findlay (as Julian Marsh)
Written by Michael Findlay (as Julian Marsh) and Roberta Findlay (as Anna Riva)
Still Photographer: John Amero (as Ellsworth Dinsmore)
Cast: Eve Bork, Michael Findlay (as Robert Wester), Ron Scardera (as A. Dick Feeler), Linda Boyce (as Lena Brice), John Amero (as John Ellie), Roberta Findlay (uncredited), Uta Erickson (uncredited)
An American Film Distributing release

A Thousand Pleasures (1968)
Directed by Michael Findlay (as Julian Marsh)
Written by Michael Findlay (as Berla L. Moke)
Still Photographer: John Amero (as Ellsworth Dinsmore)
Cast: Janet Banzet (as Marie Brent), Uta Erickson (as Artemidia Grillet), Michael Findlay (as Robert Wuesterwurst), John Amero (as Duke Ellsworth), Roberta Findlay (as Anna Riva)
An American Film Distributing release

The Ultimate Degenerate (1969)
Produced by Michael Findlay (as Julian Marsh) and Roberta Findlay (as Anna Riva)
Directed and written by Michael Findlay (as Julian Marsh)
Camera: Roberta Findlay (as Anna Riva)
Casting: John Amero
Cast: Uta Erickson (as Artimida Grillet), Michael Findlay (as Robert West), Earl Hindman (as Leo Heinz), Janet Banzet (as Marie Brent), Kim Lewid (as Kim Turner)
An American Film Distributing release

The Corporate Queen (1969)
Directed, produced, and written by John Amero and Lem Amero
Camera: John Amero
Costumes: John Brock Benson
Cast: Renay Clair, Uta Erickson, Janet Banzet (as Marie Brent), Ron Scardera (as Tony Vito)
A Victoria Films release

Lovers By Appointment (1969)
Directed, produced, and written by Jack Bravman and John Amero
Camera: John Amero
Cast: Linda Boyce, Bob Sumner, Steve Gould, Janet Banzet (as Marie Brent)
A Producers Releasing International release

Everything for Everybody (1969)
Directed, produced, and written by Jack Bravman and John Amero
Camera: John Amero
Cast: Janet Banzet (as Marie Brent), Bob Sumner, Steve Gould, Linda Boyce
A Producers Releasing International Ltd. release

The Ballers (1969)
Directed by Jack Bravman (as Wizard Glick)
Camera: John Amero (as John Meroa)
Cast: Sam Bueno, Donna Grande, Linda Lust
A Boss Distributors release

JOHN AMERO FILMOGRAPHY

Roommates Sociable (1969)
Directed by Jack Bravman (as Wizard Glick)
Camera: John Amero (as John Meroa)
Cast: Rosa Madre, Tulip Moyst, Linda Lust
A Boss Distributors release

Janie (1970)
Directed by Jack Bravman
Production Manager: John Amero (uncredited)
Camera: Roberta Findlay (as Anna Riva)
Sound: John Amero
Cast: Linda Vair (as Mary Jane Carpenter), Peer St. Jean, Michael Findlay (as Richard Jennings), Tina Kraslow
A Cine Flicks International Ltd. release

Bacchanale (1971)
Directed, produced, and written by John Amero and Lem Amero
Camera: John Amero

Editor: Lem Amero
Sets: LaRue Watts
Costumes: John Brock Benson
Cast: Uta Erickson, Darcy Brown, Ron Scardera, Linda Boyce, Chuck Federico, Steve Gould
A Distribpix release

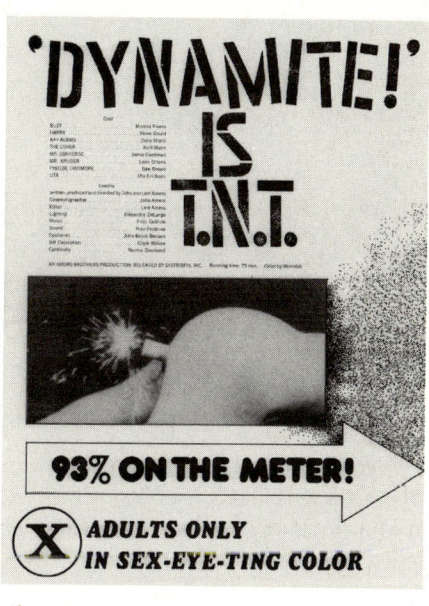

Dynamite (1972)
Directed, produced, and written by John Amero and Lem Amero
Camera: John Amero
Editor: Lem Amero
Costumes: John Brock Benson
Cast: Monica Rivers, Dolly Sharp, Uta Erickson, Jamie Gillis (as Jamie Goodman), Darcy Brown (as Dee Brown), Steve Gould, Kurt Mann
A Distribpix release

Pepper (1973)
(aka **Checkmate**)
Directed and produced by John Amero and Lem Amero
Written by LaRue Watts

AMERICAN EXXXTASY

Cast: David Savage, Marc Stevens, Brian Haines, Kurt Mann, Dan Lanning (as Dan Raymond)
A P.M. Productions Inc. release

Camera: Roberta Findlay
Editor: Lem Amero
Cast: Diana Wilson, An Tsan Hu, J.J. Coyle, Don Draper, Caren Kaye, Kurt Mann, Steve Gould
A Mid-Broadway Productions release

Every Inch a Lady (1975)
Directed, produced, and written by John Amero and Lem Amero
Camera: Roberta Findlay
Editor: Lem Amero
Sets & Costumes: LaRue Watts, Fabian Stuart
Cast: Darby Lloyd Rains, Harry Reems, Andrea True, Jamie Gillis, Marc Stevens, Erica Eaton, Kim Pope, Kurt Mann, Dr. Infinity
A Mature Pictures Inc. release

Michael, Angelo, and David (1976)
Directed, produced, and written by John Amero (as Francis Ellie)
Camera: Michael Findlay (as Oscar Riva)
Editor: Lem Amero (uncredited)
Negative Cutter: Bob Weiner

Kiss Today Goodbye (1976)
Directed, produced, and written by John Amero (as Francis Ellie)
Camera: Michael Findlay (as Oscar Riva)
Editor: Lem Amero (uncredited)
Sets & Costumes: LaRue Watts, Fabian Stuart
Negative Cutter: Bob Weiner
Cast: George Payne, Lew Seager, David Savage, Erica Eaton, Kurt Mann
A P.M. Productions release

Point Me Toward Tomorrow (1977)
Directed, produced, and written by John Amero (as Francis Ellie)
Camera: Michael Findlay (as Oscar Riva)
Editor: Lem Amero (uncredited)
Sets & Costumes: LaRue Watts, Fabian Stuart

JOHN AMERO FILMOGRAPHY

Negative Cutter: Bob Weiner
Cast: Lee Richards, Giuseppe Welch, Roger Schultz, Dan Lanning (as Dan Raymond)
A P.M. Productions release

Christopher Street Blues (1977)
Directed, produced, and written by John Amero (as Francis Ellie)
Camera: Michael Findlay (as Oscar Riva)
Editor: Lem Amero (uncredited)
Negative Cutter: Bob Weiner
Cast: Lew Seager, Lee Richards, Giuseppe Welch, Roger Schuler, Dan Lanning (as Dan Raymond)
A P.M. Productions release

Sets & Costumes: LaRue Watts, Fabian Stuart
Negative Cutter: Bob Weiner
Cast: George Payne, Jack Wrangler, Bob Meehan (as Adam DeHaven), Kurt Mann, Genie Josephs (as Anna Freed)
A P.M. Productions release

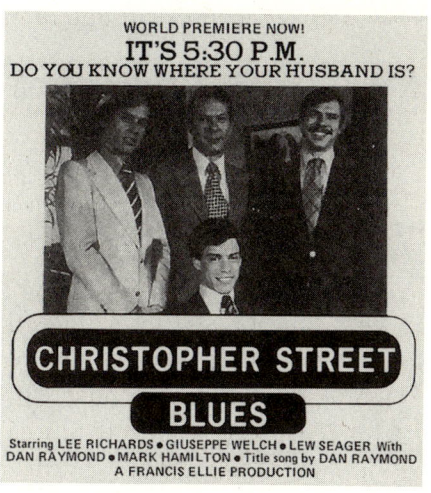

Men Come First (1979)
Directed, produced and written by John Amero (as Francis Ellie) and Lem Amero (as Francis Ellie)
Camera: Larry Revene
Editor: Lem Amero (as Ella Fay)
Sets & Costumes: LaRue Watts, Fabian Stuart
Negative Cutter: Bob Weiner
Cast: George Payne, Brian Granger, Roy Garrett, Kurt Mann, Bob Meehan (as Adam DeHaven)
A P.M. Productions release

Navy Blue (1979)
Directed, produced and written by John Amero (as Francis Ellie) and Lem Amero (as Francis Ellie)
Camera: Larry Revene
Editor: Lem Amero (as Ella Fay)

Killing Me Softly
(aka **Killing Me Gently**) (1979)
Directed, produced and written by John Amero (as Francis Ellie) and Lem Amero (as Francis Ellie)
Camera: Larry Revene (as Larry Stradling)
Editor: Lem Amero (uncredited)

Sets & Costumes: LaRue Watts, Fabian Stuart
Negative Cutter: Bob Weiner
Cast: Jack Wrangler, Giuseppe Welch, David King, Stanley Richards, John Kovaks, Kurt Mann, Bob Meehan (as Adam DeHaven)
A P.M. Productions release

In Search of the Perfect Man (1980)
Directed, produced and written by John Amero (as Francis Ellie) and Lem Amero (as Francis Ellie)
Camera: Larry Revene
Editor: Lem Amero (as Ella Fay)
Negative Cutter: Bob Weiner
Cast: Giuseppe Welch, Scorpio, Michael Stone, Shawn Gregory, Dr. Infinity
A P.M. Productions release

The Death of Scorpio (1981)
Directed, produced and written by John Amero (as Francis Ellie) and Lem Amero (as Francis Ellie)
Camera: Larry Revene
Editor: Lem Amero (uncredited)
Sets & Costumes: LaRue Watts, Fabian Stuart
Negative Cutter: Bob Weiner
Cast: Scorpio, Giuseppe Welch, Shawn Gregory, Michael Stone
A P.M. Productions release

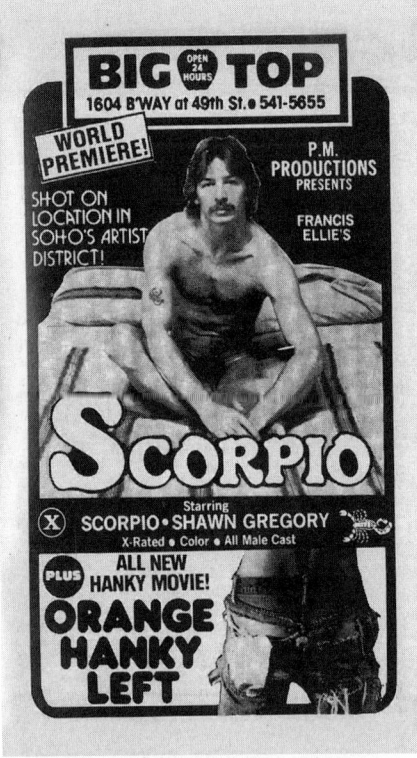

Blonde Ambition (1981)
Directed and produced by John Amero and Lem Amero
Written by LaRue Watts
Camera: Roberta Findlay, Larry Revene, John Amero (uncredited)
Editor: Lem Amero

JOHN AMERO FILMOGRAPHY

Art Direction: LaRue Watts, Fabian Stuart
Set Design: Bobby Lacrosse
Cast: Suzy Mandel, Dory Devon, Jamie Gillis, Eric Edwards, Wade Nichols (as Wade Parker), Molly Malone, Erica Eaton, Erica Havens (as Jeanne Joseph), George Payne, Kurt Mann, Pat Finnegan (as Patricia Dale)
A Mature Pictures release

R.S.V.P. (1984)
Directed by Lem Amero
Produced by John Amero
Written by LaRue Watts
Assistant Director: Billy Slobodian
Camera: Larry Revene
Editor: Lem Amero
Sets & Costumes: LaRue Watts, Fabian Stuart
Cast: Adam Mills, Linda Wiesmeier, Veronica Hart, Ray Colbert, Harry Reems, Katt Shea, Lola Mason, Georgina Spelvin
A Chuck Vincent / Platinum Pictures release

Passage Thru Pamela (1985)
Directed by Lem Amero (as Leslie Brooks)
Produced by John Amero, Jack Bravman and Bunny Atlas (as Stuart Brooks)
Written by John Amero and Lem Amero (as Derek Thurston)
Camera: Steven Kamen (as Sven Nuvo)
Editor: Lem Amero (as Firth DeMule)

Boots & Saddles (1982)
Directed, produced and written by John Amero (as Francis Ellie) and Lem Amero (as Francis Ellie)
Camera: Larry Revene
Editor: Lem Amero
Sets & Costumes: LaRue Watts, Fabian Stuart
Cast: Jack Wrangler, Scorpio, Joe Ryder, Roy Garrett
A P.M. Productions release

JOHN AMERO FILMOGRAPHY

Sets & Costumes: LaRue Watts, Fabian Stuart
Cast: Kimberly Carson, Sharon Kane, Barbie Dahl, Frank Serrone, Johnny Nineteen, Joey Santini, "Pamela"
A Bunnco / VCA release

Wimps (1986)
Directed and produced by Chuck Vincent
Written by Chuck Vincent and Craig Horrall
Camera: Larry Revene
Editor: James Davalos, Chuck Vincent (as Marc Ubell)
Casting: John Amero
Cast: Tracey Adams (as Deborah Blaisdell), Veronica Hart (as Jane Hamilton), Louie Bonanno, Jim Abele
A Platinum Pictures release

Student Affairs (1987)
Directed and produced by Chuck Vincent
Written by Chuck Vincent and Craig Horrall
Camera: Larry Revene
Editor: James Davalos, Chip Lambert, Chuck Vincent (as Marc Ubell)
Casting: John Amero
Cast: Tracey Adams (as Deborah Blaisdell), Veronica Hart (as Jane Hamilton), Louie Bonanno, Jim Abele
A Platinum Pictures release

Sensations (1988)
Directed and produced by Chuck Vincent
Written by Chuck Vincent and Craig Horrall
Camera: Larry Revene
Casting Consultant: John Amero
Cast: Veronica Hart (as Jane Hamilton), Krista Lane (as Rebecca Lynn), Blake Bahner, Jennifer Delora, Rick Savage
A Platinum Pictures release

Big Mack (1988)
Directed, produced, and written by John Amero and Lem Amero
Executive Producer: Bill Perry
Camera: Joe Vasquez
Editor: Lem Amero (as Firth DeMule)
Sets & Costumes: LaRue Watts, Fabian Stuart
Cast: Rory Miller, Scott Thomas, Chip Henson, Keith Ardent (as Coleman Jones), Bob Steele
A P.M. Productions release

Breakfast in Bed (1990)
Produced by Gary P. Conner
Directed by Ernest G. Sauer
Written by Don Shiffrin
Camera: Larry Revene
Line Producer: John Amero
Cast: Marilyn Chambers, Michael Rose, Courtenay James, Angela Schreiber, Mark Stolzenberg
A Private Screenings production

Affairs of the Heart (1992)
Produced by Gary P. Conner
Directed by Ernest G. Sauer
Written by Mike MacDonald
Camera: Larry Revene
Line Producer: John Amero
Cast: Amy Lynn Baxter, Michael Montana, Angela Nicholas, Danny Bergen, Robin Byrd
A Private Screenings production

Miracle Cures: Secrets of Alternative Healing (1994)
Directed by Clifford Fagin
Produced by John Amero
Supervising Producer: Forrest Murray
Associate Producer: Colette Connor
Camera: Larry Revene
Editor: Oliver Cukor
Production Manager: Ethan Prochnik
Host: Olympia Dukakis
An NBC two-hour primetime special

AMERICAN EXXXTASY

INDEX

Page references in **bold** refer exclusively to illustrations.

10 174
13 Nuns 166
42nd Street 45, 157
Adams, Tracey 184
Adventure 146
Affairs of the Heart 207, 220
All That Heaven Allows 59
All That Jazz 66
Allen, Woody 145
Amero, Bobby 25, 55
Amero, Gladys 9-14, 67, **105**
Amero, Hilda 15, 19, 31
Amero, Joan 15, 19, 31, 209
Amero Sr., John 9-16, 31, 32
Amero, Lem 6, 7, 10-12, 13-17, 19, 20, 23-26, 29, 31, 33, 40, 41, 43, 44, 50, 51, 53, 55, 57-59, 61-67, 69-82, 84, 89, 90, 93, 95, 97-104, **105**, **107-109**, **113**, **115**, **117**, 121-127, 137, 139, 141-150, 155-160, 164, 167-172, 174, 175, 177, 180, 181, 183-195, 197-203, 206, 209, 211
Amero, Nelson 10
An, Tsan Hu 126
Andrews, Julie 21
Ann-Margret 94
Antonioni, Michelangelo 97
Anything Goes 73
Aras, Vito K. 76, 143, 144
Arno, Norm 131-139
Atlas, Bunny 130, 186-190
Avedisian, Martin 54, 56
Babin, Ron 101
Bacall, Lauren 203
Bacchanale 6, 97-103, **113**, 121, 122, 140, 215
Bad Girls Go to Hell 54
Ballard, Jack 51
Ballers, The 90, 214
Banzet, Janet 59, 63, 75, 79, 83-87, **111**
Barrett, Pat see Banzet, Janet
Barry, John 145
Baxter, Amy Lynn 207
Behind the Green Door 128, 207
Bennett, Rita 60-66, 76
Benson, Jack 61, 80
Berkeley, Busby 155
Berle, Milton 12
Bernstein, Elmer 145
Berserk 122
Bicycle Thieves 82
Bilgrey, Felix 83, 84, 127, 146
Blonde Ambition 6, **116**, 148-160,

166, 182, 195, 218-219
Blonde on a Bum Trip 89
Blondie 154
Body of a Female 6, 40-51, 54, 57-59, 61, 65, 66, 74, 75, 78, 85, 87, **108**, **109**, **111**, 163, 209, **212**, 213
Bolla, R. see Kerman, Robert 152
Boots & Saddles 178, 179, 219
Bordello see *The Lusting Hours*
Borden, Lorraine 67, 125, 170
Borden, Stan 67, 68, 77, 78, 84, 168
Boyce, Linda 86, 90, 95, 97, 100
Brandt, Bernard B. 68
Bravman, Jack 89-92, 94, 186, 189, 191
Breakfast at Tiffany's 59
Breakfast in Bed 207, 220
Brenner, Joe 47-50, 54, 57, 58
Brent, Marie see Banzet, Janet
Britt, Sheila 75
Brown, Darcy 62, 64, 97, 98, 101, 123
Buckley, Jim 84
Burns, Michael 97
Campbell, Audrey 38, 41
Carpenter, Mary Jane see Vair, Linda
Caruso, Enrico 94
Castro, Fidel 186
Chamberlain, Judy 20, 43, 44, 71, 72
Chamberlain, Richard 203
Chambers, Marilyn 128, 129, 207
Changes 66
Channing, Carol 141
Checkmate see Pepper
Chess Murders, The see Pepper
Chorus Line, A 166
Christopher Street Blues 168, 217
Cider House Rules, The 204
Circle of Lust see *Lusting Hours, The*
Clark, Lenny 96, 102, 121, 122, 124-127, 131
Clift, Montgomery 28, 52, 53, 208
Clooney, Rosemary 174, 175
College Girls 124
Comancheros, The 31
Connor, Colette 167, 195, 203-206
Connor, Gary 207
Conti, Rose 60
Corporate Queen, The 78-84, 87, 98, **111**, **112**, 121, 139, 146, 214
Courtney, Nan 72, 73, 75
Covino, Chris 182, 184
Coyle, J.J. 100
Crawford, Joan 15, 43, 79, 122
Cronkite, Walter 25, 27

Cruise, Tom 192, 208
Cunningham, Joanna see Bennett, Rita
Curse of Her Flesh, The 6, 84, 214
Curtiz, Michael 31
Cyrano de Bergerac 184
Damiano, Gerard 66, 139, 140
Darlene, Gigi 41, 124
Davenport, Tiv 141
Davis, Bette 15, 43
De Sica, Vittorio 97
Death of Scorpio, The 218
Debbie Does Dallas 6, 132
Deeley, Heather 151
Deep Throat 6, 101, 103, 121, 122, 128, 140, 158
Defector, The 53
DeHaven, Adam see Meehan, Bob
DeHaven, Gloria 152
Delemos, George 54, 56, 66
DeMille, C.B. 157
Derek, Bo 174
Detsky, Seymour 129, 130
Devil in Miss Jones, The 6, 132
Devon, Dory 151, 154
Diary of a Swinger 54, 56, 59-69, 71, 74, 76, 81, 87, **112**, 121, 213
Dickens, Charles 203
Dietrich, Marlene 198
Diller, Phyllis 104
Diversions 151
Donahue, Troy 75
Donna Reed Show, The 30, 36
Dors, Diana 151
Downey Sr., Robert 54
Dr. Infinity see Aras, Vito K.
Duff-McCormick, Cara 60, 64
Dukakis, Olympia 7, **120**, 204, 205
Durling, Ronald 60
Durning, Charles 184
Dynamite 121-125, 215
Eaton, Erica 143, 146, 153, 166, 167
Edge of Night, The 152
Edwards, Blake 174
Edwards, Eric 147, 152, 154
Erickson, Uta 80, 84, 86, 87, 90, 97, 98, 100-102, 122, 124
Evans, Jimmy 205, 206
Eveready Hardon 124
Every Inch a Lady 6, 139-149, 160, 162, 166, 216
Everything for Everybody 90-92, 214
Fagin, Cliff 204
Farber, Howie 102, 103, 124

221

AMERICAN EXXXTASY

Farewell Scarlet 147
Federico, Chuck 55, 56, 62, 64, 65, 68, 69, 74, 75, 77, 80, 83, 88, 93, 103, **117**, 136, 142, 147, 157, 164, 165, 167, 171, 179-181, 184, 185, 191, 196, 199-203, 206, 211
Fellini, Federico 97
Findlay, Mike 6, 7, 32-35, 37, 38, 40-47, 49, 50, 57, 59, 67, 68, 72, 74-80, 83-87, 89, 93, 94, 98, **111**, 121, 124, 125, 160-171, 173, 177, 180, 209, 211
Findlay, Roberta 6, 34, 35, 38, 41-49, 57, 59, 67, 68, 72, 74, 75, 77, 83-87, 93, 94, 98, 99, 101, **109**, **111**, 121, 124-127, 140, 141, 143, 153, 155, 160, 164, 170
Finian's Rainbow 72
Finnegan, Patty see Sumner, Patty
Fitzgerald, F. Scott 183
Flack, Roberta 177
Foley, James 94
Forbidden Games 82
Fosse, Bob 33, 153
Franklin, Joe 94
Freed, Arthur 15
Freud: The Secret Passion 53
From Here to Eternity 52
Gable, Clark 146, 182
Garfield, John 182
Garson, Greer 11, 146
Giannini, Artie see Erickson, Uta
Gillis, Jamie 122, 142, 152, 155
Girl on Nightmare Island, The see Lusting Hours, The
Glass Menagerie, The 16
Glen or Glenda 78
Glick, Wizard see Bravman, Jack
Godfrey, Arthur 27
Golden Boys of the SS 193
Goldstein, Al 84
Goldwurm, Jean 82, 84, 127
Gone with the Wind 149, 152, 153
Gould, Nancy **120**, 171, 181, 191, 199, 201, 206, 211
Gould, Steve 51, 76, 77, 90, 91, 93, 98, **120**, 171, 181, 191, 199, 201, 206, 211
Grable, Betty 62, 98
Grahame, Gloria 157, 158
Granville, Bonita 79
Granville, Renay Clair 79, 80, 83
Gray, Dolores 30
Greatest Show on Earth, The 157
Griffith, Andy 30, 95
Guest, Christopher 60
Guys and Dolls 62, 98
Haines, Brian 162
Hamill, Les 143
Hanks, Tom 195
Hard, Rock 162
Harlow, Jean 54
Harrison, Rex 21
Hart, Veronica **118**, 182

Have Gun Will Travel 25
Hayworth, Rita 32
Hefner, Hugh 195
Hello, Dolly! 141
Hepburn, Audrey 192
Hepburn, Katherine 44
Herrmann, Bernard 101
Hickey, Bill 59
High Rise 128, 130
Hill, Benny 150
Hindman, Earl 87
Hitchcock, Alfred 52, 99, 142, 164
Home Improvement 87
How to Marry a Millionaire 149
How to Succeed in Business Without Really Trying 55
Hudson, Rock 192
Hunter, Ross 167
Huston, John 53
I Confess 52
I Love Lucy 25
I Shot Andy Warhol 82
Imitation of Life 59
In Search of the Perfect Man 218
Janie 94, 215
Jenny, Neil 98
Jewel Box Review, The 104
Jockstrap Strangler, The see Killing Me Softly
Johnson, Beef 162
Jorgensen, Christine 78
Josephs, Genie 151, 172, 174
Juliet of the Spirits 97
Kane, Sharon 187, 188
Kassner, Herb 130
Keller, Nancy see Gould, Nancy
Kelly, Gene 16, 171
Kerman, Robert
Kerr, Deborah 28
Killing Me Softly 175-177, 217-218
King Rat 52
Kiss Me Quick 65
Kiss of Her Flesh, The 84
Kiss Today Goodbye 166, 167, 216, **217**
Kitten in a Cage 76
Klaw, Irving 46
Klein, Adam 203, 205
Klein, Paul 195, 196, 203, 205-207
Kops, Ulla see Erickson, Uta
Kristal, Hilly 154
Lady Madonna 189
Lake, Sam 95, 127-129, 131, 146, 148, 158, 177
Lang, Fritz 32, 43
Lanning, Dan 168
Last Semester, The 76
Leighton, Ava 130, 158
Lennon, John 23, 144, 203
Lennon, Sean 144
Leonard, Gloria 151
Letterman, David 195
Lewid, Kim 87

Lord, Walter 34
Love, Billy 123
Lovelace, Linda 129
Lovers By Appointment 90-92, 214
Lubitsch, Ernst 43
Lusting Hours, The 6, 74-78, 80, 213
Mack, Big 193, 194, 220
Magnificent Obsession 59
Malone, Molly 152
Mandel, Suzy 150, 151, 153-156
Mann, Kurt 104, **116**, 123, 133, 134, 140, 152, 157, 158, 167, 185, 211
Margolis, Stanley 153
Marsh, Julian see Findlay, Mike
Mary Hartman, Mary Hartman 167
Mason, Perry 25, 27
Masters, George 94
Matchmaker, The 88
Mawra, Joe 78
McLeod, Richard 76
McQueen, Steve 73
Meehan, Bob 152, 172
Memories Within Miss Aggie 139
Men Come First 217
Metzger, Radley 121, 128, 158, 186
Michael, Angelo and David 161-167, 216
Midler, Bette 192
Midnight Cowboy 95
Mills, Adam 182
Milton Berle Show, The 12
Miracle Cures: Secrets of Alternative Healing **120**, 203-207, 220
Mishkin, William 46, 47
Mme. Olga's Massage Parlor 78
Mona: The Virgin Nymph 100
Monroe, Marilyn 52, 94, 151
Moonchildren 60
Moonstruck 204
Moore, Dudley 174
Moore, Mary Tyler 59, 203, 204
Morali, Jacques 152
Morgan, Chesty 134
Morowitz, Arthur 102, 103, 124, 180
Morris, David 155
Morse, Robert 55
Mrs. Barrington 147
Murray, Forrest 203, 204
Murrow, Edward R. 27
Music Box Mine 93, 121
Naked City 30, 32
Navy Blue 171-175, 194, 217
Nesting, The 157
Nichols, Wade 152
Nielsson, Kjell 136-139, 145, 147-149, 153, 156, 158, 159
Night to Remember, A 34
Nights of Cabiria 97
Niles, Mary Ann 153
Nineteen, Johnny 188
Novak, Harry 66
Olga's House of Shame 6, 38, 78
On the Town 171

222